TOURISM IN INDIA

TOURISM IN INDIA

By

Vijay Kumar Gupta

Tourism in India

ISBN : 978-81-212-0124-7

First Published 1987, reprint 2017 in India by
Gyan Publishing House
5 Ansari Road, Daryaganj,
New Delhi - 110002
Phones: 011- 47034999, 9811692060

E-mail: books@gyanbooks.com
website: gyanbooks.com

Printed at : Sagar Color Scan, New Delhi.

PREFACE

Tourism in India is an important factor to maintain communal harmony and peace in our country. India is a country of different faiths and religions. Tourism is a medium of National Integration and to keep up people close to each other in solving their traditional and religious differences.

Tourism has double benefits. First of all National Integration and the second is the source of transaction in trade and business for progress and prosperity of each other. A tourist of North goes to South, finds something new for him. He laerns local traditions, culture, festivals and religious worships. It widens social, political and cultural activities as well as outlook of a person.

India is a treasure of natural surroundings, scenic beauties, historical monuments, hill ranges,; pilgrimage places, colourful picnic spots and dancing festivals. From Kashmir to Kanya Kumari we can see ourselves memorable Hindu and Jain Temples, Buddhist Pagodas-Monastaries, big Mosques, fine churches, historical monuments, hill stations and picnic spots.

After independence, the tourism in India has been developed rapidly in a well planned manner which has become very popular. Old monuments are being maintained nicely and properly. They have been given their original shape. Many new picnic spots have been located. They have been illuminated and decorated in colourful manner so as to attract tourists and give them amusement in a proper way.

To attract tourists, the tourist department of other states have spent a large amount on the places of interest to give more comfort to the tourists. With modern amenities and comfort for their stay, apart from hotels, tourist cottages, bungalows, huts, rest-houses have been built. Transport facilities have been extended. Now there is no difficulty in reaching from one place to other. Air, Rail and Road services are easily available in the important cities of India.

This book is especially useful for the persons who wish to see India and its culture. Hope that they will not miss any point of interest while visiting one place to other. This book is also useful for the tourist Students.

The book is in your hands, containing all necessary informations about places of interest, how to reach there, where to stay etc. The book provides information, province and region-wise, as mentioned in contents "Tourism in India" at a Glance'. I have tried best to provide necessary information which tourists would like to have in this small book, but there are chances to slip matters of other importance. Any suggestion from readers will be welcome.

121 (MS) Timarpur
Delhi-110007

V.K. Gupta

TOURISM IN INDIA AT A GLANCE

JAMMU-KASHMIR : LEH AND LADAKH

JAMMU

According to legend, the city of Jammu was founded by Raja Jamboolochan in 9th century. In 1832, Gulab Singh merged Jammu and Kashmir into one state under the Dogra rule, which acceded to India in 1947.

This city stands on the bank of the river Tawi, surrounded by lakes, hills and ancient temples. It has a great artistic tradition.

Jammu is the winter capital of the state of Jammu and Kashmir, and gateway of the Kashmir valley.

Places of Interest

Jammu has several places of interest which may be conveniently visited in one day in the following sequence :

Bahu Fort : Distance 4 kms. Situated on a rock face on the left bank of the river Tawi, this is the oldest fort, constructed by Raja Bahulochan over 3000 years ago. There is a temple dedicated to the goddess Kali inside the fort.

Raghunath Temple : Distance 5 kms. Situated in the heart of the city, surrounded by a group of other temples. This temple is dedicated to Lord Rama. The inner walls of the main temple are covered with gold sheet on three sides.

Ranbireshwar Temple : This temple is dedicated to Lord Shiva. There are twelve Shiva temples.

Ranbir Canal : Distance 3 kms. The canal branches are off from the river Chenab at Akhnoor, 32 kms. from Jammu. It has icy cold water round the year.

Dogra Art Gallery : Situated near New Secretariat. Collection of 600 paintings. Closed on Mondays. No admission fee.

General Information

Altitude : 1000 ft. or 305 meters.

Clothing : Woollen in winter, Cotton, Silk or light tropical in summer.

How to Reach

Air Service : from Delhi to Srinagar via Amritsar, Chandigarh and Jammu. Direct Air Service is also available from New Delhi to Srinagar.

Rail Service : Jammu Mail—Daily.
Himgiri Express—Sunday, Monday, Thursday.
Super Fast—Tuesday, Saturday.
Sealdah Express—Daily.
Shalimar Express—Daily in summer.
Jhelam Express—Daily.
Madras Janata Express—Daily.
Amritsar Passenger—Daily.

Where to Stay

Public Sector Accommodation :

1. Tourist Reception Centre, Jammu.

Hotels :

Asia, Ph. 46373-75
Cosmo, Ph. 5520
Mansar
Natraj
Picnic
Mohindra
Standard
Suresh
Broadway, Ph. 43636
Jammu, Ashok
Ph. 42084, 46154
Premier Ph. 42975
Indra
Ambassador
New fort view
Amrit

Lodges :

Air line, Ph. 47099
Aroma
City Top
Darpan
Gagan
Green View Gulmohur
Jagan Lodge
Kashmir
Kiran, Ph. 42814
Mohan Lodge
Nagina Lodge, Ph. 42929
Naz Nek
Palace, Ph. 46209
Prince
Rachna
Rajesh
Tawi View, Ph. 47301
Amar
Amber Lodge, Ph. 42303
City View
Diamond
Gem
India Pride
Jandiyal, Ph. 42225
Khorana
Maharaja, Ph. 46853
Mohindra
Narulla, Ph. 5659
New Kwality
Plaza, Ph. 47488
Priya, Ph. 42508
Raj, Ph. 44630
Star
Vima, Ph. 43103

Retiring Rooms :

1. General Bus Stand
2. Circuit House, Canal Road

Transport

1. Metered Taxis are available at a number of important places in the city.
2. Mini buses, Auto Rickshaws.
3. J & K Road Transport city bus service.

Excursions

Akhnoor : 32 kms. Picnic spot on the river Chenab. Regular bus service is available.

Batote : Altitude 1560 meters. 113 kms. on the Jammu, Srinagar highway. Regular bus service. Accommodation at Tourist Bungalow. A health resort.

Kud : Altitude 1738 meters. 105.6 kms. on the Jammu-Srinagar highway. Accommodation at Tourist Bungalow.

Mansar Lake : 80 kms. Picnic spot and a sacred place for Hindus. Most of the Shiva Lingmas that automatically arose. It enjoys high reputation as a tirath. Regular bus service from Jammu. Accommodation at Pilgrim Shelters.

Patni Top : Altitude 2024 meters. 112 kms. A peaceful resort on Jammu-Srinagar national highway with all modern amenities for the tourists. Accommodation in 14 Deluxe Double Room Huts, Tourist Bungalows, Tourist Hotels.

Ramban : 148 kms. Important halting station on Jammu-Srinagar highway. Accommodation in Tourist Bungalow.

Ram Nagar : 102 kms. Buses available from Jammu and Udhampur.

Sanasar : Altitude 2079 meters. 129.2 kms. from Jammu and 19 kms. from Patnitop. Slightly away from National High Way. A place for a quite holiday. Regular bus service from Jammu. Accommodation at Tourist Huts, Tourist Bungalows.

Shudh Mahadev : Altitude 1225 meters. 120 kms. from Jammu. A holy place. A few kms. away south of Patnitop, Pilgrimage. Pilgrims visit this place on the full moon night of Sawan (July-August) and worship a Trishul Trident and a mace supposedly belonging to Bhim. Accommodation at Pilgrim Shelters.

Surinsar Lake : 42 kms. Picnic spot. Regular bus service. Shiva Khori 88 kms.

Shiva Shrine : Regular bus service upto Barak and from there on foot.

Vaishno Devi : 62 kms. A venerated Hindu shrine. Regular bus service upto Katra 48 kms. and the remaining distance has to be covered on foot or by pony. Accommodation at Tourist Bungalow at Katra, Pilgrims Hotel and dormitories, Tourist Retiring Centre. Accommodation and bedding available at Dharamshalas at the Darbar. Private accommodation available in hotels, guest houses and sarais.

SRINAGAR

Srinagar is spread on both the sides of the river Jhelum in the heart of Kashmir valley. The city gives impression of a gem nestling in the midst of lofty mountains, green meadows, rivulets and lakes. It is the summer capital of the state of Jammu and Kashmir which became part of the Indian Union in 1947.

Srinagar requires three days for complete sight seeing. Some of the important places are as under :—

Chashma Shahi : 9 kms. A testfully laid garden in terraces with a spring of cool, refreshing digestive waters. The original garden was laid out by Shah Jahan in 1632 A.D. The gardens are illuminated by night which command a magnificent view of the Dal Lake below and surround mountain ranges. Accommodation is available in 22 deluxe and 33 other huts of one, two and three bed rooms.

Dal Lake : 0.5 kms. This lovely lake lies to the east of the city at the foot of Shridhara (Zobarwan) mountain. The Shankaracharya hill is to the south and Hari Parbat, on its west. The lake is 6×3 kms. and is divided by causeways into four parts, Gagribal, Lokutdal, Boddal and Nagin. The Lokutdal and the Boddal each have an island in the centre, called Rup Lank and Sona Lank, respectively. Rup Lank is known as 'Char Chinar' as well.

Hari Parbat : 5 kms. The hill of Sharika, in the north-eastern part of Srinagar, is sacred for the Hindus. There are almond orchards around it. In spring when the blossoms are out, these orchards make a lovely sight. Permission is required to visit the fort from Director of Tourism.

Harwan : 3.5 kms. from Shalimar Bagh on the hill side south of the village remarkable remains of ancient ornamented-brick pavements of Buddhist period have come to light.

Hazratbal : 7 kms. Hazratbal shrine is situated on the western shore of the Dal Lake opposite to Nishat Bagh and commands a grand view of the lake and mountains. A sacred hair of the Prophet Mohammed is preserved here.

Jama Masjid : 5 kms. It is a typical example of Indo-Saracenic architecture.

Nishat Bagh : 11 kms. situated on the banks of the Dal Lake.

Nagin : 8 kms. The smallest but most lovely part of Dal Lake. Facilities for water skiing and swimming are available here.

Pari Mahal : 10.6 kms. situated on a spur of mountains. It is close to Chashmashahi. The road and monument are well and the place is illuminated by night.

Pather Masjid : This stone mosque is in the heart of the city, opposite to Shah Hamdan Mosque.

Shah Hamdan Mosque : Situated on the banks of the river Jhelum. This is one of the oldest Mosque in the city.

Shalimar Bagh : 15 kms. Beautiful garden of vistas and shallow terraces. It has four terraces, rising one above the other. Indian Tourism Development Corporation runs a sound and light show in this garden from May to October.

Shankaracharya Temple : 0.5 km. one thousand feet high. An early morning climb to the top offers a magnificent view of the valley and the snowy peaks of Pir Panjal range.

Transport

Deluxe sight seeing coaches are being run by the State Road Transport Corporation. For this, tourists should contact Tourist Reception Centre, Srinagar. There are about 70 private travel excursion agents, registered with the Tourism Department. Taxis are also available.

Where to Stay

Western Style Hotels :

Aziz, Ph : 77675
Brown Palace, Ph : 73856

Gulmarg, Ph : 71331

Broadway, Ph : 71211-13
The Centure Lake View
Ph : 77601 — 73175
Lake Side Resort
Ph : 78446

Madhuban, Ph : 72478
Neru's, Ph : 73641

Pamposh, Ph : 75601-2
Sabeena, Ph : 78046

Shahnshah, Ph : 73015-16

Sunshine, Ph : 71708
Zobarwan, Ph : 71441-42

Nedou's, Ph : 73015-16
Oberai Palace, Ph : 71241-46
Pari Mahal, Ph : 71235-36
Sah Abas, Ph : 77789-74158
Shangrila, Ph : 75671-72894
Tramboo, Ph : 73918
Hotel, Zamrud Ph : 75263

Other Hotels :

Angels, Ph : 78804
Bharat Hindu, Ph : 73598
Bombay Gujarat, Ph : 73596
Chinar, Ph : 73694
Dawn, Ph : 75616
Elora, Ph : 75414
Fayaz, Ph : 71512
Grand, Ph : 73242
Hill Star, Ph : 72512

Holy Night, Ph : 74608
International, Ph : 78604
Kabir, Ph : 78429
Kashmir Khalsa, Ph : 77029
Khyber
Lion Star, Ph : 71162

Malabar, Ph : 76736
Manoranjan, Ph : 78966
Mazda, Ph : 72842
Moti Mahal, Ph : 77880

Neelam, Ph : 72412

New Park, Ph : 74230 77770
New River View, Ph : 72491

Opeon, Ph : 72683
Pacific
President
Rachana, Ph : 72200
Ritz, Ph : 72498
Sailors, Ph : 73182

Ashoka, Ph : 78428
Bi-zone
Chanakya, Ph : 73879
Crown, Ph : 72763
Dreamland, Ph : 77822
Embassy, Ph : 78152
Gaylord, Ph : 74319
Hill Skit, Ph : 76615
Holiday Heaven Ph : 72282 75888
Horison, Ph : 74821
Jawahir, Ph : 78448
Kapoor
Kashmir Valley
Kohinoor
Majestic, Ph : 76519 72505
Mamta, Ph : 73388
Mayur, Ph : 78635
Metro, Ph : 77126
Naya Kashmir, Ph : 74282
New Mahalaxmi, Ph : 76286
New Rigadoon, Ph : 76313
New Shalimar, Ph : 74427 73339
Orion, Ph : 72431
Paradise, Ph : 78667
Panjab, Ph : 74163
Ragina, Ph : 72568
Shaheen, Ph : 75248
Shiraz, Ph : 75460, 73696

Surti, Ph : 72811	Surya, Ph : 78778
Taj, Ph : 73156	Tourist, Ph : 78152
Venus, Ph : 73324	Willard
York, Ph : 72218	Zero Inn, Ph : 77904

House Boats :

House Boats are available at river Jhelum, Dal Lake and Nagin Lake. There are two living rooms, two bed rooms with attached bathrooms, hot and cold running water. Shikaras are also available for sight seeing.

Guest Houses :

Apart from above, there are 74 guest houses. The names of the guest houses with phone numbers are as under :—

Alankar, Shiva Pora	Alfa Continental, Old Gagribal
Alharma, Old Gagribal	Apna Ghar, Khayam Road.
Archana, Rajbagh, Ph : 73898	Arora, Dalgate
Atlas, Nagin, Ph : 74618	Bazaz, Raj Bagh, Ph : 71228
Bengal Lodge, Dal Gate	Bhat, Zero Bridge
Bliss Lodge, Amira Kadal	Blue Star, Court Road
Bud Shah Lodge, Ph : 77070	Claridges, Kohna Khan
Continental, Magarmal Bagh	Dar, Rajbagh
Degal, Wazir Bagh	Eden, Rajbagh Ph : 78484
Elephanta, Khayam Chowk	Firdous, Rajbagh
Blamour, Naqsh Pora Ph : 712711	Green Acre, Rajbagh
Green Hill, Old Gagribal Ph : 7290	Habib, Wazir Bagh
Hampton, Iqbal Park	Hill Green, Old Gagribal
Himalaya, Sonawar : 78694	Hira Mahal, Abi Guzar
Hollywood, Alachi Bagh Ph : 77896	Holy View : Nishat
Imperial : Lal Mandi	India, Kohna Khan
Indian, Rambagh Ph : 74143/74970	Indo Kashmir, Gogi Bagh
Jabeen, Rajbagh	Jhelum View, Pandrethan Ph : 75840
Kamal Kunj, Rajbagh Ph. : 78517	Kanwal, Khayam Road
Kartar, Sonawar	Kashmir, Kohna Khan
Kashmir Pine, Wazir Bagh	Khyaban, Ex. Rajbagh
Koh-Sheen, Zero Bridge	Kotay, Bhagat Bungalow
Libra, Raj Bagh	Light Guest House, Magarmal Rd. Ph : 78835
Lords, Raj Bagh	Maharaja, Dalgate

Maole, Magarmal Bagh Ph : 76761
Meghdoot, Dalgate
Mehraj, Gupkar
M E Lodge, Zero Bridge Ph : 72505
Nagina, Naqshpora
Nagin View, Kadin Saheb Ph : 75133
National, Zero Bridge
Natraj Lodge, Maisuma
New Bombay Bishamber Nagar Ph : 71121
New Dimple, Rajbagh
New Happy House, Rajbagh
New Nagin View Bhagwanpora
New Sunshine Lodge, Hazuri Bagh
Nishat View, Rajbagh
Panorama, Rajbagh
Paradise, Magarmal Bagh : Ph : 77281
Raj Bagh, Rajbagh
Rajdoot, Miskeen Bagh
Riyaz, Bishamber Nagar
Rock Castle, Nishat
Roma, Kohna Khan
Sagina Lodge, Wazir Bagh : Ph : 74882
Sajad, Rawalpora
Sapna, Karan Nagar
Samrat, Old Gabribal Rd. Ph. : 76763
San's Lodge, Amira Kadal
Shalimar, Naqshpora
Shan, Shere Kashmir Colony Ph : 77858, 73157

Accommodation is also available in the following places :

1. Chashmashahi Hutments.
2. Budshah Hotel, Ph : 76063
3. Tourist Reception Centre, Hotel Block, Ph : 76107
4. Lall Rukh Hotel, Ph : 72378
5. Mormitory in Tourist Hotel, Ph : 77305

Excursions

After visiting local places at Srinagar, visitors can go to the other important places as mentioned below :

Achabal : Altitude 1677 meters. 58 kms. via Anant Nag. There is a fine garden in Moghul style with groves of trees, water cascades and fountains. Achabal has a camping ground. On way in Awantipur 29 kms. from Srinagar, famous for the ruins of ancient temples. Accommodation at Tourist Bungalow.

Aharbal : 51 kms. from Srinagar. This gigantic and impressive waterfall is formed by Veshav river coming down from a height of 24.4 meters. Accommodation at Tourist Bungalow, PWD Rest House is also available.

Kungwattan : A charming woodland meadow is 5 kms. ahead from Aharbal. Kounsernag Lake which generally remains frozen and carved with icebergs till late June is 11 kms. further ahead. The entire area is a trekkers paradise.

Chavari Sharif : 30 kms. on the road to Yusmarg. The ziarat or shrine of the famous patron saint of Kashmir, Sheikh Nooruddin, popularly known as Nunda Rishi.

Dachigam Wild Life Sanctuary : 21 kms. Originally a royal game preserve, this sanctuary is now protected and provides shelter to the Himalayan black bear, brown bear, musk deer and the hangul or Kashmir stag. Tourists are required to obtain special permission from the Chief Wildlife Warden.

Ganderbal : 19 kms. Situated on the bank of river Sindh. Height 5200 ft. The turfy banks and shady chinars, afford excellent camping and mooring sites. Tourist Huts are also available.

Kokarnag : Altitude 2012 meters. 70 kms. Famous for the curative properties of its springs. A botanical garden with a variety of roses. Accommodation at Tourist Bungalow and Tourist Huts.

Manasbal : 32 kms. from Srinagar on circular tour to Wullar Lake. Manasbal is a panoramic lake, laden with lotus during summer and a bird watchers paradise. Tourist Bungalow is available.

Martand : 64 kms. from Srinagar on a plateau. The most impressive ancient ruins in Kashmir.

Mattan : 61 kms. on the Pahalgam road. The spring here is an important place of pilgrimage for Hindus.

Pampore : The Karewas above and beyond Pampore are the only places in World except Spain where Saffron is grown.

Sonamarg : Altitude 2740 meters 83 kms. Sonamarg has a wild mountain beauty. A good base for trekking. Accommodation at Rest House, Tourist Huts, Tourist Bungalow.

Thajiwas : 4 kms. from Sonamarg. A small valley at the foot of the chief source of the river Jhelum. Accommodation at Tourist Bungalow.

Wullar Lake : 60 kms. The great fresh water lake, the largest in India, is an important feature of the hydrographic systems of Kashmir. Wullar Lake has a picturesque setting and is surrounded by mountains.

Yusmarg : 40 kms. A shall open valley in the hills of the Pir Panjal range. Giant pines and firs cover the mountain slopes on either side. Ponies available for trips to near-by places. Accommodation at Rest House, Tourist Huts.

Note : Pampore, Avantipur, Anantnag, Achabal, Kokarnag, Martand and Varinag all lie in a line.

PAHALGAM

This valley is very attractive, situated at the junction of the lidder and Sheshanag and deep in thick pine and fir-covered mountains. Originally it was small village of shepherds. It has grown into a hill resort. There are exhilerating treks into forests and very good fishing is available in the mountain streams.

Pahalgam is also a base for the pilgrimage to the sacred cave of Amarnath and trekking through beautiful woodlands and alpine meadows of its side valleys.

How to Reach

Pahalgam's distance is 96 kms. from Srinagar and well-connected by road.

Where to Stay

1. Tourist Huts.
2. Tourist Bungalows.
3. Dormitory.

Hotels :

Central
Hill Park 79
India
Mount View 21
Pahalgam 26
Plaza 39
Shepherds 74
Wood stock 27
Grand View 73
Hill View
Mansion 46
Natraj 25
Pine View 70, 42, 60
Raj Palace 38
Volga 46

Excursions/Treks

Amarnath : Altitude 3962 meters. 46.7 kms. (three and half days trek), The cave of Shri Amarnath is believed to be the abode of Lord Shiva. The people worship the Lingam of Lord Shiva which is formed by water-dropping through the limestone roof of the cave. Yatra, each year in the month of Sawan (July-August). The state government makes arrangements for the Yatra.

Route : Pahalgam to Chandanwadi 16 kms. Altitude 2895 meters. Pony trek as well as a Jeepable road with very steep gradients. There is Rest House and Pilgrim Shelter at Chandanwadi. Chandanwadi to Sheshnag 11.3 kms. Altitude 3574 meters, Pony trek. There is a fresh water lake. One can camp at Zojipal or a little ahead are Wawjan where there is a Rest House and Pilgrim Shelters. Sheshnag to Panchtarni 13 kms. Pony trek. Accommodation at Rest House, Pilgrim Shelter. Panchtarni to Amarnath cave 6.4 kms. Altitude 3879 meters.

Baisran : A glen in the pure and fir forests commanding a charming view of the valley, about 152 meters upon the mountain side and a couple of kms. from the Bazar.

Kolohoi Glacier : 35.6 kms. (three days trek).

Route : Pahalgam to Aru, 11 kms., Pony trek. Altitude 2408 meters. The path winds through woods to the charming meadows of Aru. There the river lidder disappears at Gurkhumb and re-appears after about 27 meters. A broad grassy mountain slope. Camp or stay at Rest House.

Aru to Lidderwatt 11 kms. pony trek. Altitude 3048 meters. A meadow in dense forests and a picturesque camping ground. Trek from here to the Sindh Valley camp or stay in the Rest House. Kolohoi glacier 13 kms. pony trek from lidderwatt upto the base of the glacier, 3200 meters.

Mamlesvara : One and a half km. down the river from the bridge, there is a small ancient stone temple of Shiva Mamlesvara.

Shikargarh : One day trek.

Sonamarg : Lidder Sindh valley. 74 kms., five days trek.

Tarsar lake : 13 kms. from lidderwatt or 35 kms. from Pahalgam via Aru, three days trek. There are delightful camping sides at Sekiwas about 2.4 kms. from lake.

Tulian lake : One day trek via Baisaran.

GULMARG

The Charming hill resort of Gulmarg was once called Gaurimarg in honour of Gauri, Lord Shiva's wife. Gulmarg offers a magnificent view of Nanga Parbat, one of the highest mountains in the world and is an excellent winter sports centre. 56 kms. from Srinagar and well approachable by road. Altitude, 2730 meters.

Where to Stay

1. Huts.

Hotels :

Gulmarg Inn	Highland Park
Kingsley	Nedous
Tourist	Woodland
Yamberzal	New Tourist Bungalow

Transport

Luxury coaches of Road Transport Corporation are available from Airport to Srinagar. Luxury coaches are also available from Tourist Reception Centre, Srinagar to Tangmarg and from Tangmarg to Gulmarg.

Taxis are also available.

Visitors can go to Gulmarg from Tangmarg by ponies.

Skiing Facilities : Skiing is an important and popular sport of the Gulmarg. Imported Ski equipment is available on hire from the shopkeepers at Gulmarg.

Excursions

Alpathar Lake : 13 kms. at the foot of the main Apharwat peak and behind the ridge separating them from Khilanmarg. The icy waters of the lake which remain frozen till the middle of June, carry floating snow.

Banibali Nag : 2926 meters. A little lake formed by landslides above the Ferozpur nallah and five hours journey from Gulmarg.

Kantar Nag : 4039 meters (three days trip). A lakelet on the top of the mountain.

Khilanmarg : 4 kms. carpeted with flowers. Khilanmarg is a 40 minute uphill journey from Gulmarg. It offers an unrivelled spectacle of the peaks and the widespreading waters of Wullar and other lakes.

Lienmarg : The path to lienmarg weaves through forests of pine and a succession of glades.

Ningal Nallah : 10 kms. This stream flows from the snow-bed and springs near Apharwat and Alpathar and cuts through picturesque pine forests.

Ziarat of Babreshi : A Muslim shrine 5 kms. from the middle gap on the east of the Gulmarg valley. The path leads down through thick forest. The ziarat or tomb is that of Baba Payam-u-Din, a Muslim saint. Both, Muslims and Hindus make offerings here.

Golf : It has an 18 hole golf course which is the highest green golf course in the world. Gulmarg is a golfers' paradise during summer.

Winter Sports : Gulmarg 2653 meters above sea-level is the only ski resort in the high Himalayas.

LADAKH

Ladakh, the land of unsurmountable mountains and fascinat ing monastaries, lies beyond the Kashmir valley, Ladakh, the abode of rare kiang and highland yak, Leh is the capital city, lies at the tri-junction of the historic 'silk route' from Sinkiang to west Asia and to the plains of India. Situated at 3500 meters in the hills of Karakoram range. 7 kms. off the banks of Indus. The famous land of the Lamas and Gumpas 434 kms. from Srinagar. It takes two days to reach from Srinagar by bus with a night halt at Kargil. Indian Air Lines also operates an air service from Srinagar to Leh and Wednesdays, Fridays and Sundays. Leh is a town of small lanes and by-lanes.

KARGIL

Places of Interest

Panikhar, Tongola, Parkochik, Shafat, Rangdim, Pensila, Abran, Tungri, Sani, Padam, Bardam, Mune, Phunkthak, Stongade, Karaska, and Zungkhul.

Where to Stay

Hotels :

High lands	Hotel d'Zojila
International	Green Land
Nun Kun	Suruview
Argali	Deluxe
Evergreen	Lylo
Marjina	New Light Hotel
Popular Chache	Sushila
Yaktil	

Other Accommodations :

1. Tourist Bungalow, Dran
2. Tourist Bungalow, Kargil
3. Tourist Bungalow, Mulbek
4. Tourist Bungalow, Panikhar
5. Tourist Bungalow, Padum Zanarkar
6. Circuit House, Kargil
7. PWD Rest House, Samoo, Rangdum and Bodh Kharbu

LEH

Leh is a town of small lanes and bylanes which is thronged by tourists for seeing the 'last shangrilla' the 'hermit kingdom'.

The Jammu and Kashmir Road Transport Corporation operates daily buses between Srinagar and Leh with a night halt at Kargil. Jeeps and Taxis are also available.

Following are the important places to be seen :—

Leh Khar Palace : The palace stands like a sentinal overlooking the town. Inside, there are old wall-paintings depicting the life of Lord Buddha.

Leh Monastery : The monastery dominates both the palace and the town. The monastery houses a solid golden statue of the Lord Buddha.

Leh Mosque : The mosque an exquisite work of Turk-Iranian architecture, stands majestically in the main Bazar.

Tsemo Gompa : One of the royal monasteries, located near the palace and is known for statue of Chamba Buddha in a sitting posture.

Where to Stay

Hotels :

Indus	King la chein	Khangari
K. Sur	Charmis	Shambala
Tsomola	Ibex	Lung se jung
Omasila	Ra-rab	Sodhan
Tibet	Choskore	Himalaya
Khardongla	Yak Tail	Barch
Delux	Dragoa	Dreamland
Hills View	Khababs	Khayal
Punchokhing		

Guest Houses :

Firdous	Kailash	Kangla
New Putelop	Samkar	Indus
Lasermo	Moonland	Sheldon
Snow View	Toldan	Zimskhang
Choskor (Achi)	Gia	Glacier
Gompa	Green View	Indus
Iqbal	Joldan	Kham Lodge
Lasermo	Loung Snow	Lingte
Malpak	Moon Land	Nazr View
Old Ladakh	Otsal	Padamkhar
Palace View	Palace View (Kidar)	Pal Rainbow
Parwana	Pyog	Sahila
Shalimar	Shelzimkhan	Shera
Skalzung	Snow View	Stream View
Taj Teri	Tak	Tamba
Two Star	Warila	Zimskhang

Other Accommodations :

Tourist Bungalow, Khaltsi
Tourist Bungalow, Leh
Tourist Bungalow, Sakli
Tourist Bungalow, Saspol

Excursions

Buses ply daily from Leh to most of the monasteries during summer. Taxis and jeeps are also available.

Alchi Gompa : 135 kms. from Leh and 5 kms. off the Saspol village. This roving monastery consists of six temples which contain a chorlen, seated Buddhas and exquisite paintings.

Choglansar : A place of full of flowers and plants which are grown fantastically at such high altitude. Polo and golf grounds offer the adventures, a rare opportunity of such sporting activities.

Hemis Gompa : 49 kms. The biggest monastery in Ladakh. On entering the valley, one sees this grand specimen of great architectural feat on a green hill. Colourful flags flutter on the four pillars in the courtyard against the background of white walls and blue sky. Every year in June, a colourful festival, marking the birthday of Guru Padam-sambhava is held here.

Lamayuru : 125 kms. on the Leh Srinagar road. This is the oldest monastery. It has fascinating caves carved out of the mountain.

Likir Gompa : A few kms. away from Alchi, ascenic road passing through rocky mountains and the river, takes you to this Gompa.

Mulbek Monastery : 190 kms. on the Leh Srinagar highway. This monastery has a huge image of Buddha carved out of rock on the side of the road.

Phiyang Gompa : 20 kms. on the Leh Srinagar road. This Gompa possesses excellent statues and tanks.

Shankar Gompa : 3 kms. The only monastery built on plain. It has a formidable collection of miniature status of pure gold and a number of wall-paintings.

Shey Palace and Monastery : 15 kms. This is the summer palace of the erstwhile rulers of Leh, surrounded by picturesque gardens. Built in 1945, the palace has the largest victory stupa, topped with pure gold. There is a spectacular double storeyed statue of Chamba or Maitreya Buddha, in a sitting posture.

Spituk Monastery : 8 kms. on the Leh Srinagar highway, built on a small hill top over looking the Indus river, is the seat of the head Lama.

Stakhana Monastery : Completely isolated, an unmetalled road stretching away from the main road, leads to stakhana monastery—one of the oldest in Ladakh.

Thiksay Monastery : 19 kms. on way to Hemis. It has twelve storeye and consists of 10 temples, 60 resident lamas, and a nunnery. The Chambers are full of statues, stupas, tankas, ancient swords and Tantric wall-paintings.

Note : For further details, visitors should contact the following tourist offices of the J & K Govt.

1. Director of Tourism, Srinagar : Ph : 72449
2. Dy. Director of Tourism, Jammu Dn. Ph : 5324
3. Tourist Office, Chandralok Building, Janpath, New Delhi : Ph : 355373
4. Tourist Office : World Trade Centre, Cuff Parade, Colaba, Bombay : Ph : 216249
5. Tourist Office : Air Lines House, Lal Darwaza, Ahmedabad : Ph : 20473
6. Tourist Office, 12, Chowranghee, Calcutta, Ph : 225790
7. Tourist Office : Lal Bahadur Stadium, Room No : 30 Hyderabad : Ph : 63276
8. Tourist Office : 2, Court Road, Amritsar : Ph : 43276

For Complaints :

Director of Tourism, Tourist Reception Centre, Srinagar.

HIMACHAL PRADESH

Himachal Pradesh is God's own country. The life of a simple hill folk is bound inextricably with a faith that is so enduring and which finds expression in various festivals celebrated round the year with a reverence of only the most devout.

SIMLA

Situated in the North-West Himalayas, Simla, the summer-capital of India during the pre-independence era, is now the capital of Himachal Pradesh. This town is spread over the ridge measuring about 12 kms. Simla is perhaps the biggest hill station of the world at its height of 2100 meters above the sea-level. A place of peace and pleasure now. At one time its base ridge had the thickest forests of the area. And resorts like Mushobra, Kufri, Naldehra, Chharabra, Fagu also grew around it.

In 1904 was built the Kalka-Simla railway, making the town easily accessible through a comfortable communication link. Simla is a tourist resort in real meaning. The Simla's best season is autumn. The air is fresh with flowers. Winter in Simla is known as the season of long moon nights. The air is incomparable.

Simla is connected with Air, Rail and Road. Nearest Airport is Chandigarh, 120 kms. away from Simla. Broad gauge railway line upto Kalka and thereafter narrow gauge line. By road connected with Delhi, Chandigarh, Kullu, Manali, Kasauli, Dharamshala, Chail, Ambala and many other towns of Punjab and Haryana.

For sight seeing local buses, taxis are available. Special tours to Kullu, Manali, Chail, Narkanda, Kasauli are organised by the H.P. Tourism Development Corporation. For details please contact: Tourist Office, The Mall, Simla : Ph : 3311 and 3956.

Where to Stay

There are so many hotels nearby Mall Simla.

Places of Interest

Jakhu Hill : 2 kms. Height 2455 meters. Simla's highest peak Offers a panoramic view of the town and the mountains. Hanuman temple, approach from ridge near Church.

Glen : 4 kms. Height 1830 meters. Most popular picnic spot. Streams flowing through dense forest. Approach near Cecil Hotel and Kennedy House.

Summerhill : 5 kms. Height 1983 meters. A picturesque suburb of Simla which offers shady walks in quiet surroundings. Situated on the Simla-Kalka railway line.

Kamana Devi : 5 kms. Height 2145 meters. A 15 minutes climb from Bailleanganj, one of the most popular picnic spots which commands a unique view of Simla, Jutogh, Summerhill, Tara Devi.

Sankat Mochan : 7 kms. Height 1875 meters : Motorable. HanumanTemple, commands an excellent view of Simla.

Tara Devi : 8 kms. Height 1851 meters. By rail and car. A temple on the hill-top.

Mushobara : 13 kms. Height 2149 meters. Motorable. Popular picnic spot which offers ideal walks amidst forests of oak and pine. Accommodation at Rest House, 3 kms. from Mushobara.

Tattapani : 51 kms. Height 655 meters. Bus Service. Popular for hot sulpher springs. Accommodation in PWD Rest House.

Kufri Bungalow : 18 kms. Height 2633 meters, Motorable. 2 kms. above Kufri. Excellent picnic spot.

Fagu : 22 kms. Height 2510 meters. Motorable. Affords an extensive view of the two opposite valleys. Accommodation, Tourist Bungalow.

Excursions

Naldehra : 22 kms. from Simla. Motorable. The well groomed nine hole golf course is perhaps one of the finest and most sportings in India. Accommodation at Tourist Bungalow and Huts.

Narkanda : 65 kms. from Simla. Motorable. Commands a unique view of the eternal snow line and the dense forest.

Chail : 45 kms. from Simla. Motorable. A tiny resort in the Shivalik region which combines the charm and beauty of a remote and peaceful mountain resort. The well-kept cricket pitch is supposed to be the highest cricket ground in the world and most scenic. Accommodation available in the Palace Hotel, Himneel and others.

Kiari Bungalow : One of the finest places on the Simla-Kalka National High way at 26 kms. from Simla.

Barog : 55 kms. from Simla. A place of scenic charm and beauty. Accommodation is available in Hotel Pine Wood and in the Rest House.

Kasauli : 77 kms. from Simla. One can see the grandeur of mountains covered with snows. Accommodation is available in Roscommon Tourist Complex.

DALHOUSIE

75 kms. from Pathankot. One of the finest hill-station in India from point of view of beauty, climate and its picturesque surroundings. Dalhousie is the summer-resort, lines on the outer slopes of Dhaula Dhar Range of Himalayas, and gate-way of Chamba. Best season, April to June and September to November.

How to Reach

Air : Nearest airport Amritsar.

Rail : Nearest railhead Pathankot. Direct rail service from Bombay, Calcutta and Delhi for Pathankot is available.

Road : Connected by road with Amritsar and Pathankot, one can go by road by car or by bus from Delhi and Chandigarh also. The distances are as under :—

from Delhi	563 kms.
from Chandigarh	252 kms.
from Amritsar	188 kms.
from Pathankot	75 kms.

Buses of H.P.S.R.T.C. and P.S.R.T.C. plying on these routes. H.P.T.D.C. Deluxe coaches also arranges conducted tours for visitors.

Where to Stay

Western Style Hotels :

Aroma-N-Claire	Crag's	Grand View
Mount View		

Indian Style Hotels :

Dalhousie Club	Green	Kohnoor
Mehra's	Metro	Spring
Glory	Lall's	Fair View

Other Accommodations :

Tourist Bungalow	Elgin Hall
PWD Rest House	Youth Hostel
Circuit House.	

Places of Interest

Dalhousie itself is a charming place. It has lovely picnic spots of Kalatop 8000 ft. Dain Kond and plains of Khajiar 6000 ft. Khajiar is 22 kms. from Dalhousie. Approachable by jeep. It has small lake in the middle with a floating island. Accommodation at PWD Rest House, Dak Bungalow and Youth Hostel surrounded by dense pine wood trees.

CHAMBA

At an altitude of 2500 ft. above sea level. 56 kms. from Dalhousie and 117 kms. from Pathankot. 14 kms. from Khajiar, jeepable road. It has number of richly carved temples and ancient ruins. Vishnu and Shiva temples are the main attractions. Chamba is famous for chappal, shawls and leather-works. Best season is April to June and September to November. Accommodation at Tourist Lodge, Circuit House, Dak-Bungalow and Youth Hostel. Reservation through Reception Officer, Tourist Bureau, Chamba.

Places of Interest

Subash Bauli : Picnic spot.

Jandri Ghat : Place of rulers of erstwhile Chamba state is located, surrounded by tall pine trees is a place of worth-visiting.

Bhuri Singh Museum : Treasurer of Chamba's cultural heritage. It has paintings of Kangra and Basoli Schools.

KULU

On the important spot of Himalayas is Kulu, known as valley of Gods, having numerous temples. Kulu valley offers a scenic charm from peaceful wooded glades and rivers through the rocks. The colourful festival of Kulu is Dussehara.

How to Reach

Air : Connected by air service with Delhi and Chandigarh. The nearest airport is Bhunter 10 kms. from Kulu.

Rail : Nearest railhead is Pathankot 270 kms. and Chandigarh 255 kms.

Road : Connected by regular bus service with Chandigarh, Simla and Pathankot.

Where to Stay

Ashok Travellers Lodge	Beas View
Central	Empire
Ramnik Guest House	Kailash
Tourist Bungalow	PWD Rest House
Alluminium Huts	Circuit House

Places of Interest

Bajura	14 kms.
Banjar	51 kms.
Bijli Mahadev	*11 kms.*
Devi Jagannath temple	*4 kms.*
Katrain	9 kms.
Kosidhar	14 kms.

MANALI

38 kms. from. Kulu. 7000 ft. above the sea-level. Famous hill station. River Beas flowing below the city. High Mountains towering above the river. The city is surrounded by pine-woods. This place is very much suitable for health resort. Fine and beautiful picnic spot. Cool in summer. It is a centre of walks, climbs and treks. At a distance of 3 kms. there are hot springs of Vasistha. The water of springs in Parvati valley is the hottest in the world and above the boiling point. Rice can be boiled within 20 minutes in it after tying in a piece of cloth. The atmosphere of this valley is calm and peace.

How to Reach

From Kulu, buses are easily available for Manali.

Where to Stay

Ashok Travellers Lodge
Tourist Cottages
New and Old Tourist Bungalow
Youth Hostel
Rest House
Log Huts
Hamta and Birchview huts
Tourist Lodge
Hotel Beas

Private Accommodation (Guest Houses)

Sunshine
New Hope
Wood Lines
Snow Lines
Johu Banon
Pine Wood
Himalayan
Bombay
May Flower
Hill Top
Green

MANDI

Mandi is an important trading centre, situated on the Pathankot-Kulu Road. It is the gateway to Kulu, Manali, Lahul and Spiti. Mandi is also on the Kulu-Simla Road via Bilaspur. Accommodation at Tourist Lodge.

JOGINDERNAGAR

57 kms. from Mandi. Terminal of Pathankot-Jogindernagar Railway. One can visit Barot, Shanon and Bassi Power Houses from here.

NAGGAR

Situated on the banks of Beas river 1000 ft. above sea-level. Excellent view of the valley and Rohtang Pass and snow covered peaks from here. Museum of art and paintings of famous painter, Nicholas Roerich is here. Naggar has some ancient temples. Accommodation at Rest Houses. Reservation through the Tourist Bureau, Naggar.

DHARAMSHALA

Situated on the other side of Chamba. Head Quarter of Kangra Distt. It is an important place and hill station 90 kms. from Pathankot. Dharamshala is in two parts i.e. Lower and Uppar Dharamshala, at a distance of 8 kms. between each other. There are several picnic spots. At a walking distance, there is a Bhagsunath Water Fall. Dal Lake is main attraction for annual function, held in September.

How to Reach

Direct bus service links Dharamshala with Pathankot, Jalandhar, Nangal, Kalka and Mandi.

Where to Stay

Hotels :

Shimla Hotel, Kotwali Bazar
Bhagsu Sun-n-Snow
B. Mehra
Dhauladhar
Rose

Other Accommodations :

Circuit House
Dak Bungalow
Civil Rest House, Kotwali Bazar
Tourist Bungalow above Kotwal Bazar
Sessions House -do-
Soldiers Rest House
Zila Parishad Rest House
Two private bungalows at upper Dharamshala

Dharamshalas :

Arya Samaj Mandir
Singh Sabha Gurdwara
Sanatan Dharam Mandir

Places of Interest and Excursions

Bhagsunath : 10 kms. picnic-spot with cold water spring and water falls.

Dal Lake : 10 kms. at an altitude of 6026 ft. beautiful lake surrounded by trees and hills.

Dharamkot : Picnic Spot.

Triund : At an altitude of 9000 ft. having snow and valley both. Accommodation at Forest Rest House.

Kareri : Situated at an altitude of 6500 ft. Beautiful picnic spot having green oaks and pines.

Chamunda Devi : Famous Chamunda Devi temple is here.

Kangra : Fort and the famous Goddess Vajreshwari Devi Temple are the worth-visiting places. 17 kms. from Dharamshala.

Jwalamukhi Temple : Most important and famous in Northern India, the Jwala Mukhi Temple is 55 kms. from Dharamshala. Big fair in April every year.

Palampur : All sides of Palampur are surrounded by gardens. 38 kms. from Dharamshala. Worth seeing place here is Nangal Khud. Accommodation at Rest House.

Baijnath : 65 kms. from Dharamshala, 16 kms. from Palampur, famous temple of Vaidyanath is located at Baijnath. Accommodation at Rest House.

Kasauli : Situated at an altitude of 6322 ft. from sea-level. 77 kms. from Kalka. Kasauli is a charming and quiet place for relaxation.

How to Reach

It is connected by road with Chandigarh, Kalka, Solan and Simla. Regular buses are available.

Where to Stay

Alasia Hotel	Kasauli Club
PWD Rest House	Dak Bungalow
Municipal Rest House	

LAHUL AND SPITI

12 kms. Beyond Manali are the Lahul and Spiti valleys which are snow field glaciers and barren mountains. Keylong is the Head quarter of Lahul and Spiti, an oasis of green fields. Accommodation at Tourist Lodge and tents provided by H.P. Tourism Development Corporation.

PUNJAB

Punjab is a land of five rivers—Jhelum, Chenab, Ravi, Beas and Satluj. It is surrounded by Himalayas in the north, Pakistan in west, Rajasthan and Delhi in south and UP in east.

CHANDIGARH

Situated at the foot of the Shivalik range. Chandigarh is a modern city divided in sectors. Each Sector is self-contained in all respects. It has a large lake with beautiful picnic-spot. Boating facilities are available here. Rose and Rock garden are worth seeing places.

How to Reach

Air : Indian Air Lines service connects Chandigarh with Deihi, Amritsar, Jammu and Srinagar. During season Kulu flight from Delhi also halts at Chandigarh.

Rail : Chandigarh is directly connected with Delhi and Amritsar by rail.

Road : Regular buses plying from all important cities to Chandigarh. The road distance between Chandigarh and the following cities is as under :—

Amritsar	230 kms.
Bombay	1753 kms.

Dehradun	230 kms.
Delhi	248 kms.
Dharamshala	250 kms.
Hardwar	264 kms.
Kulu	277 kms.
Manali	315 kms.
Nangal	102 kms.
Pathankot	267 kms.
Simla	117 kms.

Where to Stay

Oberoi Mount View	Sector 10
Aroma	Sector 22
Pankaj	Sector 22

Other Accommodations :

Govt. Sarai	Sector 23
Indira Holiday Home	Sector 24
MLA Hostel	Sector 3
Panchayat Bhavan	Sector 18
Sainik Rest House	Sector 21
YMCA	Sector 11
State Guest House	Sector 6 and 18
Eagles New Rest House	Sector 11

Dharamshala :

Sood Dharamshala :	Sector 22

Restaurant :

Kwality	Aroma	Embassy
Ladina	Anna Purna	Moti Sagar
Larks	Piccadely	India Coffee House

All are located in Sector 17 and 22

Excursions

Hindustan Machine Tools	Pinjore
Pinjore Garden	
Nangan Dam	110 kms.
Bhakra Dam	120 kms.
Anandpur Sahib	85 kms.
Rupar	45 kms.
Gurdwara Fatehgarh Sahib	50 kms.
Sirhind, Rosa Sharif	50 kms.
Chamkaur Sahib	
Mansa Devi Temple	11 kms.

AMRITSAR

It was founded by the fourth Sikh Guru Ramdas in 1579. Amritsar has religious and historical importance. Amritsar is also a commercial centre. There are several factories of different trade such as carpets, shawls, blankets, sugar and distillery. Golden Temple is the main attraction of pilgrimage not for the Sikh community but for all. Places of other interests are Jallianwala Bagh and Durgiana Temple.

How to Reach

Air : Indian Air Lines connects Amritsar with Delhi, Chandigarh, Jammu and Srinagar. Air service is also available for Kabul from Amritsar.

Rail : Amritsar is connected with Delhi, Kalka, Pathankot, Bombay, Varanasi and Calcutta.

Road : Connected with Delhi, Ferozpur, Jammu, Ambala, Chandigarh and Jalandhar.

Distances between Amritsar and other cities are as under :—

Bombay	1846 kms.
Delhi	459 kms.
Srinagar	509 kms.
Calcutta	1928 kms.
Chandigarh	230 kms.
Ambala	257 kms.

Where to Stay

Western Style Hotels :

Amritsar International : City Centre
Airlines, Cooper Road
Mrs. Bhandari's Guest House, 10, Cantonment
Astoria, Queens Road

Other Hotels :

Grand, G.T. Road	Imperial, Queens Road
Volga Queens Road	Aroma -do-
Skylark, Link Road	Ritz, 45 The Mall

Victoria Palace : near Railway Station
Prince -do-
Ashoka, Court Road

Other Accommodations :

Circuit House, Court Road
Canal Rest House, -do-
PWD Rest House, -do-
Sainik Rest House, Opp. G.P.O.
Youth Hostel : Mall Mandi

Dharamshalas :

Guru Ram Das Sarai, Opp. Golden Temple
Dhanwantkaur Dharamshala, Opp. Railway Station

There are a number of Restaurants, Dhabas and eating houses near and around Golden Temple.

PATIALA

65 kms. from Chandigarh and 60 kms. from Ambala. Its massive forts, magnificent palaces and modern buildings, gardens, create a young atmosphere. It is connected by rail and road with all the important cities of Punjab. Moti Bagh Palace and its museum are worth-visiting places. Accommodation is available in Baradari Palace Guest House and Civil Rest House.

Bhakhara Dam : Highest Dam in the world and more than three times of the height of Qutab Minar at Delhi.

Nangal Dam : Small Dam for Hydel Channels.

Govind Sagar : Covering 100 sq. kms. in the storage of water of Satluj in a vast lake, called Govind Sagar named after Guru Govind Singh. Entry pass is required for visitors. Nearest Air Port is Chandigarh and nearest railway station is Nangaldam, 11 kms. from Bhakhara Dam. It is connected with Delhi, Ambala, Patiala, Jalandhar, Pathankot and Chandigarh by road. Punjab Roadways Buses ply on this route. Accommodation is available at :
Guest House East and West, Naya Nangal, Sector 7
Satluj Sadan Rest House No 1 and 2
Tourist Bungalow, near Main Market.
Nangal Lodge.

Excursions

Gangwal Power House, 21 kms.
Kotla Power House, 30 kms.
Anandpur Sahib, 21 kms.
Naina Devi Temple

Hoshiarpur : This town is known for wooden toys and musical instruments. There is a historical temple—Thakur Dwara Ram Titwali. 65 kms. from Jalandhar by road.

Ludhiana : Important Industrial Centre of Punjab. Famous for cotton and woollen hosiery. Ludhiana is on National High way.

HARYANA

The State where you will chance upon a kaleidoscope of deep-rooted culture, fascinating traditions and delightful sensations there, are not unliked with the sophisticated ease of the 20th century.

HODAL

The Hodal complex has often been described as a landscapists delight. In this 14 acre stretch, imaginatively designed camper huts and motel wings, use of plantess for display and decoration alongwith a small lake for pedal boats have been provided. Special attractions at Hodal include Elephant and Camel rides, 14 friendly geese to watch, along with a chance to see a snake-charmer at his best. Accommodation at Dubchick 92 kms. from Delhi on the Delhi-Agra Highway in Faridabad district.

BADKHAL

The most popular tourist destination around Delhi, growing immensely popular over the years with its water spot facilities. Boating and angling facilities are already available. Badkhal is also popular for its bath complex, where swimming, sauna and massage facilities have been provided. Accommodation at Maur, 32 kms. from Delhi (5 kms. from Delhi-Agra high way) in Faridabad district.

SURAJKUND

A centre of great tourist interest. A historic amphitheatre sunpool dating back to the 10th century A.D. stands here. The pool is said to have been built by Raja Suraj Pal of the Tomar dynasty. The rocky terrain, golf, croquet, a lake for beating and angling add to its popularity. Prestigious Hotel Raj Hans stands adjacent to the old motel. Besides the air conditioned accommodation, bar and restaurant. Surajkund Raj Hans provides swimming billions, golf club and boating facilities. 8 kms. from Delhi in Faridabad district.

SOHANA

56 kms. from Delhi in Gurgaon district on Delhi-Alwar Highway, atop the Sohna Hill. In the days of yore, gold was collected from the sohna of streams around the town. Hence the name Sohna. From the hill top, Sohna commands a panoramic view of the vast green-fields and rugged country—side around. At night especially it is fascinating to gaze at the vividly lit-up villages, that have mushroomed at the foot of the hill. Dropped in green, the huge undulating lawns dotted with ornamental trees, and huts quietly watching through the veil of colourful creepers, make your eye-balls immobile. Damdama

lake, one of the biggest in Haryana is taily an angler's paradise. Accommodation at Sohna Tourist Resort. Ph : 56

DHARUHERA

70 kms. from Delhi in Mahendra Garh District on Delhi-Jaipur Road, an ideal highway resort, located in the sandy tract bordering with Rajasthan, the Jungle Babbler is a real oasis in the desert to protect you from dusty billows and harsh sun-light. Those who want to run away from the hum-drum routine, Dharuhera with its attractive landscape and surrounding greens is a beautiful breather. Accommodation at jungle bubble, Ph : 25.

SULTANPUR BIRDS SANCTUARY

46 kms. from Delhi, a little away from National High way No. 8 in Gurgaon district on Gurgaon Farakhnagar road. A find of Peter Jackson, the world famous authority on birds, here is a bird watchers' delight. The sanctuary offers more than 100 different species of migratory birds coming from Europe and Siberia. Accommodation at Guest House, Ph : 42.

PANIPAT

92 kms. from Delhi on National Highway No. 1. The three decisive batttles of Panipat, immortalised Panipat history. Though the burns of invaders' greed and the ravages of time have left little historic wealth for posterity. Panipat is not exactly berett of centres of tourist interest. Pandavas Qila, a mound yielding grey and black wares is, believed to be the oldest site of interest. Its existence has been attributed to the Mahabharata Times. The Kabuli Bagh Mosque was built in 1528 A.D. by Babur to commemorate his victory at the first battle of Panipat. Later Humayun is believed to have added a masonry platform to this structure. The Dargah of Bu Ali Shah Qalandar, a deeply venerated Sufi saint, also the tomb of Mukarrab Khan, and the famous Urdu poet Hali. The tomb of Ibrahim Khan Lodi, the last of Delhi Sultans stands in an austere enclosure. It is protected monument. One km. east of Panipat stands the Salarjung Gate. It was built by Faiz Nawab Sadak in memory of S[illegible]rjung, the Nawab of Hyderabad. The Kala Amb memorial marks the site of the black mango tree, under which Sada Shiv Rao Bhan watched his forces suffering defeat at the 3rd battle of Panipat in 1761. Accommodation at Skylark.

KURUKSHETRA

Holy land of King Kuru, the land of the epic Mahabharata

and the land where Lord Krishna gave Arjuna, the doctrine of Karma. Of the innumerable holy centres here, Sannihet Sarovar is said to be the most sacred pilgrims lake, a dip in its holy waters to pay shradh for the departed souls, and bathe here on days of eclipse to absolve themselves of sin. The Brahma Sarovar, believed to have built by king Kuru, is another holy tank. The devout gather here at the Kumbh fair, in days of eclipse and the moonless nights to pray for salvation. The Lakshmi Narain Temple stands, close by Jyotisar is the site where the Akshay Bat—the holy Banyan tree—stands.

It is said Lord Krishna gave Arjuna the immortal sermon of Karma—Bhagvad Gita—at this site. A temple marks the spot. Sthaneshwar Mahadev is the temple where the Pandavas prayed to Lord Shiva and invoked His blessings before the Mahabharata war. The waters of the tank here are said to have healing powers. The Mausoleum of Sheikh-Chilli—a Muslim saint—is a protected historical monument. Adjacent to it, lie the Harshavardhan gardens. The Kurukshetra University is a reputed seat of learnings, from where much research on the archaeological wealth of the State is carried on.

KARNA LAKE

Karna is situated in Uchana, 124 kms. from Delhi on National Highway No. 1 in Karnal district. A cluster of bottles—brush bowing in silent benediction, long stalks with colourful bracts of bouganvallia touching those placid waters. Boats waiting to serving you away out a stretch of emerald waters—that is the beauty of Karna Lake.

Karna Lake is a place where you throw off your worries in the enchanting environs, where you come face to face with peace and tranquility. Surely, this is hoe paradise. Accommodation at a motel. Ph : 2179.

PINJORE

270 kms. from Delhi and 22 kms. from Chandigarh on National Highway No. 22 in Ambala district between Kalka and Chandigarh.

Steeped in myth and legend and originally conceived by Fidai Khan, a trusted lieutenant of Aurangzeb, the Mughal gardens at Pinjore are now alive with coloured lights, running water channels and fountains. Keeping up traditions set by Fidai Khan, is a new Budgetrigar Motel. Standing parallel to the Golden Oriole restaurant, the new motel holds up a mirror to Fidai Khan's historic structures. Accommodation at Budgetrigar Motel. Ph : 455 : 559.

DELHI : NEW DELHI

Delhi, the capital of the Republic of Indian Union, possesses the most central and geographical position due to close-up situation from all important parts and cities of the country. The city is situated on the western bank of river Jamuna and the other side is protected by the ridge. Thus, it holds an unrivalled strategic location in the country. Delhi had been the capital since long of several rulers due to its central and strategic situation. All the rulers preferred it to be the capital and so also the British in 1911, decided to make Delhi the Capital instead of Calcutta which was formerly the Capital. Delhi is the most important railway centre, being the head quarter of the Northern Zone of Indian Railways and is excellently served by all other zones. Delhi enjoys the benefit of modern airport at Palam which connects it with important cities of India as well as the world. All roads go to other states through Delhi.

How to Reach

Air : Delhi is an international Airport and connects with important cities of India. Apart from Indian Airlines and Air India, regular daily air services by other countries.

Rail : Delhi is connected with all the important towns of India by rail, such as Bombay, Calcutta, Madras, Bangalore, Jammu, Hyderabad etc. All important trains pass through Delhi.

Road : Regular bus service is available from ISBT Delhi for Agra, Alwar, Amritsar, Bharatpur, Chandigarh, Jaipur, Jammu, Hardwar, Mathura, Mussoorie, Nainital, Patiala, Simla. Distances between Delhi and other cities are as under :—

Agra	203 kms.
Allahabad	603 ,,
Almora	373 ,,
Amritsar	447 ,,
Bhakhara	354 ,,
Bharatpur	190 ,,
Chandigarh	238 ,,
Jaipur	306 ,,
Khajuraho	596 ,,
Kulu	502 ,,
Mathura	147 ,,
Mussoorie	269 ,,
Nainital	318 ,,

Simla	343 kms.
Srinagar	876 ,,
Udaipur	663 ,,
Varanasi	738 ,,

Where to Stay

Hotels in New Delhi :

1. Ashoka Hotel, Chankyapuri, New Delhi, Ph. 600121, 600412
2. Hotel Air Lines, Opp : New Delhi Railway Station, Ph. 517571
3. Hotel Akbar, Chanakyapuri, New Delhi, Ph. 370252, 673251
4. Hotel Alka, 16/90, Con.Circus, New Delhi, Ph. 344328, 320778
5. Hotel Ambassador, Sujan Singh Park, New Delhi, Ph. 690391
6. Hotel Anand, 2547, Chuna Mandi, Paharganj, New Delhi, Ph. 524670
7. Hotel Asian, International, Janpath, New Delhi, Ph. 321636
8. Hotel Blue Sky, 9780, Dr. Ram Manohar Lohia Marg, Paharganj, New Delhi, Ph. 523094
9. Hotel Bright, M-85, Con.Circus, New Delhi, Ph. 350444
10. Hotel Broadway, Asaf Ali Road, New Delhi-2, Ph. 273821
11. Hotel Cleridges, 12, Aurangzeb Road, New Delhi, Ph. 370211
12. Hotel Continental, 24, Regal Bldg, New Delhi, Ph. 310011
13. Hotel Diplomat, 9, Sardar Patel Marg, New Delhi, Ph. 372003
14. Hotel Ekta, 2204, Rajguru Road, Multani Dhanda Paharganj, New Delhi, Ph. 525201
15. Hotel Gautam Deluxe, 16/2105, D.B. Gupta Road, New Delhi, Ph. 560200
16. Hotel Groves, 3/17, Asaf Ali Road, New Delhi, Ph. 271981

17. Hotel Hans (P) Ltd. 15, Bara Khamba Road, New Delhi, Ph. 46861
18. Hotel Hari Bani, 70, Mahatma Gandhi Marg, Lajpat Nagar, III, New Delhi, Ph. 525452
19. Hotel Holiday Inn, (Agar) 17, Parliament Street, New Delhi, Ph. 310318
20. Hotel Janpath, New Delhi, Ph. 350070
21. Hotel Imperial –do– Ph. 311511, 311707
22. Hotel Kabir, 4-C, Bhagwandass Marg, Ram Nagar, New Delhi, Ph. 523429
23. Hotel Lodhi, Lajpat Rai Marg, New Delhi, Ph. 619422
24. Hotel Maharja, Opp. Vishal Cinema, New Delhi, Ph. 591516
25. Hotel Marina, Con. Circus, New Delhi, Ph. 344658
26. Hotel Maurya Sheraton, Diplomat Enclave, New Delhi, Ph. 370271
27. Hotel Natraj, near Imperial Cinema, Chitra Gupta Road, New Delhi, Ph. 522699
28. Hotel Nirula, L Block, Con.Circus, New Delhi, Ph. 352419
29. Hotel Oberoi Intercontinental, Dr. Zakir Hussain Marg, New Delhi, Ph. 699571
30. Hotel President, 4/23-B, Asaf Ali Road, New Delhi, Ph. 277836
31. Hotel Qutab, Sri Aurobindo Marg, New Delhi, Ph. 660060
32. Hotel Rajdoot, Lal Bahadur Shastri Marg, New Delhi, Ph. 616404
33. Hotel Ranjit, Maharaja Ranjit Singh Marg, New Delhi, Ph. 266001
34. Hotel Satkar, Green Park, New Delhi, Ph. 644572
35. Hotel Siddhartha, 3, Rajendra Place, New Delhi, Ph. 5712501
36. Hotel Sobti, 2397, Hardhian Singh Road, Karol Bagh. New Delhi, Ph. 569035
37. Hotel Taj Mahal, 1, Man Singh Road, New Delhi, Ph. 386162

38. Hotel Tourist, Ram Nagar, New Delhi, Ph. 516581
39. Hotel Vikram, Mahatma Gandhi Marg, Lajpat Nagar, New Delhi, Ph. 625639
40. Hotel Vishal, Opp. New Delhi Railway Station, New Delhi, Ph. 527629
41. Hotel Vivek, 1541, Main Bazar, Pahar Ganj, New Delhi, Ph. 523015
42. Bawa Holiday Inn, 34, Ring Road, Lajpat Nagar IV, New Delhi.
43. Bawa Holiday Home, 21, Feroz Gandhi Road, Lajpat Nagar III, New Delhi.
44. Hotel Surya Deluxe, A/23, Vishal Enclave, Rajouri Garden, New Delhi,
45. Hotel Samrat, Chanakyapuri, New Delhi, Ph. 605186

Old Delhi :

46. Hotel Bhagirath Palace, Bhagirath Palace, Ch. Ch. Delhi, Ph. 236223
47. Hotel Eagle, Fatehpuri, Delhi, Ph. 235745
48. Hotel Flora, Dayanand Road, Daryaganj, New Delhi-2, Ph. 273634
49. Hotel Gajraj, 11/695, Bagh Dewar, Opp. Old Delhi Railway Station Delhi-6, Ph. 2510976
50. Hotel India, Opp. Old Delhi Railway Station Delhi-6, Ph. 2512706
51. Hotel Neeru (P) Ltd., 10, Subhash Marg, Daryaganj, New Delhi-2, Ph. 271357
52. Hotel New Royal, 1643, S.P. Mukerji Marg, Delhi-6, Ph. 2513233
53. Hotel Park View, Fatehpuri, Delhi-6, Ph. 2511483
54. Hotel Regal, S.P. Mukerji Marg, Delhi-6, Ph. 2526197
55. Hotel Taj, Jama Masjid, Delhi, Ph. 260773
56. Hotel Taj Mahal, 747, Church Mission Road, Delhi, Phone : 2514055
57. Hotel Vikrant, 741, Church Mission Road, Delhi, Ph. 2512216
58. Hotel De-Romana, Subhash Park, Jama Masjid, Delhi, Ph. 266031

59. Hotel Oberai Maiden's, 70, Sham Nath Marg, Delhi-54.
60. Hotel Prince, S.P. Mukerji Marg, Delhi, Ph. 2529230
61. Hotel Amrit, S.P. Mukerji Marg, Delhi, Ph. 2528370

Dharamshalas :

1. Laxmi Narain, Fatehpuri, Delhi-6
2. Marwari Dharamshala, Jogiwara, Nai Sarak, Delhi-6
3. Bissomal Dharamshala, —do—
4. Pannalal Madhav Pd. Bazar Sita Ram, Delhi-6
5. Jhabbanlal, Teliwara, Delhi-6
6. Pyarelal Dharamshala, Charkhewalan, Chawribazar, Delhi-6
7. Bholumal Dharamshala, —do—
8. Kammomal Kucha Bulaqi Begum, Esplanade Road, Delhi-6
9. Lachhumal, —do—
10. Agarwal Bhavan, Shakti Nagar, Delhi-7.
11. Ram Rup Dharamshala, Main Bazar, Subzi Mandi, Delhi-7.
12. Mammo Devi Dharamshala, Kucha Kattushah Dariba Kalan, Delhi-6
13. Beriwali Dharamshala, Kucha Patiram, Delhi-6
14. Naya Mandir, Jain Dharamshala, Dharampura, Delhi-6
15. Rohatagi Bhavan, Masjid Khajoor, Katra Khushal Rai, Delhi-6

Places of Interest

Red Fort : Situated near Chandni Chowk, Formerly Royal Palace, built by Mughal Emperor Shah Jahan in ten year's time.

Jama Masjid : Opp. Red Fort. The imposing structure of Jama Masjid was erected by the Mughal Emperor, Shah Jahan.

Jain Mandir : Known as Lal Mandir is situated just opposite Red Fort.

Gurudwara Sis Ganj : At a distance of one furlong and near fountain built in the memory of Guru Tegh Bahadur.

Shanti Vana : Situated on Mahatma Gandhi Marg, is the Samadhi of late Prime Minister Shri Jawaharlal Nehru.

Vijay Ghat : Situated near Shanti Vana, is the Samadhi of Shri Lal Bahadur Shastri, the late Prime Minister of India.

Raj Ghat : Samadhi of Father of the Nation, Mahatma Gandhi.

Jantar Mantar : Situated at Connaught Place, New Delhi. It is an astronomical observatory built by Raja Jai Singh of Jaipur.

Shri Lakshmi Narayan Temple : Situated at Mandir Marg, New Delhi. Generally known as Birla Mandir. It is a tourist attraction.

Parliament House : Situated on Parliament Street, New Delhi. Provides accommodation for Lok Sabha and Rajya Sabha.

Old Fort : Situated on Mathura Road, New Delhi, near Pragati Maidan.

India Gate : Situated on Rajpath, New Delhi. War memorial 130 ft. high. The lawns and water channels adorned with lovely fountains illuminated with coloured lights at night give a fairy land touch to the place.

Humayun Tomb : Mathura Road, New Delhi. The example of Mughal architecture of unsurpassed skill in mason's craft. Dergarh Nizam-ud-din Aulia is also worth-visiting place, just near the tomb.

Qutab Minar : 238 ft. high tower is the main attraction for tourists at Delhi.

Zoo : Situated near old fort, Mathura Road, is a treasurer of different kinds of animals and birds.

Museums

1. National Museum, Janpath, New Delhi.
2. Nehru Memorial Museum Library, Teen Murti House, New Delhi.
3. Gandhi National Museum and Library, Opp. Raj Ghat, New Delhi.
4. Dolls Museum, Nehru House, Bahadur Shah Zafar Marg Mathura Road, New Delhi.
5. Bal Bhawan and National Children's Museum, Kotla Road, New Delhi.
6. National Philatelic Museum, Dak Tar Bhawan, New Delhi.

7. Tribal Museum, New Link Road Jhande walan, New Delhi.
8. Tibet House, 16 Zorbagh, New Delhi.
9. Air force Museum, Palam.
10. Crafts Museum, Thapar House, Janpath.
11. Gandhi Smarak, Rajghat.
12. Indian War Memorial Museum, Red Fort.

Bazar

* Chandni Chowk, the Oldest Bazar of Delhi is the main trade centre of cloth, medicines, electrical goods, sanitary goods, books, famous sweet shops are there.
* Connaught Place is a well planned market of New Delhi.
* Karol Bagh has also become a main Shopping Centre after independence.
* Sadar Bazar is the whole sale Trade Centre of General merchantise goods, plastic goods, hosiery etc.

UTTAR PRADESH

Uttar Pradesh has always been the religious and cultural heart-land of India. This religious sect set its feet firmly on Indian soil. The rich and varied land of Uttar Pradesh has plenty of places related with the birth places of Lord Rama, Lord Krishna and Jain Tirthankars.

AYODHYA

This holy city, one of the most ancient cities of India, is situated on the banks of river Saryu. It is only 1.6 km. from Ayodhya railway station and 8 kms., from Faizabad, Distt. H.Q. It is most important city for Hindu and Ja in Pilgrims. It is the birth place of Lord Rama and the capital of his kingdom. It is also held in great esteem by Jain pilgrims. Out of the 14 Kulkars or munis, seven were born here.

How to Reach

Air : Nearest Air Port Lucknow.

Rail : On the Lucknow Mughal Sarai Route.

Road : Well connected by Road with all the major cities.

Where to Stay

1. U.P. Tourist Bungalow. Station Road Phone. 36
2. Railway Retiring Room.
3. Dharamshala.
   1. Birla Dharamshala Ph. 41
   2. Kanak Bhawan Ph. 24
   3. Chhamalal Ph. 24
   4. Manas Trust
   5. Jain Dharamshala Ph. 24
   6. Janki Mahal Trust Ph. 32

Places of Interest

1. Gulab Bari
2. Guptar Ghat
3. Maqbara Ramshi
4. Kichhonchha
5. Bharat Kund
6. Janam Bhumi
7. Hanuman Garhi
8. Kanak Bhawan
9. Nageshwar Nath Temple
10. Mani Parbat
11. Tulsi Chowk
12. Kaleramaji Temple
13. Amawa Temple
14. Jain Temple
15. Gurdwara Brahma Kund
16. Tulsi Garden
17. Naya Ghat etc.

VARANASI

A crescendo of temples rises from the waters edge, the air is filled with the soothing chant of saffron cled priests. Everywhere there is the unceasing stream of pilgrims in search of propriety in this life, Nirwana in the next. This is Varanasi, the city which enshrines the very essence of Hinduism.

As the sacred river Ganga flows down the snow clad Himalayas into the vast plains, half way between Delhi and Culcutta is curves into a gentle crescent. And along this crescent lies Varanasi. Said to be the first created spot on earth, and according to legend, in existance for over thousand of years.

Beyond the Ghats and the temples lie Varanasi's colourful narrow lanes throbbing with a rhythm of their ocon, spilling over with exquisite silk brocades, the products of generations of skilled weavers.

How to Reach

Indian Airlines flies to Babatpur airport which is 22 kms. from Varanasi and 40 kms. from Sarnath. Direct flights from Agra, Delhi, Calcutta, Khajuraho and Kathmandu well connected by Train and Bus services.

Where to Stay

Varanasi has a range of comfortable hotels including the Taj and Ashoka Group's Hotel, Varanasi Ashoka. Also a tourist Bangalow. There are a number of Dharamshalas.

Places of Interest

A moving spectacle both at sunrise and at sunset. The rounded umbrellas of the priests break up the serried lines of the steps leading down to the water's edge. At down, pilgrims, waist deep in water, offer salutations to the sun before taking the cleansing dip. At dark, lighted oil lamps and flowers brighten the water's surface as there are set aflot.

Manmandir Observatory : An interesting astronomical structure near Dashashwamedha Ghat built by Maharaja Sawai Jai Singh II in 1693. The instruments are made of brick and some are corsed with plaster. Fascinating yantra symbols may be seen. Well built on a north-south axis, is the Samrat Yantra, a triangular quomon where upper lines stop upwards the polar star and chakra yantra.

Alamgir Mosque : 6 kms. originally Beni Madhav ka Dharahara, 17th century Hindu structure, built by Scindia, it was destroyed by emperor Aurangzeb. The Mosque that he raised in its place is an unusual mixture of Hindu and Muslim architecture. The lower portions and the enclosure walls are of entirely Hindu design and the mosque, Islamic.

Kashi Vishwanath Temple or Golden Temple : 3 8 kms. A golden spiralled temple rebuilt in the 18th century. Dedicated to Lord Shiva, the presiding deity of Varanasi. The shikhar (or spire) was covered with a tonne of gold plating by Maharaja Ranjit Singh in 1835.

Gynavapi Mosque : 3.8 kms. built by Aurangzeb on the site of the Vishweshwara Temple in the 17th century on the foundation and the rear of the mosque can still be seen specimens of ancient Hindu Temple sculpture.

Bharat Mata Temple : 1.7 kms. this is a temple dedicated to 'Mother India' which instead of any customary goddess houses a relief camp of India carved in marble. The temple was inaugurated by Mahatma Gandhi.

Durga Temple : 6 kms. built in the north Indian Nagar style, this temple is dedicated to the Goddess Durga, the consort of Lord Shiva. The 18th century shrine has unique composition of small spires covering at the summit.

Tulsi Manas Temple : 6 kms. this temple has the whole of Ramayana engraved on the walls alongwith murals depicting the life of Lord Rama, an incarnation of Lord Vishnu.

Banaras Hindu University : 9 kms. this great seat of oriental learning was founded by Pandit Madan Mohan Malviya. It is among the longest residential universities in Asia with an area of about 2000 acres. Located on campus is the near Vishwanath Temple, a splendid Shiva shrine in marble. Also the Bharat Kala Bhawan which has an excellent collection of Indian painting, sculpture and terracotta figurines.

Excursions

Ramnagar Fort : 17.5 kms. Residential place of the former Maharaja of Varanasi on the other bank of Ganga. The Darbar Hall and the Royal Museum display a unique collection of palanquins, furniture, arms, weapons, and costumes.

Sarnath : 11 kms. More than 2500 years ago, after years of severe penance and deep meditation, Gautama Siddhartha attained enlightenment and became the Buddha. It was at the Deer Park at Sarnath that he delivered his first sermon. Sarnath went on to attain fame as the cradle of Buddhism. Two hundred years later, Emperor Ashoka erected several stupas here. Much of the glory of this city has been marred by wake of conquerors but enough still remains to make a visit to Sarnath a sacred experience.

One of the great monument, the Dhamekh Stupa is said to mark the spot where Lord Buddha set the wheel of Law in motion. Dharamrajika, another Stupa, is now in ruins, dismental by king Jagat Singh of Varanasi, in the 18th century, for the building material. Excavations around the main shrine have innumerable remains of stupas, shrines and monasteries built by devotees.

The Archaeological Museums at Sarnath : Displays many *Buddhist Sculptures. The statue of* the Buddha setting the wheel of law in motion and the lion capital of the

Ashoka Pillar are housed here symbolising the ideals of peace and righteousness, the lion capital is today the national emblem of India.

Mula Gandha Kuti Vihara : It was built in 1931 by the Mahabodhi Society. Here are enshrined sacred Buddhist relics discovered at other sites of sub-continent. Frescoes depicting scenes from the life of the Buddha are the work of the renowned Japanese artist Kosetsk Nosu. Other monuments of interest here include the Chaukhandi Stupa, the Chinese Temple, the Jain Temple and the Tibetan Temple.

Chandravati, a famous Jain religious place is 30 kms. from Varanasi. Rajdari-Deodari falls and the Chandraprabha wild life sanctuary (70 kms.) are other charming excursions from Varanasi.

JAUNPUR

It is 58 kms. on the banks of river Gomati, the city was founded in the mid 14th century, as the capital of the Sharqui kingdom. Jaunpur was once a rich and powerful state and the Sharqui kings were great builders. The whole region is dotted with Mosques and fortresses built in the Afghan style of architecture distinguished for its lofty fontal arch. Using material from Hindu Shrines, these monuments present a unique juxtaposition of the Islamic and Hindu schools of architecture. Jaunpur is also well known for its perfumes and incense.

Jaunpur fort is one of the earliest medieval forts of northern India. Though longly destroyed, the huge ornamented gateway built by Akbar is an impressive sight. Atala Masjid is the oldest mosque of the area. Built in 1408, on the site of an old Hindu Temple, the inner sanctum is notable for its filigree stone screen work. Jhanjhari mosque belongs to the early 15th century of the original mosque, only the decorated main arch remains today.

Also to be seen are the Fort Mosque, the Khalis Mukhlis Mosque, the Jami Mosque, the Lal Darwaja Mosque, the bridge across the Gomti, the Sheikh Bashas Mosque and the Shifla Temple.

MIRZAPUR

It is 89 kms. from Allahabad and 74 kms. from Varanasi via Mughalsarai. Famous for its hand knotted carpets, this district has a most picturesque river front studded with Ghats, richly carved temples, impressing forts and thick forests. Mirzapur is developing as a great industrial centre. Many major power projects and factories are located in this region.

Chunar Fort : 47 kms. on the bank of the river Ganga, this historic fort commands the highway to Bengal. During the 16th century it was the scene of many fierce battles between the Pathans and the Mughals. It was here that the Afghan ruler Sher Shah Suri defeated the Mughal Emperor Humayun. Each successive conquerer, further expanded the Fort. Akbar built the western gate. Aurangzeb added the Alamgir Mosque. The British used it as a prison for royal rebels.

Vindhya Devi Temple, Ashtabhuja Devi Temple, Sakteshgarh Fort, Vijaigarh Fort, Aghori Fort, Sidhnath ki Dari Sirsi, Lalkhawa, Ahraura Fort are other places of interest. Tanda Falls, Jargodam, Rihand Dam, Wyndham Falls are picnic spots and excursions.

Taxis and Buses are available from Varanasi.

AGRA

According to an ancient legend, the name of Agra is derived from Agra Vans, of the twelve groves of Brijmandala, where teenager Lord Krishna is said to have sported with his companions. Situated on the banks of Yamuna, this town was chosen by the Emperor Babar as a base for the Mughals. Most of his early descendents preferred to stay on, and for a century and a quarter, Agra was the new centre for an empire which matched the brilliance and power of its contemporaries, the ottamans of Turkey and the Suffaries of Iran. The Mughal court and capital outdazzled its European Contemporaries too.

Today, imposing tombs and deserted fortress cities underline the morality of man and the immortality of his art and aesthetic vision.

Akbar was the empire builder and statesman par-excellence. The robustness of his mind and spirit was bound to be translated into stone.

How to Reach

Connected with major Tourist Centres with air, rail and bus services. Buses, taxis, scooters, tongas and rikshaws are available for local sight seeing U.P.S.T.D.C. also provides air conditioned taxis.

Where to Stay

Stay at U.P.S.T.D.C. Tourist Bungalow. Western Indian style Hotels and Dharamshalas are available.

Places of Interest : Agra Fort

3 kms. History has been in change face. No mere place for

refuge and protection. Akbar built his vigour into his buildings, like the Jahangir Mahal with its courtyards, ornamental brackets and columns. The impregnable ranports of the Agra fort, an engineering feet in themselves, express ilascent empire's determination to survive little else that Akbar built survives today. Shah Jahan, his grandson, who continued using the forr gave it his distinctive touch. Exquisite and delicate marble structure, replace the red sandstone ones. The British rules, always in drive of their predecessors, the Mughals, home left their mask too in the shape of army barracks and graves for fallen heroes.

Itmad-Ud-Daulah's Tomb : 6.2 kms, the Tomb of Itmad-Ud-Daulah an important courtier and father of Nur Jahan, Jahangir's queen. Newer possibilities of marble are being discovered here. The predictability and rigidity of geometric designs are replaced by the fluidity and lyricisn of floral patterns.

Taj Mahal : Monument to the lone between the beautiful queen Mumtaz and the Mughal emperor Shah Jahan, its builders.

The Taj by full moon is worth-changing any intinery for.

Sikandra : 10 kms. Move alongwith history and stop at the crossroads the reign of Jahangir. Akbar has begun his own tomb at Sikandra and his son Jahangir completed it. Jahangir is given little credit for his architectural contributions. But the seeds that flowered in Shah Jahan's reign had began to germinate during the life time of his father. Marble had begun to be used not just as a building material as in the last two storeys of Sikandra but its potential as a decorative element was discovered. It was effectively used for inlay as in the Sikandra Gateway.

Fatehpur Sikri : 37 kms. West of Agra, stands Akbar's ceremonial capital—Fatehpur Sikri. The rambling remain today stress the magnitude and range of resources, both artistic and material, that Akbar had at his command. Artisans and styles were imported from the provinces. Innovations and imaginative experimentation had a field day. There are mural paintings in the houses of Mariam-uz-Zamani. Examples of abundant carvings decorate the quarters of his Turkish consort. Richly ornamented pillars, brackets, balconies and niches mark other buildings in this complex. But the representation of various architectural styles leads to no tension. For biding this city into one unifying theme is Akbar's aesthetic concept. Red sandstone, easily and locally querried, is used uniformally. And as is the Indo-Saracenic style of building with its use of pillars, beams and brackets.

MATHURA-VRINDABAN

It is 54 kms. not far from Agra is Mathura, the setting for a different sort of legend. The birth place of Lord Krishna, it has for centuries attracted the devotees and the curious people.

Mathura, linked in the people's mind with the frolics and antics of a naughty, butter stealing flirtations and loveable god, the perfect place for mythologies to grow colourful and alive. Festivals like Diwali, Holi and Janamashtami, the birth of Lord Krishna are celebrated with gusto. Through the ages, the pious and the rich have built temples here, giving Mathura the quality of a living folk museum.

Vrindaban : 63 kms. especially sacred, has temples dating 17th to 18th century like those of Govind Dev and Radha Vallabha, Rangji and Shahji.

There are other temples in Mathura, the Dwarkadhish and Gita. The Vishram Ghat, where Lord Krishna rested after killing the tyrant king Kansa, is a famous bathing place.

The Mathura museum is worth-visit for its houses, a fascinating collection of sculpture from a far back as the 5th century B.C. Mathura nurtured a major school of art named after it, using locally querried material, a school of free standing sculpture developed which produced the first images of Lord Buddha. Mathura had acquired the status of a rival capital under king Kanishka who started his own era beginning A D. 78. The Manryan Sunga, Kushana and Gupta period sculptures are well represented. All around Mathura are places, associated with Lord Krishna. Gokul 9 kms. from Mathura where Lord Krishna spent his childhood. Goverdhan 25 kms. where he placated the rain god Indra. Nand Gaon56 kms. his fathers' town, where a 12th century temple survives.

And it has had enough of history, there is the teeming keoladio Bird sanctuary at Bharatpur 54 kms. from Agra. Every year the Siberian Geese alongwith other birds from north Asia and the USSR come to Bharatpur.

LUCKNOW

Lucknow formed a part of the ancient kingdom of Kosal and there is a tradition that the town was named Lakshamanvati or Lakshamanpur.

A cosmopolitan city now and the capital of Uttar Pradesh, this city of gardens, once famous as a city of Nawabs, still breaths on oriental atmosphere, reminiscent of Mughal glory, The hub of modern part of the city is Hazratganj the most fashionable shopping centre. This city has many historical and palatical buildings, monuments and beautiful parks. It has been and continues to be a city of easy pace, refined taste, and carries a tradition of sophisticated courtesy and etiquette, which never fails to impress visitors and makes a testing mark on them.

How to Reach

Air : Indian Air Lines connected with Delhi, Patna and Calcutta.

Rail : Lucknow is on the main route of the Northern and North-Eastern Railways.

Road: Lucknow is connected by road with all the major cities of the country.

Where to Stay

Western Style Hotels :

1. Clarks Avadh, 8, M.G. Marg, Hazratganj Ph. 40131-7, 49669
2. Carlton, Shahnajaf Rd. Ph : 44021-5
3. Capoors Hotel, Hazrat Ganj Ph : 43958

Other Hotels :

1. Ellora, 3, Lal Bagh Ph : 31307
2. Awadh Lodge, Tilot House, 1, Ram Mohan Rai Marg Ph : 43821
3. Madan Hotel, Charbagh Ph : 57682
4. Gulmarg, Amin-Ud-Daula Park Ph : 31227 29
5. Deep Hotel, Hussainganj Crossing Ph : 32537-49207
6. Bengali Hotel, Charbagh, Ph : 50892.
7. Hotel Tourist, B.N. Road, near Jai Hind Cinema Ph : 45313
8. Central Hotel, Aminabad Jhandewala Park. Ph : 42525
9. Yatri Hotel, Vijai Nagar, Ph : 49803
10. Hotel Vaishali, Sri Ram Road Aminabad Ph : 44382
11. Hotel Raj, Hussainganj, Ph : 44232
12. Hotel Charan International, 16 Vidhan Sabha Marg, Ph : 32516
13. Darpan Hotel, 19, Hewett Road Ph : 44216
14. Kaushala Hotel, Aminabad Ph : 43241

15. Kohinoor Hotel, Ph : 32846
16. Vishnu Gopal Hotel, 19 Hewett Road Ph : 40670
17. Hotel Apsara, Latouche Road Ph :

Other Accommodation

1. Railway Retiring Room, Northern Rly. Charbagh
2. -do- North-Eastern Railways
3. Hotel Gomti, U.P.S.T.D.C. 6, Sapru Marg, Ph : 32257
4. Y.M.C.A.R.P. Marg, Ph : 47227

Dharamshalas :

1. Sital Dharamshala, Naka Hindola.
2. Chhedi Lal Dharamshala, Aminabad.
3. Lala Bhola Nath Dharmshala, Chowk.
4. Ganga Rd. Dharamshala, Chowk.
5. Vinayak Dharamshala, Naka Hindola.

Places of Interest

1. *Shah Najaf Imam Bara* : 200 meters : Shah Najaf or Najaf-e-Asharaf derives its name from Najaf, a city in Iraq where Tomb of Hazrat Ali is built. In this mausolium are buried the remains of Ghazi-ud-Din Haider and his wives including Mubarak Mahal who was a stronghold of independence fighters.
2. *Bara Imam Bara* : 5 kms. Great or Asafi Imam Bara was built by Nawab Asaf-ud-Daula in 1784 and ranks among the greatest architectural achievements of the Muslim period. Exepting the galleries in the interior, there is no wood work any where. The interior vaulted hall measuring 162 ft. long, 53 ft. broad and 50 ft. high, is said to be one of the largest apartments of its kind.
3. *Roomi Darwaza* : 5 kms. Roomi Darwaza or Turkish Gate is said to be fascimile of one of the gates of constantinopoli. It can stand comparison with any similar structure in point of beauty and splendour. This colossal gateway is situated close to the great or Asafi Imambara and was built in 1784 as a relief work during the terrible famine of 1783.
4. *Hussainabad Imambara* : 6 kms. beyond the Roomi Darwaza to the west, Hussainabad or the Chhota Imambara was built and endowed by Muhammed Ali Shah as a burial place for himself. Inside the gate there is a large courtyard where a rectangular raised

tank occupies much of the central space and is spanned by a small bridge on either side of the courtyard is a small imitation of the Taj Mahal. In one of them lies buried Zinat Asuja, the daughter of Muhammed Ali Shah and in the other are preserved the remains of her husband. The main building of the Imambara is a domed structure with numerous turrets and minarates. The walls of the mausolium are decorated with verses in Arabic.

5. *Jama Masjid* : 6 kms. The great mosque. Jama Masjid, lying to the west of Hussainabad Imambara also owes its origin to king Muhammed Ali Shah who started its construction but could not live to see it completed. It was completed by Malika Jahan Begum. It is an enormous of considerable grandeur.
6. *Clock Tower* : 5 kms : close to the Hussainabad tanks, stands the clock tower which was begun in 1880 and completed in 1887 at a cost of Rs. 1,17,000 from the funds of the Hussainabad Trust. It is 221 feet in height and 200 feet square at the base. It is equipped with one of the largest clocks.
7. *The Picture Galary* : 5 kms. facing the Hussainabad is a Baradari, also built by king Muhammed Ali Shah. It has been subsequently repaired and improved and is now used as a picture galary for the portraits of the rulers of Avadh.
8. *Lakshman Tila* : 5 kms : it is believed that this was given to Lakshman, brother of Lord Rama, as Jagir and a small habit developed at this spot, which was known as Lakshman Tila and the adjoining area as Lakshmanpur. Much later after the advent of Muslim rule, this Tila was occupied by Shahpir Muhammed and it was then known as 'Pir Muhammad Ka Tila'. Aurangzeb constructed a mosque at the place known as Tila Pir Muhammad, which still stands today.
9. *Residency* : 3 kms. Residency was built for the British Resident in 1780 1800. Originally it was a very extensive and beautiful building, but it received heavy, shelling when in and around the Residency some of the fiercest battles of 1857 uprising were fought. It is now in a dilapidated state, and the marks of cannon-shots can be seen on every wall still standing.

The main house stands on the top of mound overlooking the River with wide Varandahs a guard tower, and numerous underground rooms. All around are well maintained terraced lawns and gardens.

10. *Nadan Mahal* : 3 kms. Abdur Rehman was exalted as Jagirdar of Avadh with capital at Lucknow during the reign of Akbar. Abdur Rehman is buried in Nandan Mahal Maqbara, which is one of the oldest building in the city.
11. *Martyrs Memorial* : 3 kms. opposite the Residency on the bank of Gomti is a Martyrs Memorial, constructed to commemorate the memory of the Martyrs of India's struggle for freedom. The Memorial was opened on 15th August, 1957. It is a high conical structure made of marble.
12. *National Botanical Research Institute* : 1/2 km. this institute is housed in the old Sikandar Bagh, which derived its name from one of the Begums of Wajid Ali Shah, Sikandar Mahal.

    In 1857, Sikandar Bagh was also one of the centres of fierce fighting. The garden has now been taken over by the Government of India and houses the National Botanical Research Institute.
13. *Zoo* : 1 km. the Zoological Garden of Lucknow, situated in the Banarasi Bagh was founded in 1921 as a memorial to the visit of the Prince of Wales. The serpentarium containing a great variety of snakes, the aquarium, the children's park fitted with latest equipments for children, the elephant joy ride, and children train are some of the attractions of the Zoo.

SRAVASTI

Capital of a kingdom in the hoary past is located at a distance of 40 kms. from Bahraich on the North-Eastern Railways. Itsmodern name is Saheth Maheth. It is bifurcated by a motorable road, one side being Saheth and the other Maheth. Both sides contain the ruins and relics of Jain and Buddhist temples, forts and stupas. Bhagwan Mahavira during His *Tapas* period and later as Tirthankar visited Sravasti many times.

How to Reach

Air : Nearest Air Port—Lucknow/Gorakhpur.

Rail/Road : 21 kms. from Balrampur railway station. Bus service is easily available.

Where to Stay

1. PWD Inspection House, Distt. Behraich.
2. Burmese Temple Rest House, Saheth Maheth.
3. Chinese Temple Rest House, Saheth Maheth.

4. Jain Dharamshalas.
5. Maya Hotel.
6. Raj Guest House, Balrampur.
7. Burmese Dharamshala, Balrampur.
8. P.W.D. Inspection House, Balrampur.

KAUSHAMBI

It is 50 kms. from, Allahabad, accessible by cars and buses, Thereafter tongas carry the pilgrims to the destination. It was the seat of an ancient kingdom with Maharaja Udayan, famous for his beloved Vasavadatta, who were great devotees of Lord Mahavira. The Lord undertook a fast for 5 months and 24 days and broke it at the hands of a handcuffed slave girl named Chandana who offered him half cooked brans of urd pulse, her food for the day. Chandana, on her release from bondage joined the order as a nun and followed him.

How to Reach

Air : Air port Allahabad.

Rail : Nearest Railway Station—Allahabad.

Road : Regular bus service from Allahabad. Taxis are also available.

Where to Stay

1. Tourist Bungalow 35, M.G. Marg Allahabad Ph. 53640
2. P.W.D. Inspection House, Kaushambi.

Places of Interest

1. Ghasitarama Monastery, The Stupa Palace.
2. Fortifications.

KAMPIL

Kampilya called Kampil today, is a village in tehsil Kasganj of Furrukhabad Distt., situated near the banks of the Ganga. In the ancient times, it was the seat of an emperor. During the epic period, it was the capital of king Drupad, the father of the renowned queen Draupadi, married to the five Pandava brothers of Mahabharata fame. It was the birth place of the 13th Tirthankar-Brahlanchhan Vimal Nath. It was graced by the visit of Lord Mahaviar. The neighbouring ruins and mounds contain the relics and sculptures of Jain civilisation. Every year a *Jain mela* is held for five days in the month of March.

How to Reach

1. *Air* : Nearest Air Port Kanpur 180 kms.
2. *Rail* : Nearest Railway Station, Kaimganj 10 kms.
3. *Road* : Well connected by Road with major cities.

Where to Stay

1. P.W.D. Inspection House.
2. Sri Vimal Nath Shwetambar Jain Dharamshala.

PRAYAG

Prayag or Allahabad is situated on the banks of Triveni—the confluence of Ganga. Jamuna and the invisible Saraswati. It is considered as one of the holiest pilgrimage, by Jains and Hindus. Pabhosa or Prabhashgir in Allahabad Distt. is only 4 kms. away from Kaushambi. It is regarded as one of the most sacred pilgrim centre of Jainism. On the hill of Pabhosa, was born 6th Tirthankar named Padam Prabhu who performed *Tapas* and attained enlightenment.

How to Reach

Air : Allahabad.

Rail : Well connected with all major cities of India.

Road : Allahabad is connected by good roads with Agra, Calcutta, Delhi, Kanpur, Lucknow, Khajuraho, Lumbini and Varanasi.

Where to Stay

U.P. Tourist Bungalow, 35 M.G. Marg, Allahabad.

Hotels :

1. Barnet Hotel
2. Royal Hotel.
3. Finard Hotel.
4. Yatrik Hotel.
5. Ashok Hotel.
6. Mansarovar Hotel.

Other Accommodation :

7. Y.M.C.A.
8. P.W.D. Inspection House.
9. Circuit House.
10. Railway Retiring Room.
11. Dharamshala.

Excursions

1. Ayodhya
2. Bhita
3. Chitrakoot
4. Garhwa
5. Kaushambi
6. Macpherson Lake
7. Sheo Kuti.

SANKISA

30 kms. from Kampil in Farukhabad Distt., Sankisa was an ancient cultural centre of Jainism. Remains of very old velies sculptures and idols of Jains have been excavated. It is held in great reverence due to the *Tapas* and further enlightenment of Vimal Nath, the 13th Tirthankar.

How to Reach

Air : Agra or Delhi.

Rail/Road: 11.3 kms. from Parkhava Railway Station by Rd.

Where to Stay

P.W.D. Inspection House, Fateh Garh.
Distt. Farruhhabad Ph. 75852.

Ahichhatra : In Bareilly District, near the town of Ram Nagar this place was 'Tapobhumi' of 23rd Tirthankar, Parshva Nath. While in deep meditation, He was attacked by notorious demon Shambhar. The cobra king Ahi provided an umbrella (Chhatra) by his hood and he attained enlightenment. It is a very holy pilgrimage of Jains.

Paras Nath Kila : 5 kms. from small township of Burhanpur, in Tehsil Nagina, Distt. Bijnor, on the ruins of an ancient Jain city called Parasnath Kila.

BUNDELKHAND

JHANSI

Jhansi is the principal town in Bundelkhand region which revive memories of heroic young Rani Lakshmi Bai who fought battle against Britishers in 1857. The walled city was founded by Raja Bir Singh Deo who built its fort on a rocky hill in 1613 A.D. Around Jhansi is studded with the remains of numerous Vaishnava, Shiva and Jain Temples, a few of which date as far back as Gupta Times, some belongs to the post-Gupta period and a large number of Chandela times. The most outstanding of the Gupta period temple is the Vishnu Temple of Deogarh which was built of large blocks of dressed stone, red in colour. The monuments belonging to the post-Gupta period are some rock sculptures including the Saptamatrik, the ruined temple of Varaha and the great Jain Temple which the most important structure of that period and lies, with some thirty other Jain shrines, inside the precincts of what was the fort of Deograh. Some of the pillars and columns in or near *these temples are of exquisite workmanship the most important* temples built during the times of Chandellas are at Deogarh,

Chandpur, Dudhai, Madanpur, Bar, Banpur, Siron, Budhni, Barwasagar, Sarkar, Pachwara, Khisni Khurd and Bangawan. Medieval Muslim structures are but a few in the district such as the Bansa (of the times of Feroz Shah Tughlak) at Lalitpur, the mosque in the ruined fort at Erich and Dargah (Tomb) near the lake at Talbehat. Bundela buildings include the palace and temple at Banpur and the temple at Vijaipur.

How to Reach

Air : Nearest Airport is Gwalior 98 kms.
Rail : Junction Station on Bombay-Delhi route.
Road: Situated on National Highway Nos. 25 & 26.

Where to Stay

Western Style Hotel :

1. Jhansi Hotel, Civil Lines Ph : 1360

Indian Style Hotels :

2. Ashok Hotel, Civil Lines Ph : 761
3. Prakash Hotel, -do- Ph : 964
4. Sipri Hotel, Sipri Market
5. Shiljeet Hotel, -do-

Other Accommodation :

1. Shri Ram Lodge, near Khandere Gate
2. Railway Retiring Room
3. PWD Inspection Bungalow
4. Circuit House, Ph : 527

Dharamshalas :

1. Narayan Dharamshala, Jhokan Bagh
2. Gopal Dharamshala, near Subzi Mandi
3. Baldeo Dharamshala, Civil Lines, Station Road.
4. Amba Wali Dharamshala, Rani Mahal
5. Sindhi Dharamshala, -do-

Places of Interest

Rani Mahal : Residence of Rani Laxmi Bai at present museum.

Jhansi Fort : Belongs to Rani Laxmi Bai.

Gardens : Govt. Garden, Narain Bagh, Rani Laxmi Bai Park.

Other Places : Raghunathji ka Mandir, Manik Chowk, Murli Manohar Mandir, Subzi Mandi, Kali Temple, Bhoot Nath Temple, Laxmi Mandir,

Hanuman ji ka Mandir, Chetar Toria, Idgah, Bisat Khana, Mosque, Gurdwara, St. Marks Church, Isagarh Church, St. Francis Church.

Jhansi is connected with the following cities :

1. Delhi 416 kms.	Bombay 1128 kms.
2. Calcutta 1236 kms.	Madras 2169 kms.
3. Khajuraho 178 kms.	Lucknow 340 kms.

Babina : A flourishing town on Jhansi-Sagar National Highway about 22 kms. south of Jhansi, from where at a distance of 11 kms. lies Dukhwadam on the Betawa. This side is bordered with jungle-clad hills and the reservoir form a charming piece of water. Accommodation at Inspection House near Dam.

Barwa Sagar : A small town 24 kms. on the road going from Jhansi to Mauranipur. Bus and railway service are available. A fine old fort is situated here on an eminence and commands an excellent view of the large lake and surrounding land-scape. About 5 kms. west of town there is an old maind crowned with a tower which contains an image of Shiva and Parbati.

Chandpur : Situated adjacent to the road which goes from Jakhlanu to Dhaura via Bant, half way between Dudhai and Deogarh, being 11.3 kms. to the north-west of the former and upwards 9.6 kms. to the east to the latter. The place is very rich in archaeological remains which are of Chandella and Jain origin comprises five groups ruined temples and many pieces of sculpture, some of exquisite craftsmanship. At a short distance lies another group of ruined Hindu Temples mostly dedicated to Lord Vishnu, one having an undated inscription the character of which appears to belong to the 12th century.

Erich : A small town on the right bank of the Betwa about 70 kms. north-east of Jhansi. Birth place of Prahlad, the son of Hiranyakashyap. An old Hindu fort stands in ruins on the bank of the Betwa. A representation of Hanuman carved on one of its walls about 60′ above the river and 30′ from top is still in existence.

Gurha : A small village on the left bank of the Dhasau about 15 kms. south-east of Garantha, 88 kms. east of Jhansi and 8 kms. east of Markuan which lies on the road from Garantha to Mauranipur and from here one has to walk to reach the place. The Nagonath hill, a conspicuous land mark, lies a mile north-east of the village and on its crown , there are two old temples and a shrine of Mahadeo in cave and at the foot of the hill on the eastern side there is a Chandella baithak. There is also an image of the sage Vishwamitra, which lies submerged in the Dhasan. A fair is held here in the honour of the saint on the occasion of Makar Sankranti.

Deogarh : Situated on the right bank of the Betwa at a distance of 123 kms. from Jhansi at the western end of the table land or the Lalitpur from range of hills in extremely picturesque natural surroundings. Distance of Deogarh from Lalitpur is 33 kms. The nearest railway station is Jarkhlaun about 11 kms. away.

Deogarh has great antiquarian, epigraphical and archeological importance and figured in the history of the Guptas, the Gujara Pratihars, the Gonds, the Muslim rulers of Delhi, Kalpi, Malwa, the Bundelas, the Marathas and the British. It possesses the remains of fine Vishnu temple of Gupta period and a group of old Jain Temples known as Sagar Marh.

A group of Jain Temples situated inside the fort of Karnalion the hill over looking the Betwa. Some 31 of these are still standing. The thick forest on the hill is a haunt of wild animals.

Mahoba : 140 kms. from Jhansi in Hamirpur district. It is associated with the history of the Chandellas who ruled over modern Bundelkhand from 9th to 14th cent. A.D. The tank and temple at Rahilla, 3 kms. S.W. of the city were built by the first king Rahillya, Kakora Maths is the only temple which has escaped destruction and is situated in the north-east corner of Madan Sagar. It follows the plan of Khajuraho Temples. A mark of Lingam in the middle of sanctum indicates its Shiva Character, there are also the remains of a large temple, now known as Madan Temple dedicated to Lord Vishnu.

Summer House : In the bed of the Madan Sagar are the ruins of an old building known as the summer house of Chandela Kings.

The Temple of Maniva Deva : The temple of the tutelary diety of the Chandellas stands on the northern bank of the Madan Sagar. Today it serves as a lamp post on festival occasions and is consequently known as Diwat or Alha ki Gili.

Old Chandella Forts : On the top of a hill near Kirat Sagar another remarkable monument of the same period is the tomb of Jalhas Khan, an officer of Jaichand of Kannauj who has come to arrest Brahma in his war against Prithwiraj and was slain at the passage of the Betwa.

Jains and Buddhist Shrines : Mahoba also boasted of a

number of Jaina and Buddhist Shrines. The former are survived by a number of statues mostly of the Tirthankars in the different stages of preservation on a hill adjoining the south-east bank of Madan Sagar, there are inscriptions.

Lakes of Mahoba : Chandella period would not be completed without a mention of its magnificent lakes formed by throwing massive embankments across the shallow valleys, Kirat Sagar 1 km. in circumference has to the west of the city Madan Sagar with a circuit of 5 kms. to its south and Kalyana Sagar and Vijaya Sagar. Vijaya Sagar is the largest, being not less than 6 kms. in circuit and now known as Bijai Nagar tank but Madan Sagar is the most picturesque of all. With the granite hill of Gokhar on its west and the range of *ghats* and modern temples on the north and several rocky covered with the ruin of ancient buildings in its bed, it presents a very magnificent view, the famous Kajli Mela which figures prominently in Alha is still held on the bank of Kirat Sagar in the month of Sawan.

Lalitpur : Situated on the Jhansi Bombay section of the Central Railway at a distance of 90 kms. from Jhansi. There are few archaeological remains at Lalitpur, the foremost being a small building known as Bansa. It has an inscription which bears the name of Ferozshah Tughlak and the date Samvat 1415 (A.D. 1358).

Kamla Sagar Dam : About 6 kms. south-west of Mauranipur the river Saprar has been dammed to form the Kamla Sagar reservoir which covers an area of about 10 sq. kms. There is an inspection house and a hill and a ruined for which is said to have been the residence of the legendary thief Bona, a character of Alha.

Sukhwa Dukhwa : This masonary dam on Betwa river was constructed during 1905 and is located on Jhansi Lalitpur high way. The same road goes to Matatila Dam. Bus service is available from Jhansi upto the dam. The dam is about 4000 ft. in length. There is an inspection house here which offers a panoramic view of the dam and its upstream lake.

Bhasneh : 96 kms. from Jhansi on the Jhansi Mauranipur-Gursarai Road. This place is associated with Bhasmasur, a demon king. Picturesquely situated at the foot of Vindhyan hill range there is a lake, artificial fall. Bhasmasur cave and lush green vegetation which make the place a picnicker's paradise. Inspection house is also available here.

Matatila Dam : Constructed during 1952 to 1958 on the river Betwa. The dam is located in Lalitpur district 60 kms. from Jhansi. Daily bus service is available upto the dam from Jhansi. There is a well laid out garden here with beautiful illumination arrangements which resembles Brindaban garden of Mysore. Accommodation at Inspection house.

Banda : Banda is said to have derived its name from Bandeo, the name of a sage mentioned in Hindu mythology as a contemporary of Rama. Places of interest include Nawab Ali Bahadur's palace and other buildings in an open space in the city. There is a fine tank on the road to Kalinjar which is a large sheet of water, surrounded on all four sides by masonary banks or flights of steps leading to the water edge. Beyond the Nimni Nala lie the ruins of a well built fort and palace. Of the Hindu temples here are oldest and most celebrated are the two sacred to Bameshwari Devi and Bameshwar Mahadeo.

Bagrehi : Close to the Ohan river at a distance of 18 kms. from Karwi. The village is noted as containing the sacred and picturesquely wooded Lalapur hill, the reputed residence of the sage Valmiki. At the top is a trignomatrical survey station.

Kalinjar : The celebrated hill fort and town of Kalinjar is situated at a distance of 56 kms. from Banda. The nearest railway station is Atarsa which is 38.6 kms. from here. The hill, on which the fort is built, is situated at the south-eastern edge of the plains of Bundelkhand. There are seven gates in the Kalinjar fort.

Patal Ganga, Pandu Kund, Buddhi Talao, Siddha ki Gupha, Rani ki Aman, Mirhi Bhairon, Mrigdhara, Kumbhu, The Boar Avtar, Nilkanth Temple, and the cave are some of the attractive places of tourist interest at Kalinjar.

Kalpi : 128 kms. from Jhansi on Jhansi Kanpur road. There is a fort, now in ruins, situated on the bank of the river. The western outskirt of the town along the Jamuna is a region of fine old tombs, the more important being the great tomb called 'Chaurasi Gumbaj'. In this town is situated a lofty tower, known as the 'Lanka'.

Parichha : 22.5 kms. from Jhansi on Jhansi— Lucknow road. Here the masonary dam was constructed in 1885, close to the head works is the Inspection House perched on a high mound which offers a panoramic view of the upstream lake and water-falls.

CHITRAKOOT

120 kms. from Allahabad. Situated on the banks of river Mandakini, district Banda, Tehsil Karvi, on the border of Madhya Pradesh. It is on the Jhansi Manikpur Rail Route. There is no such village or city by the name Chitrakoot. Sitapur, Kamta, Khohi, Naya Gaon and Karvi, these five cities are called Chitrakoot.

How to Reach

8 kms. from Sitapur, Karvi Station on Manikpur Jhansi Rail Route. It is connected by road.

Where to Stay

1. U.P. Tourist Bungalow.
2. Jaipuria Guest House.

Dharamshala :

1. Goenka Dharamshala.
2. Sri Ram Dharamshala.
3. Agra Dharamshala.
4. Calcutta Dharamshala.
5. Ma ki Dharamshala.

Places of Interest

1. Kamadgiri
2. Ram Ghat
3. Pramodvan
4. Janki Kund
5. Sphatik Shila
6. Atri and Sati Anusuya Ashram
7. Gupta Godawari
8. Bharatkoop
9. Marfo
10. Ganesh Garden
11. Barke Siddha
12. Koti Tirth
13. Dewangana
14. Hanuman Dhara
15. Balmiki Ashram
16. Rajapuret

HARDWAR

Under district Saharanpur, situated on the right bank of holy river Ganga at the foot of Shivalik Mountains. Hardwar has been a sacred place for pilgrimage since Puranki age. In the age of Purana it was named as Mayapuri. It was also known as Gangadwar and Tapovan. More ancient than these names is Kapilothan, as it is said that the ancestors of Raja Bhagirath were burnt at this place by the curse of sage Kapila. For their salvation, he performed Tapa and brought down Ganga from Heaven.

How to Reach

Air : A Vayudoot service ply from Bhaniawala (Dehradun to Delhi.)

Rail: Hardwar to Howrah, Bombay, Delhi, Varanasi, Lucknow, Dehradun, Mathura, Nainital, Agra and other places of tourist interest.

Road: Hardwar to Sharanpur 82 kms. Dehradun 52 kms. Meerut 141 kms. Delhi 222 kms. Ambala 210 kms. Mussoorie 100 kms. Agra 368 kms. Nainital via Karnaprayag 386 kms. Badrinath 250 kms. Yamunotri 273 kms. Gangotri 245 kms.

Where to Stay

Hotels:

1. Anand Niwas Hotel, Shravannath Ghat.
2. Arya Niwas Trust Bldg. Niranjani Akhara Road.
3. Gurdev Hotel, Station Road.
4. Gyan Niketan, Subhash Ghat.
5. Jaipuria House, Ram Ghat.
6. Palace Hotel, Shravannath Nagar.
7. New Royal Hotel, Gaughat.
8. Shanti Niketan, Har ki Pauri.
9. Upma Hotel, Subzi Mandi.
10. Vasi Dev Madras Hotel, near Railway Station.
11. Hotel Samrat, Shravannath Nagar.
12. Deep Hotel —do—
13. Alka Hotel, Gaughat.
14. Hotel Hari Niwas, Gaughat.
15. Raj Hotel Vishnu Ghat.
16. Vikrant Hotel, Gaughat.
17. Yatri Niwas, near New Ganga Talkies.
18. Hotel Savera, Nirmala Chhawani.

Other Accommodation:

1. U.P.S.T.D.C. Tourist Bungalow Haridwar.
2. Canal Inspection House Nos. 1, 2, 3 & 4, Mayapur.
3. Laljiwala Canal Inspection House, Laljiwala.
4. Zila Parishad Inspection House, near Bus Station.
5. P.W.D. Inspection House, Bhim Goda Road.
6. Forest Rest House, Ranipur.
7. Railway Retiring Room, Railway Station.

Dharamshalas:

1. Kali Kamli Dharamshala.
2. Dhandevi Dharamshala.

3. Basanti Devi Dharamshala.
4. Nanki Bai Dharamshala.
5. Bhatinda Wali Dharamshala.
6. Amritsar Wali Dharamshala.
7. Narsing Bhawan.
8. Bindraban Dharamsahala.
9. Lucknow Wali Dharamshala.
10. Suraj Mal Dharamshala.
11. Karori Mal Dharamshala.
12. Bholagiri Dharamshala.
13. Karnatak Dharamshala.
14. Madrasi ,,
15. Bikaner ,,
16. Mishara ,,
17. Gita Bhawan.
18. Goel Dharamshala.

Places of Interest

Har ki Pauri : This is the most sacred bathing Ghat at Hardwar. Every 12 years the Kumbh and every 6 years Aradh Kumbh fairs are held here. Arti of the Ganga performed everyday after sunset is worth-seeing.

Canal Centenary Bridge : This bridge near Har ki Pauri Commands a beautiful view of all the Ghats as well as the canal.

Bhim Goda Tank : This tank is on the way to Rishikesh and is about 2.5 kms from Tourist Office. It is said that while Pandavas were going to Himalayas through Hardwar Bhim made this tank with the blow of his knee.

Bhim Goda Canal Head Works : It is about half km. from the canal centenary bridge. The northern Ganga canal diverts from this place. The area has been developed into beautiful gardens.

Sapt Rishi Ashram and Sapt Sarovar : It is situated at a distance of about 6 kms. from tourist office on the way to Rishikesh. It is said that the Ganga had split herself in seven currents at this point so that the sapt (seven) Rishis worshipping there would not be disturbed.

Sadhubela : At about 5 kms. from tourist office towards Rishikesh it is a newly built Ashram.

Daksh Mahadev Temple and Sati Kund Kankhal : It is about 3.5. kms. from Tourist Office Hardwar. The mythological story about this place is that Daksh Prajapati, father of Sati (Lord Shiva's first wife) performed Yagya at this place. Daksh Prajapati did not invite Lord Shiva and Sati felt insulted. Sati burnt herself in Yagya Kund. Kankhal is one of the five sacred places around Hardwar. The five tirthas are—Ganga, Kushawart, Bilwa Tirtha, Neel Parvat and Kankhal.

Mansa Devi Temple : 3 kms. from tourist office situated on Bilwa Parbat. To go to this Temple, Uran Khatola (Rope way) is available.

Chandi Devi : 6 kms. situated on Neel Parvat on the other bank of the main Ganga river. One has to trek. 3 kms. on the hill to reach the Chandi Devi Temple. The Temples of Gauri Shanker, Neeleshvar Mahadeo and Anjani Devi are at the close distance to Chandi Devi Temple on the hill.

Other Temples of Hardwar : Shri Gorakhnath Temple and Gupha, Bilkeshwar,—Bilkeswar Mahadev Temple, Kal Bhairav Temple, Gita Bhawan, Maya Devi Temple, Vishnu Bhawan, Bhola Giri Ashram, Bhairau Nath Temple of Pashupati Mahadev, Mano Kamna Siddh Temple, Ganesh Ghat, Mayapur Mano Kamna Siddh—Hanuman Temple, Awadhoot Mandir Jwalapur Rd., Manav Kalyan Ashram, Kankhal, Narayani Shila, Maya Pur.

Rishikesh : 24 kms. from Hardwar situated on the right bank of river Ganga. It is said when Raibhya Rishi did heard penances God appeared by the name of 'Hrishi Kesh' and this area was henceforth called by the name Rishikesh has additional significance being the base commencing journey to the Himalayan shrine of Yamunotri, Gangotri, Kedarnath and Badrinath.

The yoga centres of Rishikesh have enhanced the significance of the palace, the tourist from all over the world visit this place to have lessons in yoga and meditation.

How to Reach

Air : Vayudoot Seva from Delhi to Jolly Grant near Bharawala, Dehradun Road. 14 kms. from Rishikesh.

Rail : Connected by Rail with all the important cities of India.

Road : Connected to other parts of India by Road.

Where to Stay

Western Style Hotels :

1. Hotel Inderlok Rly. Station Road.
2. Hotel Laxman Jhoola. Ph. : 289—290
3. New Tourist Lodge, near Rly. Station.
4. Hotel Rajhans, U.P.S.R.T.C. Bus Stand. Ph. : 126
5. Hotel Tapovan, near Luxman Jhoola. Ph. : 212

Indian Style Hotels :

1. Motel Menko, near U P.S.R.T.C. Bus Stand. Ph : 285
2. Tourist Travel Home, Dehradun Road.

Other Accommodation :

1. Tourist Bungalow, Muni ki Reti, Ph. : 372-373
2. P.W D. Inspection House.
3. Forest Rest House, Muni ki Reti Ph. : 31
4. Trimula Tirupati.

Dharamshalas :

1. Baba Kali Kamli.
2. Panjab Sindh Kshetra.
3. Jai Ram Anna Kshetra.
4. Shri Vithal Ashram.
5. Shivananda Ashram.
6. Geeta Bhawan.
7. Parmarth Niketan
8. Swargashram.
9. Sindhi Dharmshala.
10. Bhagwan Ashram.
11. Gopal Kuti.
12. Saharanpur Wali Dharamshala.
13. Delhi Wali Dharamshala.
14. Devki Bai Dharmshala.
15. Jeewani Mal Dharamshala.
16. Kanpur Wali Dharamshala.
17. Khurja Wali Dharmshala.
18. Jaipur Wali Dharamshala.
19. Mahanand Ashram.
20. Avadhoot Ashram.
21. Bhajan Ashram.
22. Manbhri Bhuri Mai Dharamshala.
23. Rukmani Dharamshala.
24. Pushkar Mandir Dharamshala.
25. Nepali Kshetra.

Places of Interest

Laxman Jhoola : 5 kms. from Rishikesh in North. It is said that at this place Sri Laxman performed Tapa. The Laxman Temple was built in this memory. There was a hanging jute rope bridge, without pillar, till 1889. This was rebuilt with iron ropes.

Kanva Rishi Ashram : 6 kms. from Kotdwara at the bank of river Malini. It is said that/this place Rishi Kanva lived and Shakuntala spent a few days here. A regular bus service from Kotdwara is available for this place.

Neelkanth Mahadev : This temple is situated at the height of 5500 feet above sea level and about 12 kms. from Laxman Jhoola. While going upto Neelkanth Mahadev one can have a wide angled view of Himalayan Peaks.

Other Places of Interest

Bharat Temple, Triveni Ghat, Rishi Kund, and Raghunath Temple, Pushkar Temple, Venkteswara Temple, and Chandra Mauleswara Temple, Shatrughan Temple, Laxman Temple, Laxman Jhoola bridge, Swargashram, Geeta Bhavan, Parmarth Niketan.

Distance of Some Important Cities from Rishikesh

Dehradun	42 kms.	Hardwar	24 kms.
Narendra Nagar	16 kms.	Neel Kanth	16 kms.
Mussoorie	77 kms.	Yamunotri	288 kms.
Gangotri	258 kms.	Uttar Kashi	154 kms.
Badri Nath	301 kms.		

PILGRIMAGE TO UTTARAKHAND

The Yatra to Uttarakhand starts from Rishikesh which is the seat of a large number of Ashrams and religious institutions. On way to Yamunotri, Tehri, for several years was the seat of the state of the same name. From Tehri, the road goes along the meandering Bhagirathi upto Dharasu and bifurcates to the left for Yamunotri. Buses can go upto Hanumanchatti from where a 14 kms. trek starts to Yamunotri. Yamunotri is the cradles of Yamuna and is one of the most picturesque spots in Himalayas.

Going to Gangotri, one has to trace one's way back upto Dharasu and then continue on the road along the banks of Bhagirathi to Uttarkashi, which is a town of ancient heritage as well as modernity. Lord Vishwanath is the presiding deity and the Maneri Hydro Project is the new age attraction. The road from Uttarkashi to Gangotri flanks Bhagirathi and passes through thick woods and shady groves from Gangotri, Gomukh birth place of river Ganges, is 18 kms. The trek is gradual and one of the serene beauty. From Gomukh, the more intrepid adventures can trek upto Tapovan Nandanvana etc.

Kedarnath, the abode of Lord Shanker, is the next shrine to be visited. From Gangotri, one has to come back to Tehri and then take up the road to Srinagar, Rudraprayag, Sonprayag, and Gaurikund. The 14 kms. trek from Gaurikund to Kedarnath is indeed full of beauty and splendour. Kedarnath temple is an outstanding example of fine temple architecture. Peace dwells here and nature has lavishly unveiled itself to hypnotize the visitors at the very first sight. Leaving Kedarnath on a sunny day without pangs of separation is not that easy because it is all divine and all beautiful. But one must come back to kund or Rudraprayag for onward journey to that cherished dham of Shri Badrinathji. Passing through Karnaprayag, Pipalkoti, Joshimath, one ultimately reaches Badrinath to see Lord Vishnu enshrined in an old temple set in the lap of Narayana Parbat. From the back ground peeps the lofty and magnificent Neelkanth, truly called the queen of Himalayas. Stay here for one or two days is fully rewarding. On way back to Rishikesh, the visitor carries with him cherished memories of beautiful Garhwal (Uttrakhand) beckning him to come back again and again.

And now it is not only the *Yatra* you may look forward to but scores of experiences that one may get visiting the lively confluences, shady groves and fruitladen orchards. Trek to various places, studded with peaks, glaciers, meadows and forests will equally make one believe that mature dwells in Garhwal (Uttarakhand) in its prestine glory more than it does anywhere else.

Package Tour No: I Rishikesh, Pauri, Kedarnath-Badrinath : 8 days : Route

Rishikesh, Muni ki Reti, Pauri, night stay at Pauri. Pauri to Sonprayag, Night stay at Sonprayag. Sonprayag to Gaurikund to Kedarnath, night stay : Darshan and Pooja. Kedarnath to Gupta Kashi. Night stay at Gupta Kashi. Gupta Kashi to Pipal Koti. Night stay at Pipal Koti. Pipal Koti to Badrinath, night Puja and Darshan at Badrinath. Badrinath to Karanprayag, night stay at Karnaprayag. Karnaprayag to Rishikesh back.

Tour No : II 7 days : Rishikesh : Kedarnath-Badrinath route

Rishikesh, Muni ki Reti, Deoprayag, Night stay at Deoprayag. Deoprayag to Rudraprayag to Gaurikund. Night stay at Gaurikund. Gaurikund to Kedarnath. Night stay at Kedarnath for Darshan and Puja. Kedarnath to Rudraprayag. Night stay at Rudraprayag. Rudraprayag to Joshi Math to Badrinath. Night stay at Badrinath for Darshan and Puja. Badrinath to Nandprayag. Night stay at Nandprayag. Nandprayag to Srinagar toRishikesh.

Tour No : III : 4 days : Rishikesh-Badrinath : Route

Muni ki Reti, Deoprayag to Srinagar to Pipal Koti. Night stay at Pipal Koti. Pipal Koti to Badrinath. Night stay at Badrinath for Darshan and Puja. Badrinath to Joshi Math. Night stay at Joshi Math. Joshi Math to Rishikesh.

Tour No : IV : 9 days : Rishikesh-Yamunotri-Gangotri-Gaumukh : Route

Rishikesh, Muni ki Reti, Chamba. Night halt at Chamba. Chamba to Dharasu to Sayanachatti, night halt. Sayanachatti to Yamunotri for Darshan and Puja. Yamunotri to Jankichatti. Night halt at Janki Chatti. Jankichatti to Hanuman Chatti to Uttar Kashi, night halt. Uttarkashi to Gangotri, night halt, Darshan and Puja. Gangotri to Gaumukh to Bhojwasa, night halt. Bhojwasa to Gangotri to Lanka, night halt. Lanka to Dhanolti, night halt. Dhanolti to Mussoorie to Dehradun and back to Rishikesh.

Tour No : V : 14 days : Rishikesh-Yam·notri-Gangotri-Kedarnath-Badrinath : Route

Rishikesh, Muni ki Reti, Dehradun, Dakpathar, night halt. Dakpathar Barkot, Sayanachatti, night halt. Sayanachatti to Yamunotri to Jankichatti, night halt. Jankichatti to Hanumanchatti to Barkat to Uttarkashi, night halt. Uttarkashi to Gangotri, night halt for Darshan and Puja. Gangotri to Gaumukh to Bhojwasa, night halt. Bhojwasa to Gangotri to Bhairon Ghati, night halt. Bhairon Ghati to Tehri to Rudraprayag, night halt. Rudraprayag to Gaurikund to Kedarnath, night halt. Kedarnath to Gaurikund to Gupta Kashi, night halt. Gupta Kashi to Joshi Math, night halt. Joshi Math to Badrinath, night halt for Darshan and Puja. Badrinath to Karnaprayag, night halt. Karnaprayag to Muni ki Reti back.

Tour No : VI : 9 days : Delhi-Kedarnath-Badrinath : Route

Delhi, Hardwar, Chila, night halt. Chila to Rudraprayag, to Gupta Kashi, night halt. Gupta Kashi to Kedarnath, night halt, for Darshan and Puja. Kedarnath to Rudra Prayag, night halt. Rudraprayag to Pipal Koti to Joshi Math, night halt, Joshi Math to Badrinath, night halt for Darshan and Puja. Badrinath to Srinagar, night halt. Srinagar to Devprayag to Rishikesh, night halt. Rishieksh to Delhi back.

Tour No : VII : 7 days : Rishikesh-Hemkund : Badrinath : Route

Muni ki Reti, Rudraprayag, Pipal Koti, night halt. Pipal Koti to Govind Ghat to Ghangharia, night halt. Ghangharia to Hemkund to Ghangharia, night halt. Ghangharia to Valley of Flowers to Badrinath, night halt for Darshan and Puja.

Badrinath to Joshi Math to Karnaprayag, night halt. Karnaprayag to Srinagar to Muni ki Reti.

On all the above routes buses are being run by the Garhwal Mandal Vikas Nigam Ltd. A U.P. Govt. undertaking, for further details please contact :

Manager,
Garhwal Mandal Vikas Nigam Ltd.,
U.P. Tourist Bureau, Lalitaras Bridge,
Hardwar (U.P.) Ph : 19.

HILL STATIONS IN UTTAR PRADESH

Almora : It is one of the important hill station in Uttar Pradesh. It has historical importance. It was a prominent city during Chand kingdom in 16th century. Almora is a peaceful hill station with natural beauty.

It is connected with rail and road. The nearest railway station is Kath Godam. Buses are easily available to reach there. Accommodation at private hotels.

Baijnath : 64 kms. from Almora in the north. It is a beautiful picnic spot. Baijnath Sarovar is surrounded by temples. The main attraction is Parbati Statue. U.P. Roadways buses are available to reach there.

Chakrata : It is a peaceful health resort with natural scenic beauty. One can reach there from Dehradun. It is an important military station.

Mussoorie : 33 kms. from Dehradun in north. Queen of hill stations. Situated at a height of 197 meters from sea-level. Most important health resort of northern India during summer vacations. There are several hotels to stay there. Nearest railway station is Dehradun. It is connected by road with all the important cities of India. Places of interest : Committee Bagh, Rope Way, Gun Hill, Lal Tibba, Campti Fall is also an important picnic spot, 10 kms. from Mussoorie on the way to Dehradun.

Nainital : An important and famous hill station in Uttar Pradesh. Situated in Kumaon range. Famous for health resort during summer vacations. There are several private hotels to stay. The nearest railway station is Kath Godam. It is direct connected with Delhi and other important cities of Uttar Pradesh. U.P. Roadways buses are easily available. It is surrounded by hills. There are several places to visit. Bhim Tal, Sat Tal, Nankuchia Tal and Khupa Tal are worth-seeing lakes.

Ranikhet : It is situated in the natural surroundings. Ranikhet is a cantt. area. Peaceful for health resort. It is between Almora and Nainital on the way. Chobatia Garden is full of fruits and worth-visiting picnic spot.

Oindari Glacier : Situated on the height of 3943 meters near Almora. It has natural scenic beauty and full of colourful flowers.

National Parks

Corbett National Park : India's oldest and best known wildlife habitat named after the legendry Jim Corbett with an area of 5208 sq. km. encloses the Patlidam valley of Ramganga river and foot hills of the Shivalik range. The park is the home of the tiger, gharial, crocodile, deer, elephant, panther, sloth, bear, wild bear, rhdus monkey, mongoose, python, and 585 species of birds. And for the angler there are Mahaseer Trout and Goonch.

It was established in 1935 in Nainital and Pauri Garhwal District. Nearest railway station is Ram Nagar on Moradabad-Ram Nagar branch line. Approachable by road from Delhi via Ghaziabad, Hapur, Moradabad, Kashipur, Ram Nagar and Dhikala ; 290 kms. Time of visit 15th November to 15th June. Accommodation at Forest Rest House, Tourist Hutment, Swiss Cottage, Khimauli Forest Rest House, Sarapduli Forest Rest House, Gairal Forest Rest House, Bijroni Forest Rest House.

Dudhwa National Park : The 490 kms. (sq.) Dudhwa National Park is of prime importance because of its flora, fauna and ecological spreadout. The park encompasses the forests of North Kheri Forest Division and holds abundant wildlife species. Those include tiger, panther, sambher, swamp deer, spotted deer, hog deer, barking deer, wild deer, sloth bear, nilgai, mugger, elephant, hyna, jackel, ratel, porcupine, hare, besides 400 species of birds and various reptiles. There is also good scope for fishing. Approachable from Delhi by road via Moradabad, Bareilly, Pilibhit, Puranpur, Khutar crossing, Mailani, Bhira, Palia and Dudhwa. By rail from Delhi via Bareilly to Malinijn. Dudhwa distance 430 kms. from Lucknow by road via Sitapur, Lakhimpur Kheri, Nighasoa (after crossing Sarda river by Pantoon bridge) Palia, Dudhwa, distance 215 kms. and by rail via Dudhwa distance 260 kms. By air, nearest airport is Lucknow, Tourists are advised to reach Dudhwa before sunset. Season for visit, November to May. Accommodation at Dudhwa, Bankoti, Sonaripur etc.

RAJASTHAN

JAIPUR

Capital of the state of Rajasthan, Jaipur has, over the centuries, played a stillar role in the history of this magnificent land of kings and warriors, poets, and saints, artists and craftsmen. Here in this fabulous city of broad avenues and rose pink palaces, the finest of Rajasthani traditions, in and out culture, in valour and heroic deeds, have been found, bestowing upon modern Jaipur a noble legacy. Jaipur has a long established reputation of being one of the most refined cities of India, as well as one of the best pearned.

How to Reach

By Air : Indian Air Lines Boeing flights twice daily from Delhi and Bombay.

By Rail : The daily Pink City Express from Delhi is a fast convenient train. Jaipur is also linked by direct train services to Bombay, Agra, Ahmedabad etc.

By Road : Rajasthan state transport deluxe buses and ITDC A/C buses have daily services between Jaipur and Delhi : 306 kms.

Jaipur to	Agra	230 kms.
-do-	Ajmer	138 kms.
-do-	Alwar	143 kms.
-do-	Bharatpur	174 kms.
-do-	Bikaner	329 kms.
-do-	Kota/Bundi	245 kms.
-do-	Chittorgarh	320 kms.
-do-	Sariska	105 kms.
-do-	Udaipur	407 kms.
-do-	Jodhpur	340 kms.

Where to Stay

1. Gangaur Tourist Bungalow, M.I. Road, Ph ; 60231
2. Teej Tourist Bungalow : Collectrate Road : Bani Park : Ph : 74206
3. Swagatam Tourist Bungalow : near railway station : Ph : 67360
4. Youth Hostel : Behind S.M.S. Stadium, Ph : 67576

5. Palace Hotels : Ram Bagh Palace, Raj Mahal Palace, Hotel Bissu Palace, Narain Niwas.
6. Deluxe Hotels : Clarks Amar, Welcome group, Mansingh, Jaipur Ashok.
7. First Class Hotels : Meru Palace, LBM Hotel, Rajasthan State Hotel : Hotel Khosa Kothi.
8. Midways : Midway Baharor, on Delhi Jaipur highway, 135 kms. from Delhi, 132 kms. Jaipur (2) Janta Dhaba (3) Midway Mahuwa on Jaipur Agra Road, 118 kms. from Agra, 104 kms. from Jaipur.

Places of Interest

Rajasthan Tourism has three sight seeing tours : two half days tours and one full day tour. Half-day tours cover : Hawa Mahal, Ambar Fort, City Palace, Observatory, Central Museum, Ram Niwas Gardens. The full-day tour also includes Gaitor, Nahargarh, Vidyadhar Garden, Jain Nasia, Ram Mandir, and Dolls Museum. Metered Auto Rikshaws are available throughout the city. Private taxis are also available for hire.

Excursions

1. *Ram Garh Lake* : 30 kms. from Jaipur. Idyllic lake resort. Historic Temple Janiwa Mataji. Accommodation at Jheel Tourist Village. Ph. 40449
2. *Siliserh* : 139 kms. palace on the bank of the Siliserh lake. Unique holiday resort. By train upto Alwar and then by bus to Sariska. Accommodation at Honeymoon and Deluxe suits.
3. *Sanganer* : 16 kms. The name of this historic township is today synonymous with the unique block painted fabrics that bear its name. Ornately carved Jain temples and a tower. Other nearby excursions that can be comfortably covered in a half-day are Jaigarh fort 11 kms. and Samod palace 22 kms.
4. *Jodhpur* : The magnificent fortified city of Rathore kings of Marwar is the entry point and base for the desert triangle which consists of the two other cities that were also princely strongholds with rich artistic traditions.

How to Reach

By Air : Indian air lines being flights connect Jodhpur with Delhi, Udaipur, Bombay, Aurangabad and Ahmedabad.

By Rail : Direct rail links with Delhi, Jaipur, Ahmedabad, Udaipur and Bikaner.

By Road : State transport bus service by to all major cities in Rajasthan, Jaipur 338 kms. Ajmer 208 kms. Bikaner 248 kms.

Where to Stay

1. Ghoomer Tourist Bungalow, High Court Road, Ph : 21900
2. Umaid Bhavan Palace
3. Ajit Bhavan
4. Ratanda International
5. Circuit House
6. Alpana Hotel
7. Shanti Bhavan Lodge.

Places of Interest

The fort
Umaid Bhavan
Museum and Zoo
Jaswant Thara
Mahamandir

Excursions

1. Osian : 65 kms. Ancient Temple Complex.
2. Kailana Lake : 11 kms. in Jaisalmer Road. Boating facilities.
3. Sardar Samand Palace and Lake : 55 kms. part of the royal estates.
4. Gulab : 23 kms. A Bishnoi village.

JAISALMER

In the heart of the Thar Desert, rising out of the desert scape like a fantastic mirage is Jaisalmer, city of palaces and havelis, each a poem in stone.

How to Reach

By Air : The nearest air port is Jodhpur 306 kms.

By Rail : Daily train service between Jodhpur and Jaisalmer. Maharaja's saloon, private luxury train with catering on board provided by Umaid Bhavan Palace is available for groups to Jaisalmer and back to Jodhpur. Palace on wheels include Jaislamer in its intinery.

By Road : Motorable roads. State transport bus services

connect Jaisalmer with Jodhpur 285 kms. Delhi 897 km, Ajmer 500 kms. and Udaipur 663 kms.

Where to Stay

1. Moomal Tourist Bungalow : Ph : 92—192
2. Jaisal Castle : Ph : 62

Places of Interest

1. Fort : Built by Rawal Jaisal on the Trikuta Hill.
2. Jain Temple.
3. Haveli : Salim Singh ki Haveli
4. Patwari ki Haveli.
5. Nathmalji ki Haveli.
6. Camel Safaris.

Excursions

1. Sam's Dunes : 42 kms. The beauty of the desert escape is at its best here.
2. Wood Fossil Park : 17 kms. on the Barmer Road.
3. Ladurva : 17 kms. to the west of Jaisalmer, is capital of Bhati Rajputs.
4. Amar Sagar : Enchanting picnic spot on Ladurva route with a lake and a complex of Jain temples.
5. Bada Bagh : 6 kms. A lake and groves of trees, historic spot.
6. Barmer : 153 kms. Renowned for crafts.
7. Kiradu: 35 kms. on the Hathma Siyani Road and major centre of art.

BIKANER

A city with a heroic part of brave deeds and mighty warriors.

How to Reach

By Air : Nearest air port Jodhpur 253 kms.

By Rail : Direct train services from Jodhpur, Jaipur and Delhi.

By Road : Connected to major cities motorable roads, Jodhpur, Jaipur 340 kms. Delhi 567 kms.

Where to Stay

Dhola Maru Tourist Bungalow : Ph : 5002

Places of Interest

1. Fort : most striking feature.
2. Joramal Temple.
3. Hari Mandir
4. Anoop Mahal
5. Rang Mahal
6. Bijay Mahal
7. Chandra Mahal
8. Phool Mahal
9. Museum
10. Armoury and Library

Excursions

1. Camel Breeding farm 10 kms.
2. Deshnoke : 32 32 kms. on Jodhpur road.

UDAIPUR

An enchanted city, the most romantic spot on the continent of India. Maharajá Udai Singh built his place on the very edge of lake Pichola. Udaipur has its long history of battles and heroic deeds. The history of Mewar and its Sisodia rulers is one of the most glorious chapters in the annals of Rajput history.

How to Reach

By Air : Indian Air Lines daily Boeing flights connect Udaipur with Delhi, Bombay, Ahmedabad, Aurangabad and within the state, with Jaipur and Jodhpur.

By Rail : Direct rail links with Delhi, Jaipur, Ajmer, Chittaur, Jodhpur and Ahmedabad.

By Road : State Transport bus services link Udaipur witb all the major cities of Rajasthan and Gujarat. Udaipur to Agra 630 kms. Ahmedabad 262 kms. Ajmer 264 kms. Bombay 730 kms. Delhi 670 kms. Jaipur 406 kms. and Jodhpur 275 kms.

Where to Stay

1. Kajri Tourist Bungalow, Shastri Circle : Ph : 3509
2. Lake Palace Hotel
3. Shiv Niwas Palace Hotel
4. Laxmi Vilas Palace Hotel
5. Hotel Lake End
6. Hotel Anand Bhavan
7. Hotel Chandralok
8. Keerti and Pratap country inn
9. Hotel Shikarbadi

There are some other private Hotels and Dharamshalas to stay at Udaipur.

Places of Interest

1. *Museum* : Provides a fascinating glimpses in the history of Udaipur.
2. *Pichola Lake* : A canal commands two lakes. There are two palaces in its midst, Jagmandir and Jog Niwas. Jog Niwas has been converted into Hotel.
3. *Fateh Sagar* : Lovely place for picnic. Boating facility available.
4. *Gulab Bagh* : Specious rose garden. Aravali express, a mini train, runs around the garden.
5. *Sahelion ki Bari* : The garden lies below the embark-ment of Fateh Sagar Lake.
6. *Jagdish Temple* : Udaipur's most impressive temple. Dedicated to Lord Vishnu.
7. *Bhartiya Lok Kala Mandal* : A folk art museum.
8. *Ahar* : The cenotaphs of the Maharanas of Mewar.
9. *Pratap Memorial* : An appropriate and satisfying culmination of a tour of the city would be at the Pratap Memorial, reached through the landscaped Moti Mongri gardens.

Excursions

Sajangarh : 6 kms. Densely forested area. Wild life can be seen here. Ideal picnic spot.

Jai Sumand Lake : 84 kms. Asia's second largest artificial lake. Accommodation at tourist bungalow, Udaipur, half kms. from bus stand and 9 kms. from Dingri Railway Station.

Raj Samand Lake : 65 kms. Located on the Ajmer Road. Beautiful lake. On the bank of the lake lies Kankroli, site of the Dwarkadheesh Temple.

Kumbhal Garh Fort : 64 kms. Maharana Kumbha built this magnificent fort.

Jagat : 58 kms. An ornate 10th century Ambika Mata Temple here has exquisite carvings and erotic sculptures.

Eklingi : 22 kms. The Temple of Eklingi tuterly deity of the Sisodia of Mewar, is a 15th century complex of white marble.

Nagda : 23 kms. This ancient city was the original capital of the founder of the Sisodia dynasty.

Nathdwara : 48 kms. on the highway to Ajmer. The Temple of Srinathji has drawn generations of pilgrims to it. This is one of the holiest of Vaishnava shrines in the country. Accommodation at Gokul Tourist Bungalow, Lal Bagh Ph : 85.

Rishabdeoji : 65 kms. This Jain Temple is the only one in India where offerings of saffron are made daily to the deity, the 1st Jain Tirthankara. Accommodation at Gauri Tourist Bungalow. Ph : 45. Nearest Railway Station at Kalyanpur 15 kms. Bus stand 1 km. connected with Udaipur, Bombay and Baroda.

Haldi Ghati : 40 kms. The historic site of the battle fought by Maharana Pratap against the Mughals in 1576. Accommodation at Haldi Ghati Rest House, Abu International Hilltone, Mount Hotel Palace, Samrat International.

Mount Abu : Temple Town and hill resort of Rajasthan's most unusual holiday destinations, a visual and aesthetic feast, tapped in legend, sanctified by Jain and Hindu faiths, with all the charm of a cool gateway resort.

How to Reach

By Air : Nearest air port is Udaipur 185 kms.

By Rail : Abu Road : 27 kms.

By Road : Regular state transport bus service ply between Mount Abu and Jaipur 509 kms, Udaipur 185 kms.; Delhi 764 kms., Bombay 782 kms.

Where to Stay

1. Shikhar Tourist Bungalow : Ph : 29
2. Purjan Niwas Youth Hostel.

Places of Interest

Nakki Lake : A placid stretch of water, scooped out of the rocks, according to legend by the thirsty gods, with their fingernails. The lake is pleasant centre.

Dilwara Jain Temple : Five temples situated on the crests of the Aravallis and are dedicated to the Jain Tirthankaras.

Vimal Vasahi : Modhera's Sun Temple, built by Makrana marble.

Achaleshwar Mahallen : On the way to Guru Shikhar, Mount Abu's highest point dedicated to Shiva, Mandakini a holy tank.

Gou Mukh : 9 kms. from town. A perennial flow of water flows from a rock opening.

Arbuda Devi Temple : A top a peak north of Abu, this beautiful temple chiselled out of a rock face, is approached by a flight of 20‸ steps. The view from here is breath-taking particularly at sunset.

Parks and Museums : Landscaped garden parks provide ideal picnic spots to relax in. The museum and art gallery is situated on Raj Bhavan Road.

CHITTORGARH

Symbolises the finest of Rajpur traditions, chivalry, courage, dauntless heroism and sacrifice.

How to Reach

By Air : Nearest airport Udaipur 98 kms.

By Rail : Rail links with Ajmer, Jaipur, Udaipur, Ratlam, Ahmedabad and Delhi.

By Road : Regular state transport services connect Chittorgarh with Ajmer 187 kms. Bundi 156 kms. Jaipur 320 kms. Jodhpur, Kota and Udaipur 115 kms.

Where to Stay

1. Panna Tourist Bungalow : Udaipur Road : Ph : 273
2. Janta Avas Grih : Ph : 9

Places of Interest

Fort : Sprawling over 700 acres, a top a 180 meter high hill.

Vijay Stambh : 37 meters high, nine storeyed.

Kirti Stambh : 22 meters high, dedicated to the first Jain Tirthankara, Adinath.

Rana Khumbha Palace : Jauhar place of Rajput ladies and queen Padmini.

Padmini Palace : Alauddin Khilji beheld the image of Padmini in mirror.

Mira and Kumbha Shyam Temple : Associated with the poetess queen Mira.

Govt. Museum : The Fateh Prakash Palace now houses a magnificent collection of sculptures from the fort.

Excursions

Nagri : 14 kms. North of Chittor. Ancient township of Rajasthan.

Gambhiri D..m : 27 kms.

Avri Mata Temple : 34 kms.

Jain Temples at Bhupal Sagar : 46 kms.

Ranakpur : Complex of Jain Temples.

How to Reach

By Air : Nearest airport Udaipur 114 kms.

By Rail : Nearest rail head Falna 35 kms.

By Road : Direct bus service connects Ranakpur with Udaipur 98 kms. Jodhpur 169 kms. and Mount Abu.

Where to Stay

Shilpi Tourist Bungalow : Distt. Pali.

Places of Interest

Mammothshrine dedicated to the Tirthankara, Adinath. There are two other Jain Temples, located in front of the main shrine and a Sun Temple.

KOTA

Kota is truely representative of the changing industrial map of India, for here, in this ancient stronghold of the Hada Rajputs are significent land marks of the progress of modern India. This is a centre of nuclear research of textiles and other major industries. It is also, still, a city of exquisite palaces and fine museums.

How to Reach

Air : Indian Air Lines Boeing flights from Delhi via Jaipur, four times a week.

Rail : Direct rail link with Jaipur via Sawai Madhopur, Bharatpur, Agra, Delhi and Bombay.

Road : State Highways connect Kota with Delhi 501 kms., Jaipur 246 kms., Udaipur 280 kms.

Where to Stay

1. Chambal Tourist Bungalow : Naya Pura, Ph : 6527
2. Hotel Narang, Hotel Brij, Raj Bhavan Palace.
3. There are some Dharamshalas and Municipal Sarais.

Places of Interest

Fort and Palace : Kota's fort is the city's most imposing ancient structure.

Maharana Madho Singh Museum : Situated in the palace. Treasurer home of Miniature paintings of the Kota school.

Jag Mandir and Chambal Garden : Both are ideal places to spend a quiet, relaking few hours or to picnic in Jag Mandir in the middle of a lake. Chambal gardens offer a fine view of the river and surrounded areas.

Kota's Industries : A tour of the industrial area is equally fascinating.

Excursions

Baroli : 40 kms. A spectacular 9th century temple complex.

Rana Pratap Sagar Dam : 45 kms. on the same road as Baroli.

Rajasthan Atomic Power Project : 75 kms. at this station nuclear research is being carried out.

Jhalara Patan Temple : 60 kms. Jeeps can make this journey comfortable to the ancient city of bells.

BUNDI

Bundi is a medieval town, where time seems to have stood still. Encircled by wooded hills, Bundi's fantastic palaces, and narrow winding streets are reflected in the translucent waters of the Naval Sagar Lake, Shimmering mirage-like, unchanged by time.

How to Reach

Air : Nearest air port is Kota 35 kms.

Rail : Nearest rail head is Kota 35 kms.

Road : Regular state transport bus services connect Bundi with Kota, Jaipur 214 kms., Ajmer 163 kms., and Chittor.

Where to Stay

1. Chambal Tourist Bungalow at Kota.
2. Circuit House, Dak Bunglow, Sukh MahalEl Rest House, Dharamshalas and Jain Lodge at Bundi.

Places of Interest

Tara Garh : As its name implies, this fort commanding a magnificent view from a hill top, has a uniquely shaped exterior, representing innovative architectural techniques.

Palaces : Bundi's palaces are unique even in Rajasthan state of some of the most splendid palaces and palatial residences in India.

Chhatar Mahal : Palace of towers, is guarded by massive gateways.

Chitra Mahal : Best examples of mural paintings of the renowned Bundi school.

Shikar Burj : Delightful picnic spots in the forests around Bundi are Shikar Burj.

Excursions

Menal : 70 kms. in a magnificent setting, overlooking the Menal River gorge are a group of 12th century Shivaite temples.

Bijolia : 16 kms. from Menal on the Bujdi Chittor road. 100 temples of Bijolia is a place of pilgrimage.

Bharatpur : The magnificent 18th century fort was built by Raja Suraj Mal, with double ramparts and enormous moats that gave it its reputation of invincibility. The palace has apartments embellished by patterned tills and murals. In the central wing the museum is worth a visit for its exhibits dating back to 2 A.D. Accommodation at Saras Tourist Bungalow, Fatehpur Sikri Road, Bharatpur Ph : 2169.

Keoladeo Ghana National Park : Best known as a sanctuary for rare avian species the park, once the hunting reserve of the Bharatpur rulers, stretches over a 19 sq. kms. marshly area, ideal terrain for migratory aquata birds. Bharatpur is easily accessible by road from Agra 55 kms., Delhi 184 kms., and Jaipur 176 kms. Direct train services also link Bharatpur with Mathura, Delhi, Agra, Jaipur and Bombay. The nearest airport is Agra.

Deeg : 34 kms. from Bharatpur which is also nearest rail-head. Regular bus service connects Deeg with Bharatpur. This garden resort built as a royal retreat in the 18th century by rulers of Bharatpur. There are so many interesting palaces to be seen.

For further details please contact :
Department of Tourism, Govt. of Rajasthan,
100, Jawaharlal Nehru Marg,
Jaipur.

GUJARAT

Sea girt Gujarat, the gateway into India values, rich in history, faith and culture. This is the land which gave the world Mahatma Gandhi, and where his philosophy is still a living legacy. But Gandhi's Gujarat is also an exciting holiday destination. With the country's longest line, it offers a series of beaches, exciting shopping in its textile towns, and a vibrant, modern capital, Ahmedabad. And, in ancient temple towns like Somnath, Dwarka and Modhera, the call of faith is as profound as it has been for centuries. Destination India presents here the complete Gujarat.

AHMEDABAD

Ahmedabad is now the industrial capital of the State and a graceful blend of old and new. Famous as the second largest textile centre of India. Ahmedabad is also the city where Mahatma Gandhi established Sabarmati Ashram. Today, Ahmedabad has spread beyond the confines of its mediaeval walls for across the Sabarmati river.

How to Reach

Air : Air Port Ahmedabad—connects with Bombay, Delhi and Jaipur.

Rail : Ahmedabad is connected by rail with all the major cities of India—Delhi, Bombay, Western Railway.

Road : Connected with all Major cities of India.

Where to Stay

Hotels : 1. Cama, Capital, Karnavati, Natraj, Ritz, Roopal, Siddhartha, Palace : etc.

2. Gujarat Tourism's Toran.
3. Gandhi Ashram Guest House.

Places of Interest

Sidi Sayad's Mosque : This elegant mosque is noted for its own windows of pierced stone, worked in a design of a tree with palm leaves and carving tendrids. This design has become almost a symbol of the city.

Shaking Minarets : Popular with visitors are two delightful mediaeval mosques famed for their shaking minarets. One is the Ajpur Bibi Mosque at Gomtipura and the other is Sidi Bashir's Mosque at Kalupur. Pressure exeted on the inner walls of the minarets sets them vibrating strongly.

Adalaj Vav : This 15th century stepwek is an architectural delight. 17 kms. from Ahmedabad Adalaj can be reached by road within minutes.

Shreyas Museum : This modern museum houses a collection of craft items assembled with great care and attention to detail.

Indian Institute of Management : A comprehensive education in management is provided here to students drawn from all over India.

Sarkhej Roja : The impressive 15th century Roja, which lies on the main arterial road linking Ahmedabad with Saurashtra, was erected over the tomb of a Sultan of Gujarat, Mahmud Shah Begra and his wife.

Vechar Utensil Museum : Vechar is best visited in the cool of evening. The museum houses a remarkable collection of metalware.

Hutheesingh Temple : The architectural style of this jain temple is strongly reminiscent of the white marble temples at Mount Abu.

Swaminarayan Temple : The ornate Swaminarayan Temple was constructed in the early 19th century in an entirely different style.

Rani Sipri's Mosque : This mosque is distinguished for the intricacy of the designs on its carved stone balconies and supports its windows, door ways and lintels.

Rani Rupmati's Mosque : Rani Rupmati's mosque too reveals a synthesis of Hindu-Muslim structural ideas in its layout, its arched introduce and ornate, carved stone balconies.

Teen Darwaja : This fascinating gateway with three open arches is one of the twelve which originally provided access to the walled city.

Jama Masjid : This large mosque deserves special mention for the highly effective manner in which Hindu-Muslim elements are combined in its architecture.

Sabar Mati Ashram : Among the many interesting things to be seen at the Ashram is Hirdaya Kunj, the simple home built by Mahatma Gandhi where he lived and worked for 15 years.

GANDHI NAGAR

Gandhinagar, the capital of Gujarat 25 kms. North of Ahmedabad, is the most beautiful city of the state. Dedicated to Mahatma Gandhi and named after him, the best time to visit Gandhinagar is from September to March.

How to Reach

Air : Nearest Airport is Ahmedabad 23 kms.

Railway : Nearest Railway Stations are Gandhi Nagar 2 kms. and Ahmedabad 31 kms.

Road : Ahmedabad 25 kms., Baroda 150 kms. Surat 308 kms., Bombay 540 kms., Mehsana 63 kms. Delhi 900 kms. state transport buses are available.

Where to Stay

1. Pattaikarshram, Sector No. 11.
2. Youth Hostel, Sector No. 16.
3. Circuit House, J-Road.
4. Rest House, Sector No. 21.

Vadodara

Vadodara is a city of beautiful gardens, magnificent palaces and many institutions of learning of international repute.

How to Reach

Air : Direct daily flight from Bombay.

Rail : From Ahmedabad, Bombay or Delhi.

Road : 118 kms. from Ahmedabad, 420 kms. from Bombay and 1030 kms. from Delhi via Jaipur and Udaipur.

Where to Stay

1. Circuit House, Alka Puri Rd.
2. Valmiki Bungalow Alka Puri Rd.
3. Municipal Corporation Guest House, Station Rd.
4. Dak Bungalow, Fateh Ganj Camp.
5. Railway Retiring Rooms.
6. Express Hotel, R.C. Dutt Rd.
7. Hotel Kaviraj, R.C. Dutt Rd.
8. Green Hotel, R.C. Dutt Rd.
9. Hotel Natraj, R.C. Dutt Rd.
10. Hotel Stay Well R.C. Dutt Rd.
11. Hotel Surya.
12. Hotel Ambassador.
13. Hotel Kalyan.
14. Ccronation Hotel.
15. Hotel Utsav, Navrang Cinema Compound.
16. Hotel Gaurav, Pratap Ganj.

Places of Interest

1. Maharaja Sayajirao University.
2. Sayaji Baug, Zoo, Mini Train
3. Sardar Patel Planetorium.
4. Baroda Museum.
5. Sursangar Lake.
6. Temple of Shri Gyane Dakshinamoorthy.
7. Idol of Lord Shiva.
8. Kirti Mandir.
9. Nyaya Mandir.
10. Laxman Vilas Palace.

Excursions

1. Ajwa Lake, 20 kms. from Vadodara Popular Picnic spot.
2. Dabhoi 30 kms.

SURAT

One of the oldest city of Gujarat, Surat has been a flourishing international trade centre since 14th century. Situated on the southern Bank of river Tapi, 20 kms. from Arabian Sea. Surat was the Chief Port of the Moghul Empire. This city was thrice sacked and burnt down by the Portuguese.

The city presents a charming contrast between the old and new, with historical monuments by the side of modern architectural edifices and traditional crafts with modern technology and machines.

How to Reach

Air : Nearest Airport is Baroda (Vadodara) 140 kms. from Surat. Daily flights from Bombay to Baroda.

Rail : 229 kms. from Ahmedabad 129 kms. from Baroda. Situated on the main line of Western Rly.

Road : 140 kms. from Baroda, 250 kms. from Ahmedabad well connected by Road.

Where to Stay

1. Hotal Tax Plaza.
2. Hotel Amisha.
3. Satkar Hotel.
4. Hotel Apsara.
5. Circuit House.
6. Vishram Grih.

Places of Interest

The Castle : Surat's most important historical monument.

Sardar Patel Museum : The Museum has a rich collection of more than 10,000 specimens of arts and crafts.

Rang Upavan : An open air theatre in the western part of Gandhi Baug, having capacity of 4,000. Other places of interest are the Nehru Park, Chowpaty, Ambica Temple and Revolving Restaurant.

Excursions

Dumas : 16 kms. South-East of Surat. An excellent health resort. Many cottages are available for visitors.

Hajira : Well known health resort with two santourism in the South-West of South.

Ubharat : Popular sea side resort.

Unai : 64 kms. from Surat, well developed lake side resort famous for hot springs.

RAJKOT

Rajkot is the heart of Saurashtra and one of the most important cities of the region.

Karam Chand Gandhi, father of Mahatma Gandhi lived here when he was Prime Minister of the State. Gandhiji himself spent his early years.

Popular product of Rajkot is Bandhi Saree. Patchwork, mirrorwork, bead work and silk embroidery are among the traditional handicrafts of the city. The best time for a visit is from October to March.

How to Reach

Air : Daily flight from Bombay.

Rail : 253 kms. from Ahmedabad via Viramgam.

Road : 216 kms. from Ahmedabad.

Where to Stay

1. Circuit House.
2. Sardar Baug Atithigrih.
3. City Rest House.
4. Pathik Ashram opp. Railway Station.
5. Railway Retiring Rooms.
6. Dharamshala.

Hotels :

Hotel Galaxy, Hotel Ruby, Hotel Tulsi.

Places of Interest

Kaba Gandhino Delo : This is the house where Mahatma Gandhi's father lived. Gandhi also lived in this house during his school days.

Educational Institutions :

1. Raj Kumar College.
2. Dharamendra Singhji College.
3. H.H. Katak Institute of Science.
4. A.V. Parekh Technical Institute.
5. Rashtriya Shala.

Public Garden :

1. Jubilee Garden.
2. Janta Baug.
3. Pradyuman Park.

Watson Museum :

It has an impressive collection of archaeological exhibits.

Bal Bhawan :

A unique institution for children's education through entertaining indoor and outdoor activities.

Excursions

Lake of Lal Pani and Raudera : This is a picturesque picnic spot, 4-8 kms. from the city.

Aji Dam : 8 kms. from Rajkot main service of water supply to the city.

JAMNAGAR

Jamnagar, is the Jewel of Kathiawad, is a coastal Town about 300 kms. to the west of Ahmedabad. Jamnagar is a charming blend of the old and new with its ancient monuments and broad streets. It is called Paris of Saurashtra. There are a number of ancient temples in and around the town.

How to Reach

Air : Daily Direct flights from Bombay.

Rail : From Ahmedabad.

Road : 303 kms. from Ahmedabad, 90 kms. from Rajkot.

Where to Stay

1. New Aram Hotel, Bedi Road.
2. Hotel Asiana, Super Market.
3. Galaxy Guest House, near Galaxy Cinema.
4. Dream Land Hotel, Station Road.
5. Ashoka Hotel, Station Road.
6. Chetna Hotel, Station Road.
7. Railway Retiring Rooms.
8. Bhatia Dharamshala, outside Khambhalia Gate.
9. Gokul Das Dharamshala, Subhash Market Road.
10. Johri Musafir Khana, Bedigate Road.
11. Karsandas Holu, Irwin Hospital Road.
12. Mulji Jetha, outside Khambhalia Gate.

Places of Interest

1. *Ranmal Lake* : Centre of attraction in the city. In the middle of lake is Lokhita Palace. It has a museum, fine collection of sculpture and pottery from Saurashtra. On the bank of the lake is the 'Kotha' an old arsenal. Nearby is the Digjam Acquarium.
2. *The Jain Temples* : At Chandi Bazar. Beautifully sculptured Khambhalia Gate and the Vibha Vilas Palace. Manek Bhai Muktidham, a unique cremation ground.

JUNAGADH

Junagadh literally means the old fort, and the picturesque city nestling at the foot of Mount Girnar. The city evokes memories of romance, triumph and tragedy. Junagadh is the home town of Narsi Mehta, the devout poet, saint, singer, scholar, philosopher and social reformer of the 15 century.

How to Reach

Air : Nearest airpot Keshod 65 kms.
Rail : From Bombay, Ahmedabad and Rajkot.
Road : 327 kms. from Ahmedabad. 101 kms. from Rajkot.

Where to Stay

1. Manoranjan Circuit House.
2. Dilaram Guest House.
3. Panchayat Rest House.
4. Railway Retiring House.
5. Vaibhav Hotel.

Places of Interest

1. Among five magnificent Jain Temples at a height of about 610 meters on Girnar.
2. Shrines of Ambaji, Gorakhnath and Guru Dattatreya are further upon the sacred mount.
3. Girnar attracts Jain. Hindu and Muslim pilgrims.
4. Shiva Temple and the tomb of a Muslim saint are also here.
5. On the way to Girnar is the rock with Ashoka's edicts.
6. The monument also bears inscriptions of Rudradaman and Chandergupta.
7. Nearly is the sacred pond, Damodar kenel.
8. An old Rajput palace, two stepwells and Buddhist cave are of special interest in the historic Uparkot fort.
9. On the eastern side of the town is Narsi Mehta's choro.
10. At the foot of Datar Hill is the Willingdon Dam overlooking the Vivekanand's Garden, a beautiful picnic spot which being developed as a National Park of medicinal herbs.
11. Other places of interest—Ranchhodji Mandir, Swaminarayan Temple, the Haveli Temple of Lord Krishna, Rang Mahal, Sakkar Baug with Museum and Zoo. Darbar Hall Museum, Rupayatan and the Maqbera.

Excursions

Sasan Gir : 54 kms. from Junagadh.

Tulsi Shyam Sulphur Springs : 163 kms. from Junagadh popular picnic spot, in the heart of Gir forest.

Chorwad : 66 kms. from Junagadh well developed sea side resorts.

Prabhas Patan : 70 kms. from Junagadh city, known as Somanath Patan.

Porbandar : 103 kms. from Junagadh. Mahatma Gandhi's birth place. Sudama Temple is of interest in that town.

BHAVNAGAR

Flourishing port town on the South-Eastern coast of Gujarat's Saurashtra region. Bhavnagar has a number of small, medium and large Industries Textile, Oil, Iron and Steel, Rubber, fertilizer, metalware etc. The city has also been a centre of educational and cultural activities. The best period to visit this city is October to April.

How to Reach

Air : Daily flight from Bombay.

Rail : 269 kms. from Ahmedabad via Botad.

Road : 212 kms. from Ahmedabad via Dhandhuka.
177 kms. from Rajkot via Babra.

Where to Stay

1. Atitheegrih.
2. Muirshead Majirawadi Guest House.
3. Pathik Ashram.
4. Railway Retiring Rooms.
5. Dharamshalas.

Hotels :

1. Hotel Apollo, Opp. Central Bus Stand.
2. Takhte Khurshid Hotel. near Tokhtas Mahadeo.

Places of Interest

Gandhi Smriti : This memorial comprises a library with 40,000 volumes on Gandhian thought, and social sciences, Gandhi picture Gallery, Museum and Khadi and Village Industries Emporium.

Public Gardens : Gauri Shanker Lake is a beautiful picnic spot. Kailas Vatika public garden, Bal Ghar, Vallabh Bhai Patel garden, Malik Bag, Thakkar Bapu Garden and Diamond Chowk Garden, Victoria Park botanical garden.

Burton Library and Museum : Collection of 41,000 Books, Rare coins, artefacts, Arms etc.

Excursions

Palitana : 59 kms. from Bhavnagar. The town is at the

foot of the famous Shatrunjaya Hills, most sacred place of Jain pilgrims.

Takhteshwar Temple : 5 kms. from Bhavnagar on way to Mahuva, the temple is at the top of a hillock.

Rupavani Temple : 2 kms. from city. Shrines of Rupavati Mata.

Velava, Vallabhipur, Mahuva : 70 kms. Bhavnagar Velavadeer National Park and Black Buck Sanctuary. Vallabhipur an ancient city is 35 kms. north-west of Bhavnagar. Another place of interest is Mahuva, the famous old port town 90 kms. south of city.

PALITANA

Near the river Shetrunji is Palitana, the base town that leads to Shatrunjaya Hill. A devout Jain expires to visit this hill at least once in his life time.

Palitana is well connected by rail and road from—Ahmedabad and Bhavnagar. For visitors from Bombay, Bhavnagar is the nearest air port to reach Palitana.

How to Reach

Air : Nearest airport Bhavnagar 62 kms.

Rail : On western Railway Meter Gauge line 277 kms. from Ahmedabad via Sihor.

Road : 56 kms. from Bhavnagar, 215 km. from Ahmedabad, 751 kms. from Bombay.

Where to Stay

1. Ready-money Guest House, near Power House, Palitana.
2. Dharamshalas : There are 40 Dharamshalas for Jains and Hindu Sarvajanik Dharamshalas.
3. Hotel Sumeru, Opp. S.T. Stand.

Places of Interest

1. Temple on Shatrunjaya Hill are architectural marvels.
2. The river Shetrunji flowing to the South of the hill enhances the scenic charm.
3. Most important temple is of Shri Rishbhdev, the first Tirthankar of the Jains.
4. Other important temples are Kamar Pal, Sampritiraja, Bhulavani, Ashta pada, Sahara kuta etc.

Dandi : Situated on the coast line and well known as a Salt Centre. This place has acquired a name in the history after the famous Dandi March Salt Satyagraha launched by Gandhiji in 1930.

Bardoli : Gandhiji had launched a Satyagraha known as the Bardoli Satyagraha in 1928. 287 kms. from Ahmedabad.

Ahmedpur Mandvi : An absolutely untouched beach located in Saurashtra at a distance of 12 kms. from Una Railway Station, and providing the entry to the Union Territory of Diu which is next door.

Tithal : 4 kms. from Bulsar in South Gujarat is pleasant on account of the invigorating sea breeze that is constant feature.

Somnath : One of the 12 most sacred jyotir lingas or Shiva Shrine in India. Ransacked and destroyed by Muslim invaders time and again but rebuilt at the same spot.

Dwarka : The sacred town of Dwarka, associated with Lord Krishna's life, is situated on the western most tip of the Saurashtra peninsula, like a sentinal overlooking Arabian Sea.

Dwarka is one of the four most sacred pilgrimage centres of Hinduism. The Dwarkadhish Temple is a five storeyed temple supported on 60 columns and is crowned by a soaring elaborately carved spire.

Bet Dwarka : An island near Okha port where Lord Vishnu killed the Demon Shankhsar who had become a menace.

Bhalka Tirth : Bhalka Tirth near Somnath is the place where Lord Krishna was mistaken for a deer and wounded by an arrow.

Madhavpur : Associated with Lord Krishna. The temple and the area is the place where the marriage of Lord Krishna and Rukmani took place.

Shamlaji : One of the principal Vaishnava Shrines of Gujarat. The temple is 800 years old and the sculptures of the temple are particularly fine.

Dakor : Dakor is a temple town sacred to Lord Krishna.

Modhera Sun Temple : The Sun Temple of Modhera is one of the first examples of Indian Temple architecture of its period.

Ambaji : Situated on the Arasur Hill near Mount Abu. Ambaji is dedicated to the worship of Shakti and is one of the most popular places of pilgrimage in Gujarat.

Patanji : A beautiful old town with Jain temples famous for Patola Silk.

For further details please contact :
Gujarat Tourism Corpn. Ltd.
HK-House, opp. Ashram Road,
Ahmedabad-380009.
Phone : 449683/460640.

MAHARASHTRA

Maharashtra is the composition of three states viz. Western Maharashtra, Vidarbha and Marathwada. Rukmani, (wife of Lord Krishna), Indumati (wife of Aja), and Damyanti (wife of Nal) were the daughters of Vidarbha kings. Great hero Shivaji was also from Maharashtra. Mahatma Phule, Agarkar, Tilak and Gokhale were the great personalities ot Maharashtra.

BOMBAY

Once it was a sleepy island which was discovered in 250 B.C. It was known as Mombai. Bombay came into British hand. Portuguese, as a part of dowery, gave it to British. After independence it has become a big commercial city. It has one of the natural harbours. Ships of the world touch it and go. It is one of the most important metropolitan cities of India. It is famous for film-making. There are more than 150 textile units. Being industrial city, Bombay is producing many items of our need.

How to Reach

Air : Bombay is an international air port. It is connected by air with the important cities of India as well as world. Daily air service from Delhi, Madras and Calcutta.

Rail : Bombay is connected with the other parts of India by rail service. There are two main rail heads i.e., Bombay Central and Bombay V.T. Some trains terminate at Bombay V.T. while others at Bombay Central. There are direct trains from Jammu, Chandigarh, Amritsar, Delhi, Howrah, Hyderabad, Bangalore, Madras and Trivandrum etc.

Road : Regular bus service is also available from Bombay to other important cities of India.

Road Distances from Bombay to other Cities :

Ahmedabad 554 kms.
Calcutta via Nagpur 2044 kms.
Delhi via Indore 1405 kms.
Jaipur 1170 kms.
Kodai Kanal 1946 kms.
Panch Marhi 1315 kms.
Srinagar 2280 kms.
Bhubneshwar 1747 kms.
Dharamshala 1971 kms.
Kohima 3368 kms.
Lonavala 125 kms.
Nainital 1558 kms.
Ranikhet 1596 kms.
Aurangabad 412 kms.
Kanya Kumari 1930 kms.
Delhi via Ahmedabad 1690 kms.
Jogfalls 788 kms.
Madras 1592 kms.
Pondicherry 1280 kms.
Varanasi 1613 kms.
Chandigarh 1646 kms.
Hazari Bagh 1864 kms.
Kotagiri 1360 kms.
Lucknow 1372 kms.
Ooty 1320 kms.
Simla 1754 kms.
Bangalore 1035 kms.
Coimbatore 1334 kms.
Goa 675 kms.
Kathmandu 2390 kms.
Mahabaleshwar 304 kms.
Pune 184 kms.
Almora 1645 kms.
Coonoor 1339 kms.
Kalim Pong 2434 kms.
Kozhikode 1245 kms.
Manali 1924 kms.
Patna 1886 kms.
Trivandrum 1806 kms.
Calcutta via Indore 2294 kms.
Darjeeling 3138 kms.
Hyderabad 730 kms.
Khajuraho 1243 kms.
Mount Abu 876 kms.
Shillong 3058 kms.
Bhopal 784 kms.
Dalhousie 1968 kms.
Khandala 117 kms.
Kulu 1994 kms.
Mussoorie 1645 kms.
Ranchi 1830 kms.

Where to Stay

Western Style Hotels :

1. Oberoi Towers : Nariman Point
2. Taj Mahal : Apollo Bunder
3. Taj Mahal Inter Continental, Apollo Bunder
4. Sea Rock Welcome, Land's End, Bandra
5. Holiday Inn, Balraj Sahni Marg, Juhu
6. Centur, Bombay Air Port
7. President, Cuff Parade, Colaba
8. Ambassador, Veer Nariman Road
9. Ritz, Jamshedji Tata Road
10. Poonam International, Shiva Sagar Estate, Worli
11. Furlyas, Off Arther Bunder Road, Colaba
12. Horizon, Juhu Beach
13. Air Port Plaza, Nehru Road, Vile Parle (East)
14. Bombay International, Netaji Subhash Road

15. Sun-N-Sand, Juhu Beach
16. Transit, Off Nehru Road, Vile Parle (East)
17. Oriental Palace, Khar Pali Road, Khar
18. Natraj, Netaji Subhash Road
19. Sea Green South, -do-
20. Ajanta, Juhu Tara Road
21. Sea Green, Netaji Subhash Road
22. Astoria, Jamshedji Tata Road
23. West End, V. Thackersy Marg
24. Ascot, Garden Road
25. Godwin, 41, Garden Road
26. Pali Hills, Union Park, Khar
27. Grand, Sprott Road, Ballard Estate
28. Hilltop, Poch Khana Wala Road, Worli
29. Rivera, near Hotel Horizon, Juhu Road
30. Apollo, M. Bhushan Marg
31. Imperial Palace, Telly Park Road, Andheri (East)
32. Heritage, Victoria Road, Byculla
33. Shalimar, August Kranti Marg
34. Ram Krishna, Nehru Road, Vile Parle
35. Sea Palace, P. J. Ramchandani Marg
36. Caesar's Palace, Linking Road, Khar
37. Amiga, S.V. Savarkar Marg, Shivaji Park, Dadar
38. Chatwani's International, Vaikunth Park Road, Andheri (East)
39. Sea Side, Juhu Beach
40. Parkway, Ranade Road, Shivaji Park
41. South End, Juhu Tara Road, Juhu

Indian Style Hotels :

1. Juhu, Juhu Beach
2. Diplomat, Mere Weather Road, Colaba
3. Pyrke's Apollo, M. Bhushan Marg, Apollo Bunder
4. Garden, Garden Road, Colaba
5. Kings, Juhu Tara Road
6. Siddhartha, S.V. Road, Bandra
7. Jewel Palace, Corner of 2nd and 5th Road, Opp. Municipality Baudra
8. Delamar, Sunder Mahal, Netaji Subhash Rd
9. Shelly's P.J. Ramchandani Marg, Colaba

10. Parklane, Dadar T.T.
11. Kemps Corner, Kemps Corner
12. Y.W.C.A. International Guest House, 18, Madame Cama Road.
13. Hotel in Phom, 148, P Juhu Road. Juhu.
14. High Way Inn, Vishal Apartments, near Andheri Railway Station East
15. Strand, Apollo Bunder
16. Rajdoot, Sakaria Bunder Road, near Cotton Green Station.
17. Metrople, Bank of Baroda Building, Paltan Road.
18. Lovely, Nehru Road, Santa Cruz (East)
19. Norman's Guest House, Netaji Subhash Road
20. Bentlley's, Oliver Road
21. Galaxy, Behind Electric Home, Santa Cruz (East)
22. Rupam, P.D. Mello Road
23. Suba Guest House, Opp. Cottage Industries. C. Shivaji Maharaj Marg
24. Chetak Windsor Guest House, near Nariman Road
25. YMCA International Guest House, YMCA Road. Bombay Central
26. Elphinstone, DN. Road
27. New Bengal Lodge, Sita Ram Bldg. B-Block, Div. Road
28. Bentlley's D. Road, Netaji Subash Road
29. Minerva, opp. Minerva Cinema, Bhadkamiker Road
30. Arya Niwas, Kila Chand Mansion, Kalba Devi.
31. Lawrence, Ashok Kumar House, K. Dubark Marg
32. Purnima, Asha Colony, Juhu, Sardar Griha opp. Mahatma Phule Market.
33. Narsinha Guest House, near T.V. Station.
34. Fernandez Guest House, Balmer-Lawrie Bldg. 3rd floor Ballard Estate.
35. Empire Hindu, opp. T.V. Station.
36. Girgaum Lodge, opp. Majestic Cinema.

Paying Guest Accommodation :

A list of paying guest accommodation is available with Govt. of India, Tourist Office, Bombay.

Other Accommodation :

1. Railway Retiring Room, Bombay Central and Victoria Terminus.

2. YWCA, Lady Willington Hostel, Madam Cama Road.
3. Acharuma Bhawan Hostel, Moti Bai Street Byculla.
4. Red Shield Hostel, Mereweather Road.
5. Sodality Guest House, J. Bai Road.
6. Women's Graduate Union Sasoch Dock Colaba.

Youth Hostels :

1. Bhavan's College, Versova Road.
2. Bhavans Camp, Andheri.
3. University Hostel, RA Kidwai Road.
4. Dodar College of Commerce Hostel, Sion.

Sanitoria and Dharamshalas :

1. BSNC Pooranchandji Trust, Kalba Devi Road.
2. Hargovan Anandji Desai Charities Corner Pinjira Pole Street.
3. Seth MM Dharamshalas Charity Trust CP Tank Road.
4. D. Singhavia Dharamshala Trust, Anant Wadi.
5. P. Jivandas Charity Trust, Doongersy Road.

Musafir Khanas :

1. Cumine Jafar Suleman, Wadi Bunder Road.
2. Rangri Mohalla Jamal Khana, Minar Masjid Pydhone.
3. Oswood Baug, Mazagaon.

Restaurants :

1. Gay Lord Church Gate Area.
2. Kwality Church Gate Area
3. Moca Bar Church Gate Area.
4. Ritz Coffee Bar Church Gate Area.
5. Talk of the town Church Gate Area.
6. Caravan, Sterling Cinema.
7. Cafe Royal, Oberoi Towers.
8. Flaming Hostel Bombay International.
9. Gulmarg, Shalimar Hotel.
10. Inner circle, Grand Hotel.
11. Lacozy, Hotel Amigo.
12. Moti Mahal Bandra.
13. Pasha, G. Dashmukh Marg.
14. Playboy, Caesar's Palace Hotel.
15. Rendevous, Taj Mahal Hotel.
16. Sea Lounge, Taj Mahal Hotel
17. Supper club oberoi Towers.
18. Touche, Bhulabhai Desai Rd.
19. Tanjore, Taj Mahal Hotel.

Mughlai and Tandoori

1. Algrill, Bandra.
2. Ali Baba, C. Shivaji Marg.
3. Berry's near Nariman Road
4. Copper Chimney, K. Dubesh Marg.
5. Delhi Darbar, near Regal Cinema.
6. Kabab Corner, Natraj Hotel.
7. Khaybar, K. Dubesh Marg.
8. Kwality, Colaba.
9. Copper Chimney, Worli.
10. Kwality, Worli.
11. Mocambo, P.M. Road.
12. Moghul Room, Oberoi Towers.
13. Nandi Hotel, Bandra.
14. Oscar, Pali Hill.

Chinese Restaurant :

1. Chinese Room, Kemps Corner.
2. Chopsticks, Church Gate.
3. Flora, Worli.
4. Fredericks, Colaba.
5. Guzebo Oriental, Bandra.
6. Golden Dragon, Taj Mahal Hotel.
7. Golden Gate, M. Cama Road.
8. Nanking C. Shivaji Marg.
9. Mandarin C. Shivaji Marg.
10. Kamling, Church Gate.
11. Shanghai, Colaba.
12. Sri-Hal, Colaba.

Vegetarian Restaurant :

1. Bristol Grill, P. Mehta Road.
2. Chetana, K. Dubash Marg.
3. Kubera, Church Gate.
4. Purohit, Church Gate.
5. Rasna, Church Gate Reclamation.
6. Shyadrim, M. Karne Road.
7. Samrat, J. Tata Road.
8. Satkar, Church Gate.
9. The Shilpa, Opera House.
10. Sun, Bhulabhai Desai Road.
11. Tavorn, Nariman Point.
12. Thacker's near Marine Lines Rly. Station.
13. Woodlands, Nariman Point.

Clubs

1. Bombay Gym Khana, Mahatma Gandhi Road.
2. Catholic Gym Khana, N. Subhash Road.
3. Cricket Club of India, Brabourne Stadium.
4. Chembur golf, Chembur.
5. Hindu Gym Khana N. Subhash Road.

6. Islam Gym Khana -do-
7. National Sports Club of India Hornby Ballard.
8. Parsi Gym Khana, N. Subhash Road.
9. Princess Victoria Marg Gym Khana Cooperative.
10. Radio, Arther Bunder Road Colaba.
11. Royal Western India Turf. Mahalaxmi.
12. Willingdon Sports, Khade Marg Mahalaxmi.
13. W.I.A.A. Ridge Road.
14. Wodehouse, Gymkhana, Wodehouse Road

Swimming Pools

1. Beach Candy Swimming Bath Trust Bhulabhai Desai Road.
2. Golwala's Victoria Swimming Bath.
3. Mahatma Gandhi Memorial Olympic Swimming Pool Cadell Road.
4. Mafatlal Hindu Swimming Bath Club Trust, Netaji Subhash Road.
5. Willingdon Sports Club Swimming Pool.
6. C.C.I. Swimming Pool, Church Gate.

Places of Interest

Art Galleries :

1. Jahangir Art Gallery.
2. Taj Art Gallery, Taj Mahal Hotel.
3. Aakr-Bhulabhai Desai Road.
4. Cymorza Bhulabhai Desai Road.
5. Oasis, L.J. Road.
6. Pundole, Flora Fountain.
7. Shiroms, Inside Dhanraj Mahal.

Museum :

1. Prince of Wales Museum.
2. Victoria and Albert Museum.

Zoo : Victoria Garden, Byculla.

Parks :

National Park : Borivali, 34 kms. opened in 1949 Area 5000 Acres.

Kamla Nehru Park : Near Hanging Garden.

Jawaharlal Nehru Park : At Sion a beautiful picnic spot.

Gardens :

1. Victoria Garden.

2. Feroze Shah Mehta Garden—(Hanging Garden) on Malabar Hill.
3. Joseph Baptista Garden.

Lakes :

Lake District of Bombay is famous for its picturseque surroundings. Powel Lake is 42 kms. from Bombay. Vihar is 2 kms. from Powel.

Sight Seeing :

1. Mantralaya (Secretariat).
2. Gate Way of India.
3. Marine Drive.
4. Taraporewala Acquarium.
5. Chowpatty Beach.
6. Haffkine Institute.
7. Tata Memorial Hospital.
8. Crawford Market.
9. Nehru Planetorium.
10. Randet Tehera.
11. Worli Dairy.

Excursions

Trombay Island : 27 kms. from Bombay by road. Two Oil Refineries and Bhabha Atomic Energy Estt. are here.

Aarey Milk Colony : 35 kms. from Bombay one of the modern dairies.

Kanheri Caves : 7 kms. from Aarey Milk Colony. Appx. hundred Buddhist caves are there.

Bassein : 50 kms. Historical Place.

Elephanta Caves : 10 kms. from Bombay Harbour. Famous for Brahmanical sculpture of 1000 years. ago. Regular ferry service from Gate Way of India by Motor Launch.

Karnala Bird Sanctuary : 61 kms. on Bombay Goa Road.

Hill Stations

Khandala : 120 kms. from Bombay at an altitude of 2000 ft. above sea level. A little further alongwith main road is Bhandala's finest waterfall.

Lonavala : 5 kms. from Khandala, Rye forest is the main attraction of this place. Lake Bhangerwadi and Tiger's leap have scenic grandeur. Famous caves of Karla, Bhaja and Bedsa are at a distance of 11 kms. from Lonavala.

How to Reach

Air : Nearest air port Bombay.

Rail : Both the hill resorts are on Bombay-Pune Main Line of the Central Railway.

Road : Both are connected with Pune and Bombay by road. Regular buses are available.

Where to Stay

Lonawala

Western Style Hotels :

1. Dinesh
2. Janta
3. Vishwa Bharat
4. Biji's Ingleside Inn

Indian Style Hotels :

1. Adarsh
2. Anupama
3. Chandralok
4. Firi Kunj
5. Ashoka
6. Regal
7. Shamiyana
8. Shalimar
9. Woodlands
10. Maharaja Inn
11. Matru Chhaya Lodge
12. Park Motel
13. Pitale Lodge
14. Shri Krishna Boarding.
15. Shahani Holiday Home

Khandala

Western Style Hotels :

1. Girija
2. Mayur
3. Hotel on the Rocks.

Indian Style Hotels :

1. El Taj
2. Mount View
3. Mount View Extension.

Other Accommodation :

1. Holiday Camp
2. Inspection Bungalow
3. Municipal Rest House
4. Govt. Rest House.

Dharamshalas :

1. Siddheshwar.

Sanitorium :

1. Shanilal Jamnadas Morarjee
2. Nathulal Manek Chand Parekh Arogya Bhawan.
3. Narayanji Parmanandji Trust.
4. Dawood Bohra.
5. Bande Ali Sivaji Virani.
6. Mathuradas Dwarkadas.
7. Kanju Vasanjee Munjee.
8. Diwalibai.
9. Joshi.
10. Lady Thackersey.
11. Sri Krishna.
12. Modi.
13. Kotkar.
14. Dhanbai Cawasji.

MATHERAN

Hill resort 104 kms. from Bombay. The main attractions are long, quiet walks and panoramic view from the many points.

How to Reach

Air : Nearest air port Bombay 104 kms.

Rail : Connected by rail to Neral 20.8 kms. by mountain toy train.

Road : Jeepable road from Neral via Karjat from Bombay or Pune.

Where to Stay

1.	Hope Hall Hotel, M.G. Road	Phone	53
2.	Janata Happy Home, Kasturba Road.	,,	29
3.	The Kaka Group of Hotels, Mathern.	,,	71-72
4.	Laxmi Hotel, M.G. Road.		
5.	Meghdoot Hotel, Kasturba Road.	,,	66
6.	N. Lords Guest House, M.G. Road.		
7.	Alankar Hotel, M.G. Road.	,,	10
8.	Ashok Hotel, Mallet Road.	,,	35
9.	Bombay new Hotel, Cutling Road.	,,	79
10.	Cecil Hotel, Chimoy Road.	,,	56
11.	Diwadkar Hotel.	,,	23
12.	Gujarat Bhawan Hotel, Maulana Azad Road.	,,	78
13.	Guru Hotel, Matheran	,,	54
14.	Giri Vihar Hotel, M.G. Road.	,,	31
15.	Hotel Prasanna Opp. Railway Station.	,,	58
16.	Prem Deep Lodging Kasturba Road.	,,	15
17.	Shirin Hotel, Panday Road.	,,	76
18.	West End Hotel, near Police Station.	,,	59
19.	Alexander Guest House, Madhavji Road.	,,	51-90
20.	Khan's Hotel, M.G. Road.	,,	40
21.	Lords Central Hotel, M.G. Road.	,,	28
22.	Regal Hotel Kasturba Road.	,,	43-87
23.	Royal Hotel, Kasturba Road.	,,	43-75
24.	Rugby Hotel, Kotwal Road.	,,	91-92
25.	Silvana Hotel, Acharya Are Road.	,,	20-74
26.	Woodland Hotel, Chinoy Road.	,,	71-72

Other Accommodation :

1. MTDC Holiday Resort Ph. 77
2. Scott Bungalow, Paymaster Park Ph. 88
3. Inspection Bungalow.
4. Mount District Bungalow.
5. Municipal Rest House.
6. Manik Lal Terrace.
7. Naimisharanya.

Places of Interest

1. Olympia Race Course.
2. Charlotte Lake.
3. Ram Bagh Village.
4. Pay Master Park.
5. N. Lord Garden.
6. Pande Playground.
7. Cathedral Rock Points.

PUNE

184 kms. from Bombay. It has various attractions. There are number of forts, temples and modern educational institutions. It is a centre of sports also. It has historical background. Maratha Sardar Shivaji defeated ruler of Bijapur at a distance of 24 kms. from Pune.

How to Reach

Air : Pune itself airport.

Rail : Pune itself railway station. There are a number of trains from Bombay to Pune.

Road : Direct connection with Bombay and other important cities of India by road.

Where to Stay

Western Style Hotels :

1. Saras, Nehru Stadium, near Saras Baug.
2. Amir, Sadhu Waswani Road.
3. Ajit, Deccan Gymkhana.
4. Blue Diamond, 11, Koregaon Park.
5. Ellora, Sadashiv Peth.
6. Gulmohar, Sadhu Waswani Road.
7. Jawahar, Tilak Road.
8. Pathik, Jungli Maharaj Road.
9. Poonam, Shivaji Nagar.
10. Sapana, Jungli Maharaj Road.
11. Sutalaj, AFCR Road.
12. Seven Loves, Shanker Set Road.
13. Shalimar, Sadhu Waswani Road.
14. Swati, Apte Rd. Deccan Gym Khana.
15. Shreyas, Apte Road.
16. Vishwa Kamal, Pune-Satara Road.

Indian Style Hotels :

1. Alankar Willson Garden.
2. Dreamland, Sadhu Waswani Road.
3. Metro Sadhu Waswani Road.
4. Ritz, Sadhu Waswani Road.
5. Tourist, Mangalwar Peth.
6. Pearl, Rani Jhansi Chowk, Shivaji Nagar.
7. Prince, Shanker Set Road
8. Sauman, opp, Sambhaji Park, Shivaji Nagar.
9. Shri Krishna, Somwar Peth.

Other Accomodation :

1. Railway Retiring Room.
2. W.I.A.A. Arsena Road.
3. Western India Turf Club, Solapur Road.
4. Poona Club Ltd. Bund Garden.
5. Y.W.C.A. Gurudwar Road
6. Turf Club House, Solapur Road.
7. Circuit House, Queens Garden.
8. Inspection Bungalow Queen Garden.

Dharamshala :

1. Morarji Gokuldas, Opp. Pune Railway Station.

Restaurants :

1. Moti Mahal, Deccan Gymkhana.
2. Rupali, Fergusson Road
3 Vaishali, -do-
4. Deepa, Shivaji Nagar.
5. Santosh Bhawan, Budhwar Peth.
6. Rasana Jungli Maharaj Road.
7. Ruihira Jungli Maharaj Road.
8. Shere Punjab, Opp. Alankar Cinema.
9. Latif's, Thimayya Road.
10. Kwality, East Street.
11. Poonam, Jungli Maharaja Road.
12. Preeya, Mahatma Gandhi Road.
13. Samarat, Shanker Sett Road.
14. Khyber, Jungli Maharaj Road.
15. Natraj, Shanker Sett Road.
16. Modern Cafe, Shivaji Nagar.
17. Three Coins, East Street.
18. Swagat, Kirkke.
19. Ashoka, Sadashive Peth.
20. Jawahar, Bajirao Road.
21. Ellora, Sadashiv Peth.
22. Apsara, Tilak Road.
23. Seven Loves, Shankar Seth Road.
24. Poona Coffee House, Deccan Gym Khana.
25. Raj Mohal. Mahatma Gandhi Garden.
26. Blue Nine, Mahatma Gandhi Garden.

Places of Interest

Agha Khan Palace : Mahatma Gandhi, Kasturba and

Mahadco Desai were detained here during 1942 Quit India Movement.

Mahatma Gandhi Udyan : Previous name Bund Gardens.

Chaturshringi Temple : During Navaratra a big fair is held here.

Bhandekar Oriental Research Institute : This famous institution has a collection of 20,000 manuscripts.

Glinder Drome : 13 kms. Gliding training centre.

National Defence Academy : 17 kms. at Khadak Vasala, training centre of officer cadets.

Raja Dinkar Kelkar Museum : House of collection of historical exhibits of Mughal and Maratha period.

Film and Television Institute of India : Training centre of direction, music, screen play writing, acting, editing and photography of film.

Parks :

1. Sambhaji Park, Jungli Maharaj Road.
2. University Parks, Ganesh Khise.
3. Chitaranjan Vatika Sadashiva Peth.
4. Peshwa Park, Sadashiva Peth.

Gardens :

1. Dr. Ambedkar Udyan, Station Road.
2. Empress Garden, Opp. Race Course.
3. Botanical Garden, Ganesh Khise.
4. Mahatma Gandhi Udyan.
5. Ghor Pade Udyan, Ghor Pade Peth.
6. Jaya Prakash Narain Udyan Opp. Pune Station.
7. Jijamata Udyan, Budhwor Peth.
8. Kamla Nehru Udyan, Erandwana.
9. Saras Baug Sadashiva Peth.
10. Shahu Udyan, Somwar Peth.

Shopping Centre :

1. Deccan Gymkhana, Laxmi Road.
2. Mahatma Gandhi Road.

MAHABALESHWAR

120 kms. from Pune, 19 kms. from Panchgani, 188 kms. from Kolhapur, Mahabaleshwar is a hill station at an altitude of 1372 meters above the sea level. It is cold from October to February and cool from March to May. Best season October to June. It has scenic beauty and good climate.

How to Reach

Nearest air port is Pune. Convenient rail head Pune. S.T. Buses regularly plying from Bombay and Pune to Mahabaleshwar.

Where to Stay

Western Style Hotels :

1. Anarkali
2. Blue Park
3. Deluxe.
4. Fredric.
5. Fountain.
6. Grand.
7. May Fair.
8. Motel Tree Shade.

Indian Style Hotels :

1. Ajanta Lodge.
2. Apsara.
3. Aram.
4. Bharat.
5. Dreamland.
6. Giri Vihar.
7. Blue Heaven.
8. Bombay Vihar
9. Greenland.
10. Shreyas.
11. Laxmi Lodge.
12. Nell's
13. Paradise.
14. Race View.
15. Rajesh.
16. Regal.
17. Ripon.
18. Satkar.
19. Savoy.
20. Sharma Safalya
21. Shanti Sadan.
22. Triveni Lodge.
23. Modern.

Other Accommodations :

1. Holiday Camp.
2. Govt. Rest House No. 1 and 2.
3. Hirda Forest Bungalow.
4. VIP Bungalow.
5. Lingmala Forest Rest House.

Places of Interest

1. Arthur Seat.
2. Castle Rock.
3. Savitri Point.
4. Elphinstone Point.
5. Old Mahabaleshwar.
6. Hunter's Point.
7. Connaught Peak Point.
8. Kate's Point.
9. Lingmala Water Fall.
10. Venna Lake.
11. Dhobi Water Fall.
12. Lodwick Point.
13. Elephant Head.
14. Bombay Point.
15. Carnac Point.
16. Chinaman's Water Fall.
17. Babington Point.
18. Helen's Point.
19. Wilson Point.
20. Pratap Garh.
21. Robber's Cave.

AURANGABAD

It is famous for Ajanta and Ellora caves which are 100 and 30 kms. from Aurangabad respectively. It contains several ruins.

How to Reach

Air : Direct air line from Bombay.

Rail : 375 kms. from Bombay by rail on meter guageline. Passenger have to change at Manmad Railway jn. 114 kms. from Aurangabad, then by road.

Distance between Aurangabad and other Cities

Bombay via Nasik Manmad	:	302 kms.
Bombay via Dhulia Jalgaon—Ajanta	:	580 kms.
Bombay via Pune Ahemadabad	:	415 kms.
Hyderabad	:	554 kms.
Nagpur	:	645 kms.
Shirdi	:	153 kms.
Calcutta via Jalna	:	1626 kms.
Calcutta via Allahabad—Jhansi	:	1960 kms.
Delhi via Mathura, Agra, Gwalior or Jalgaon and Ajanta	:	1323 kms.
Madras	:	1285 kms.
Bangalore via Coonoor	:	1101 kms.
Bangalore via Bijapur and Sholapur	:	1021 kms.

Where to Stay

Western Style Hotels :

1. Ajanta Ambassador, Airport Road.
2. Aurangabad Ashok, Dr. Rajendra Prasad Marg.
3. Nandanvan, Railway Station Road.
4. Welcome hotel Rama International, Chiklalthana Road.

Indian Style Hotels :

1. Ashok, Tilak Path.
2. Emphire, Juna Bazar.
3. Gitanjali Guest House, near Head Post Office.
4. Kamakshi Lodge, Behind City Police Station.
5. Natraj, Station Road.
6. Neelam, opp : Jubilee Park.
7. Oberi, Osmanpur.
8. Palace, Shahganj.
9. Printravel, Dr. Ambedkar Road.
10. Punjab National, Pan Dariba.

11. Samarth Lodge, Samarth Nagar.
12. Simla, Osmanpur.
13. Tourist House, Railway Station Road.

Other Accommodation :

1. Govt. Holiday Camp, near Railway Station
2. Subedari Guest House, near Collectorate
3. Railway Retiring Room
4. Municipal Rest House, near Railway Station
5. Youth Hostel, Padampura

Dharamshalas :

1. Samarth, near Railway Station
2. Shri Chandra Sagar, Shahganj

Restaurants :

1. Bahar, Hotel Neelam
2. Dewan-e-Am, Ajanta Ambassador Hotel
3. Kozy, Adalat Road
4. Madhuban, Welcomehotel Rama International
5. Pinky, opp : Holiday Camp

Places of Interest

Aurangabad Caves : 3 kms. Buddhist caves.

Bibi Ka Maqbara : 5 kms. Mausoleum of Dilras Banu Begum, first of Aurangzeb.

Panchakki (water mill) : 3 km. historical place.

Daulatabad : 13 km. on the way to Ellora Caves, Capital of Mohammad Tughlaq.

NASIK

Lying on the banks of the sacred river Godavari, Nasik is one of the holy cities of the Hindus. Rama, the hero of the epic Ramayana is said to have spent part of his exile here. The name of Nasik is derived from the famous incident in Ramayana, where Lakshamana cut the nose of Shurpanakha sister of Ravana. Nasik has many small and big industries coming up on the outskirts of the city. Inspite of this fast industrial growth. Nasik is still famous for its religious back grourd and is even today a renowned pilgrim centre. Simhortha Mela is held here every twelve years.

How to Reach

Air : Nasik has a small airport.

Rail : The nearest rail head is Nasik Road 8 kms. on Central Railway. Regular bus service is available.

Road : On National Highway known as Bombay Agra Road. Distance between some important cities :

Nasik to Bombay 178.8 kms.

Nasik to Aurangabad 204 kms.

Nasik to Shirdi 89.9 kms.

Nasik to Nagpur 726.4 kms.

Nasik to Pune 211.5 kms.

Regular S.T. buses ply from Nasik to Bombay, Pune, Aurangabad, Shirdi, Trimbak etc.

Where to Stay

1. Hotel Mazda, Old Agra Rd. Nasik Ph. 72910.
2. Hotel Pawan, Shivaji Road. Nasik Rd. Ph. 86430
3. Hotel Raj Shivaji Road, Nasik Rd. Ph. 86601
4. Hotel Manali Gok colony, Nasik Ph. 73310
5. Hotel Basera, Shivaji Rd, near C.B.S. Ph. 74271-72
6. Hotel Green View, Trimbak Rd. Ph. 72231-32
7. Dwarka Tourist Hotel, Deolali Naka Ph. 72241-42
8. Govt. Rest House, near Golf Club.
9. Tourist Bungalow near Golf Club Ph. 2026713/2027762
10. Rest House Nasik Rd.
11. Railway retiring rooms, Rly Station, Nasik Rd. Ph. 6274
12. Zila Parishad Rest House, opp. Railway Station Nasik Rd.

Dharamshalas :

1. Laxmi Bai Morarji Dharamshala, Panchvati.
2. Abhonkar Dharamshala, Nasik.
3. Khimri Damji Dharamshala, Panchvati.
4. Kanji Dongarsi Dharamshala, Panchvati.
5. Digamber Akhada, Panchavati.
6. Javeri Dharamshala, Ganeshvadi Nasik.
7. Kachha Saurashtra Moti Dharamshala, Panchvati.
8. Kapoorthala Dharamshala, Khothda, Nasik.
9. Gadge Maharaj Dharamshala, Nasik.
10. Vishwa Karma Panchal Sutar Dharamshala Nasik.
11. Kanji Durgsha Trust Dharamshala, Nasik.
12. Dharmanabh Maharaj Jain Shwetambar Mandir, Dharamshala Nasik.
13. Chatare Sampurna Devi Akhada Panchvati, Nasik.

14. Satya Narain Math, Nasik.
15. Mukti Dham, near Railway Station, Nasik Road.

Places of Interest

Gangapur Dam : 8.1 kms. from Central bus stand, Dam stands on the confluence of the Rivers Godavari and Kashyapi.

Pandu Leni : 6 kms. Buddhist cave, known as Pandav Lane. There are 23 caves in all.

Chambhar Loni : 6 kms. one of the many pilgrim places of the Jains.

Tapovan : 3 kms. A beautiful picnic spot.

Someswar Temple : 9 kms. A temple dedicated to Lord Shiva, situated on the banks of Godavari.

Panchavati : The Sita Gompha is situated here. Sita and Rama stayed here during exile. Ravana kidnapped Sita from here. There are many Temple worth-seeing.

Excursions

Bhandara : 92 kms. A beautiful hill resort.

Saptashringi : 53.3 kms. a Temple to goddess Sapta Shringi in a cave.

SHIRDI

Shirdi has acquired all India fame on account of its association with the renowned Saint Shree Saibaba. Pilgrim throng here all the year.

How to Reach

Air : Nearest airport Nasik 122 kms. Pune 207 kms. Aurangabad 157 kms.

Rail : Nearest and convenient rail head is Kopargaon 18 kms. of the Daund Manmad line of Central Railway Bombay-Kopargaon 303 kms. Pune Kopargaon 269 kms. Aurangabad Kopargoan 115 kms.

Road : Shirdi connected with all major cities in Maharashtra by motorable roads.

KOLHAPUR

Situated amidst lovely purple hills rising to nearby 500 meters, Kolhapur enjoys on the whole, a temperate climate. Held in high esteem for the antiquity of its sacred Shrine Mahalaxmi, it is known as 'Dakshin Kashi' or Kashi of South. About 1212 A.D. the Yadavas of Deogiri ruled over it but later it came under the rule of Bijapur. In 1659 Shivaji took possession of the city and it remained with the Marathas until annexed by the British.

How to Reach

Air : Nearest airport is Belgaum 105 kms.

Rail : It is a railway station on Pune-Miraj-Kolhapur section of the South Central Railway. Connected with all important cities.

Road : Kolhapur is situated on the Pune Bangalore Highway. S.T. buses ply from Bombay, Panaji, Miraj, Sangli, Pune, Satara, Savantwadi, Sholapur.

Where to Stay

1. Hotel Gokul, Station Road : Ph. 15192
2. Padma Guest House, Laxmi Puri Ph. 26782
3. Sangam Lodge, -do- Ph. 27104
4. Hotel Sahayadri Opp. : S.T. Stand Ph. 24581
5. New Badshahi Lodge, Laxmi Puri
6. Hotel Opal, Pune-Bangalore Road : Ph. 26044/23622
7. Hotel Samrat, near Central Bus Depot Ph. 27101
8. Hotel Davat, near Market yard Ph. 24313
9. Tourist Hotel, Station Road : Ph. 25364/25324
10. Hotel International, 517, Shivaji Park Ph. 25156
11. Hotel Rajhans, 1089, C. Ward, Bindu Chowk Ph. 26663
12. Hotel Meghana, Laxmi Puri Ph. 27193
13. Hotel Vijay lodging and Boarding, Laxmi Puri Ph. 27852
14. Hotel Tapasya, Tarabai Chowk Ph. 27213
15. Hotel Anand Malhar, Opp : Central Bus Stand Ph. 25091
16. Hotel Anand, Cozy Corner Ph. 26066
17. Hotel Pearl, New Sahu Puri Ph. 24387/24509
18. Hotel R.R. Sheraton, Ramkala Towers Ph. 26255

Other Accommodation :

1. Circuit House Ph. 24857
2. Rest House Ph. 24857

Dharamshala :

Mahalaxmi Dharamshala, near Mahalaxmi Temple Ph. 26977

Places of Interest

1. New Palace
2. Old Palace
3. Ramkala Lake
4. Shalini Palace
5. Town Hall
6. Panchaganga
7. Koti Teerth
8. Bindu Chowk
9. Ambabai Temple
10. Wrestling Arena
11. Gardens and Parks.

Excursions

1. Vishal Garh 83 kms.
2. Narsobachiwadi 40 kms.
3. Jyotiba Hill
4. Mouni Vidyapith Gargoti
5. Radhanagari 52 kms. 52 kms.
6. Bahubali 18 kms.

Where to Stay

M.T.D.C. runs a first class Hotel at Shirdi (Pilgrim Inn) Shree Sai Baba Saurthan provides all types of accommodation :

1. Sai Niwas Guest House
2. Sainath Chaya.
3. Shanti Niwas.
4. Gurusthan.
5. Bhakti Niwas.
6. Sai Prasad.
7. Samadhi Mandir.
8. Sai Udyan.
9. Dormitan
10. Sevarhan
11. Shakti Niwas Big Hall.
12. Mangal Kanyalaya, Hall.
13. Keshav Mandir.

For further details please contact :
Shree Saibaba Saurthan.
At P.O. Shirdi, Taluka Kopergaon Distt.
Ahmedanagar
Ph. 26

TRIMBAKESHWAR

One of the twelve Jyotirlinga in India. It is an important place of pilgrinage for Hindus. The river Godavari has its source here on the hill Brahmagiri. Devotees take a dip in the sacred 'Kushavati Teerth' before proceeding for Darshan of Trimbakeshwar. The temple has beautiful carvins.

How to reach

Air : Nearest airport Nasik 36 kms.

Rail : Nearest railhead Nasik Road 36.3 kms.

Road : On the state highway from Nasik to Dahanu, buses and taxis are also available from here.

Where to Stay

1. Holiday Resort, Gangadwar Road, Trimbakeshwar Ph. 35
2. Govt. Rest House.

Dharamshalas :

1. Jethabhai Dhamaji Dharamshala
2. Mulji Govindji Dharamshala
3. Hansraj Kramsi Dharamshala
4. Narmadabai Dharamshala

Places of Interest

1. Trimbakeshwar Mandir
2. Nirvrihinath Samadhi
3. Ganga Mandir
4. Shri Krishna Mandir
5. Parshuram Mandir
6. Shri Ram Mandir
7. Neel Parvat
8. Hridayeshwar Mandir
9. Narhari Maharaj Mandir
10. Jain Mandir, Gokal Das lane
11. Masjid Teli Gally.

Excursions

1. Janardan Swami Ashram 1 km.
2. Ahilya Dam half km.
3. Anjani Parvat 7 kms.
4. Harihar Fort 10 kms.
5. Vaitarna Dam 15 kms.

PANHALA

18 kms. from Kolhapur. Place of scenic beauty. Panhala is redolent with memories of Chhatrapati Shivaji Maharaj.

How to Reach

Air : Nearest airport Belgaum 123 kms.

Rail : Nearest railhead Kolhapur 18 kms.
Bombay Kolhapur 430 kms.

Road : Bombay-Panhala 414 kms. S.T. bus ply regularly between Kolhapur and Panhala.

Where to Stay

1. Holiday Resort Ph. 25364/25324
2. Rest House Ph. 24857
3. Forest Rest House
4. Tourist Cottage Ph. 27

Places of Interest

1. Sajja Kotih
2. Teen Darwaza

3. Amber Khana
4. Pavankhind
5. Sambhaji Temple
6. Ambabai Temple
7. Jyotibha Temple.

SEVAGRAM

'Village of Sevika' is a small and unpretentions village symbolizing the 'Gandhian way of life'. Gandhiji made this home in later years and many momentous political decisions taken during India's freedom struggle. Today Gandhiji's Ashram in Sevagram is a national institution and his cottage, where his personal belongings are preserved, has become a place of pilgrimage.

How to Reach

Air : Nearest airport is Nagpur 72 kms.

Rail : Sevagram is the railway station on Central Railway. Wardha Jn. is 6 kms. from here. 765 kms. from Bombay.

Road : Maharashtra State Road Transport Corpn. operates several buses from Wardha to Sevagram.

Where to Stay

1. There is no hotel at Sevagram or Paunar.
2. Seva Gram Community maintains a guest house, Rustam Guest House.
3. Holiday Camp at Wardha
4. Govt. Rest House at Wardha
5. Circuit House, Wardha
6. Railway Retiring Room Wardha Railway Station.

Places of Interest

1. Aadi Niwas
2. Bapu Kuti
3. Ba Kuti
4. Aakhiri Niwas
5. Prayer Ground
6. Mahadeo Kuti
7. Shanti Bhavan
8. Kasturba Hospital

PAUNAR

6 kms. from Sevagram is famous for the Paramdhan Ashram, founded by Acharya Vinoba Bhave who started *Bhudan Andolan* movement for landless farmers. The Ashram, over-looking the river Dham, is set in great natural beauty.

How to Reach

Air : Nearest airport is Nagpur 62 kms.

Rail : Paunar Railway Station, now known as Sehi Road, is on Central Railway. 14 kms. Wardha Jn. Paunar 773 km. from Bombay, 65 kms. from Nagpur.

Road : State transport buses halt at Paunar on the following route :

Nagpur	Wardha
Wardha	Bor Dam
Wardha	Bhandari
Wardha	Sindhi Kandri

Places of Interest

1. Paramdham Ashram
2. Paunar Chhatri
3. Gandhi Stambh
4. Bharat Ram Mandir
5. Dattapur Leprosy Colony.

CHIKHALDARA

Situated on the Southern spurs of the Govilgad hills, part of the Satpura ranges, in Amravati Distt. Chikhaldara has a mythological background also. According to a legend in Mahabharat, Bheema killed Keechaka.

How to Reach

Air : Nearest airport Nagpur 255 kms.

Rail : Nearest railhead Amravati on Central Railway.

Road : Connected to most of major cities by road.

Where to Stay

1. Holiday Camp
2. Circuit House
3. Rest House
4. Forest Bungalow.

Places of Interest

1. Devi point 1.6 km.
2. Govilgad 4.8 kms.
3. Vana Udyan 1.6 km.
4. Bir Talao 3 kms.
5. Sakkar Point 1.6 km.
6. Long Point 3 kms.
7. Kalapani Tank 1.6 km.
8. Bhim Kund 3 kms.
9. Panchbol 5.3 kms.
10. Hurricane Point 2.4 kms.
11. Prospect Point 3 kms.
12. Mozri Point 2.4 kms.
13. Vairat Point 11 kms.

AMRAVATI

Prominent educational and trade centre in Vidarbha. According to a legend Shri Krishna carried Rukmani away when she came to pray at the Amba Devi Temple before she was to be married to Shishupal against her wishes.

How to Reach

Air : Nearest airport Nagpur 155 kms.

Rail : Amravati is the terminus of the branch line of Central Railway. Badnera-Amravati 10 kms. Badnera Jn. on Bombay-Calcutta main line, Central Railway.

Road : Connected to all major cities in Maharashtra.

Where to Stay

1.	Hotel Tourist, near Railway Station.	Ph : 3873
2.	Kirti Lodge, Ralis Plot	„ 3241
3.	Hotel Natraj, Jawahar Road	„ 2536
4.	Hotel Neelam, Badnera Road	„ 2647/2791
5.	Rajendra Lodge, Jawahar Road	„ 3650
6.	Hotel Samrat, -do-	„ 3264
7.	Vidharbha Lodge, -do-	„ 2446
8.	New Bharat Lodge, -do-	„ 4422
9.	Central Lodge, Chitra Chowk	
10.	Rajasthan Lodge, Rallis Plot	„ 2324
11.	Shree Lodge	„ 3428
12.	Rest House	
13.	Circuit House	

Dharamshalas :

1. Zunzunwala Dharamshala, near Vasant Talkies.

Places of Interest

1. Amba Temple 1 km.
2. Sainath Temple and Garden 4.5 kms.
3. Mal Tekdi 1 km.
4. Tapovan lepers colony 4.8 kms.
5. Sati Dham.

NAGPUR

Capital of former central provinces and old city of Bhosle Kingdom. It is famous for its ancient monuments.

How to Reach

Air : Daily air service available from Bombay, Delhi, Calcutta and Madras.

Rail : Nagpur itself a railway Jn. on Central Railway and South-Eastern Railway. Trains are available from the following places.

Bombay	837 kms.
Pune	887 kms.
Chandrapur	194 kms.
Aurangabad	690 kms.
Gondia	130 kms.

Road : Nagpur is connected by road with the important and big cities of India.

Where to Stay

Western Style Hotels :

1. Mount Hotel Annexe Sadar Ph : 33818/32616
2. Needos Hotel, Sangam Bridge, Sitawadi
3. Hotel Skylark, 119, Central Avenue Ph : 40354/55/56

Indian Style Hotels :

1. Sheesh Mahal Hotel, Variety Chowk, Sita Wardi Ph : 31076
2. Hotel Shyam, Sita Wardi, Ph : 24076
3. Anandashram, Dhantoli

Another Accommodation :

1. Circuit House, No. 1, Ravi Bhavan Ph : 31297
2. Circuit House, No. 2, Civil Lines ,, 31488
3. P.W.D. Rest House, Sadar
4. P.M. Cottages, near Circuit House No. 1
5. M.L.A. Hostel, Civil Lines ,, 32078
6. New M.L.A. Rest House, near Reserve Bank Quarters, Civil Lines. ,, 31521
7. Y.M.C.A. Hostel ,, 22810

Dharamshalas :

1. Baldev Dharamshala, Modi lane No. 1 Ph : 25714
2. Jamnadhar Poddar Dharamshala, Meyo Hospital Road. Ph : 25917

Places of Interest

1. *Sita Wardi Fort* : Situated on the top of Sitawardi hillock.
2. *Maharaj Garden* : Birds sanctuary is here.
3. *Zoo* : Collection of architectural items.
4. *Hutatma Shankar Smarak* : Memorial of Shankar.

5. *Other Places* : Statue of Rani Laxmi Bai of Jhansi, Ambhajhari lake, and garden, Gandhi Sagar, Gandhi Garden etc.

RAMTEK

Associated with Lord Rama. Situated near a hillock. While going to Dandakaranya Rama stayed here. Famous poet Kalidasa inspired to write Meghdoot here. There are a number of temples.

How to Reach

Air : Nearest airport Nagpur 47 kms.

Rail : Ramtek is railway station on branch line of South-Eastern Railway between Nagpur-Gondia rail line.

Road : Tumser 48 kms. Bhandara 65 kms. and Gondia 96 kms. buses are available.

Where to Stay

1. Hilday Camp 6 kms from Ramtek near the Khindse Tank.
2. Rest house Khindse.

Places of Interest

1. Sri Ram Temple
2. Laxman Temple
3. Hanuman Temple
4. Memorial of Kalidasa
5. Lake.

Tadoba National Park :

Situated 150 kms. from Nagpur. Famous for wildlife sanctuary. Accommodation at Guest House, Rest House No. 1 & 2, Inspection House and Youth Hostel of Forest Department.

GOA DAMAN AND DIU

The Union Territory of Goa, Daman and Diu, comprising of three distinct districts, covers an area of 3814 sq. kms. and is inhabited by over 10 lakhs of people. Goa is accessible by road, rail and sea Goa is bounded by states of Maharashtra on the North and Karnataka on the East and South. Daman and Diu contiguous to Gujarat. Panaji is the capital of the Union Territory.

Goa famed in myth and history, snugly esconced between the Sayadri ghats to the east and the Arabian sea to the west is 65 kms. at its widest from east to west, whilest its maximum length north to south is 105 kms. The terrain is intersected by hilly spurs running down from the Western Ghats (Sahyadris) and number of streams which together with canals from an important water ways network for inland navigation and irrigation. The most important rivers are Terekhol, Chapora, Mandovi, Zuari, Sal and Talpona. The entire land covered with derdant forest, coconut, cashewnut and mango tree groves, interspread with extensive paddy fields for cultivation of rice, the staple food of the people, offers a marked and refreshing contrast to the arid hinterland.

Panaji, the capital, situated on the left bank of the Mandovi river is a picturesque town with beautiful red roofed houses built in the latin type architectural style with imposing balconies and ample varandah, also boasts of a few modern multi-storeyed buildings, well laid gardens and archives lined with gulmohur, cassia and other trees.

The nearest airport is at Dabolin 29 kms. and the rail heads at Vasco-de-Gama 31 kms. and Margao 35 kms. away. The modern interstate bus stand run by the Kadamba Transport Corporation is the hub of road transport, service by luxury and semi luxury buses.

Tourist season : October to May
November to February pleasant.

How to Reach

Air : Goa is connected by I.A. flights from Bombay, Belgaum and Bangalore.

Sea : Mogul lines operate sailings during fair weather (October to May).

Rail : Goa is connected by metre gauge line with Londa Jn. on Miraj-Bangalore line. Convenient station for Panaji is Margao.

Road : Goa is connected by road with all the major towns in India :

Ahmedabad to Panaji via Bombay, Panvel.

Mahad, Sawant Wadi : 1234 kms.

Aurangabad to Panaji via Pune, Satara, Kolhapur Sawantwadi : 706 kms.

Bangalore to Panaji via Hiriyur, Hubli, Londa, Ponda : 598 kms.

Bombay to Panaji via Panvel, Mahad, Sawantwadi 594 kms.

Howrah to Panaji via Sambalpur, Nagpur, Jalgaon, Pune : 2487 kms.

Cochin to Panaji via Mangalore, Karvar, Margao : 833 kms.

Delhi to Panaji via Agra, Indore, Dhulia, Nasik, Pune : 1895 kms.

Hyderabad to Panaji via Yagdir, Mudgal, Jungund: 757 kms.

Kanya Kumari to Panaji via Trivandrum, Mangalore, Karvar : 1133 kms.

Madras to Panaji via Bangalore, Hiruyur, Hubli, Londa Ponda : 920 kms.

Mysore to Panaji via Hassan, Jog Falls, Astoli : 696 kms.

Srinagar to Panaji via Jammu, Delhi, Nasik, Pune : 2785 kms.

Varanasi to Panaji via Allahabad, Jabalpur, Nagpur, Jalgaon and Pune : 2049 kms.

* for local transport, tourist taxis, yellow cabs, motor bike taxis and auto-rikshaws are available throughout Goa.
* Conducted sight seeing tours are being arranged by Goa Daman and Diu Tourism Development Corpn. Ltd.

Where to Stay

Hotels rates above 150/- per day :

1. Aguada Hermitage, Sinquerin, Badez, Goa
2. Fort Aguada Beach Resort, -do- Ph. 4401-8
3. Hotel Fidalgo 18th June Road Panaji, Goa: Ph. 3·20-32
4. Hotel Oberoi, Biogmalo Beach, Dabolin Air Port : Ph. 2191-92
5. Hotel Silver Sands, Colva Beach, Goa. Ph. 3645-46/3651
6. Welcome Group, Cidade de Goa, Curla, Dona Paula Goa : Ph. 3301-8
7. The Taj Holiday Village, Fort Aguada Resort. Ph. 4415-17
8. Majorda Beach Resort, Majorda, Salcete Goa. Ph. 3181-82

Hotels rates above 75/- per day :

9. Concha Beach Resort, Calangute, Goa. Ph. 56
10. Conqueiral Holiday Home, Kamotin, Wado, Candolim, Beach Goa.
11. Dona Paula Beach Resort, Dona Paula, Goa. Ph. 4256

12. Estrela Do Mar, Cobrawaddo, Calangute, Goa.
13. Hotel Nove Goa, Dr. Atma Ram Borker Road Panaji Ph. 4575-76
14. Hotel Mandovi, Panaji : Ph. 4481-85
15. Hotel Metropole, Avenida, Conassao Road Margao Ph. 3552-56, 57
16. Hotel Bata Do Sol, Baga Beach, Calangute, Goa : Ph. 3277-78
17. Hotel Delomn, Caetano de Albuquerque Road Ph. 5616
18. 'O Camarao Beach Resort, Umtawaddo, Calagute, Bardez, Goa
19. Hotel Flamingo, Rua de ourem, Panaji Ph. 4765
20. Ludoviel Tourist Home, Dando, Siquerin Bardez, Goa
21. Lapaz Hotel, Swatantra Path, Vasco-de-Gama Ph. 2121-26
22. Prainha Cottages, the sea, Dona Paula. Ph. 4004
23. Hotel Goa International Tonca, Miramar Ph. 5716-17

Hotels above 25/- at Panaji :

1. Ambika Hotel, Church Square. Ph. 4987
2. Carvasarai Tourist Unit, B-1, St. Mary's Miramar. Ph. 5339
3. Guirnaka Guest House, near Ashok/Samrat Theatre. Ph. 2119
4. Hotel Campal near Agencies Square, Campal. Ph. 4531
5. Hotel Aroma, Cunha Rivera Road. Ph. 4249/4811/3519/5657
6. Hotel Aroma, Hotel Neptune, Malaca Road. Ph. 4447/5727
7. Hotel Dun Hill Palace, Ruade Ourem. Ph. 3476
8. Hotel Rivera, Rua de Ormuz. Ph. 4118
9. Hotel Rivera, Hotel Sona, Rua de Ourem. Ph. 4426
10. Hotel Sona, Hotel Solmar, D.B. Bandodkar Marg. Ph. 4555-56
11. Hotel Sangam, Mola. Ph. 2307
12. Hotel Dolphine, Panaji Old Goa Road Saopedro : Ph. 4189
13. Hotel Vihar Lodging and Boarding, near Head Post Office.
14. Keni's Hotel, 18th June Road. Ph. 4581-86

15. Liberty Guest House, near Don Basco High School. Ph. 3219
16. London Hotel, Miramar
17. May Fair Hotel, Dr. Dada Laidya Road near Mahalaxmi temple. Ph. 5952
18. Minerva Lodge, near LIC Office, Corte de Octerio. Ph. 3584
19. Mandovi Pearl Guest House, Behind Tourist Hotel. Ph. 3928
20. Noah's Ark, Bamboo Motels, Vereen Reis, Magos. Ph. 5770/4860
21. Prakash Lodge, Opp, Azad Maidan. Ph. 5676
22. Royal Beach Hotel, Mirmar
23. Temprence Guest House, Afonsa de Albuquerque Road. Ph. 3268
24. Vistar Hotel, Alfonsa de Albuquerque Road. Ph, 3247
25. Lord's Guest House, near Cine El Dorado. Ph. 3857
26. Central Lodging, Behind General Post Office. Ph. 4992
27. Hotel Mipal, Ribander Goa. Ph. 5007/5794

Hotels Rate Below 25/- per day :

28. Bharat Lodge, near Head Post Office. Ph. 4862
29. Belvilla Lodge, Miramar.
30. Church Side Lodge, near Immaculate Church.
31. Deluxe Lodge, 31st January Road.
32. Goa Lodge, Rua Afonso de Albuquerque. Ph. 3152
33. Glemar Lodge, near Cine National Theatre.
34 Gujarat Lodge, 18th June Road. Ph. 3931
35. Girosal Lodge, near Govind Bldg.
36. Hotel Rupublic Opp. Seeretorist. Ph. 4630
37. Hotel Imperial, near Old Bus Stand.
38. Hotel Madhavashram, near Hotel Mandovi. Ph. 4823
39. Hotel Venite, 31st January Road. Ph. 5537
40. Kiran Lodging and Boarding, near Sachivalaya. Ph. 4820
41. La Vista Lodge, near Patto Bridge. Ph. 4765
42. Matruchaya Lodging and Boarding, near Municipal Garden. Ph. 4889
43. Miresh Lodge, Ram Niwas, Agacaim, Panaji Road.
44. National Guest House, near Cine Eldorado

45. New Gujarat Lodge, Rua Heliodoro Salgado. Ph. 3767
46. New Punjab Lodging and Boardig near Municipal Garden. Ph. 3475
47. Naguesh Bhavan, Dr. Atmaram Borker Road. Ph. 5676
48. Palace Hotel, Behind Sectt. Ph. 4210
49. Rameshwar Hindu Lodging and Boarding, near Mahalaxmi Temple. Ph. 4776
50. Rajesh Lodge, 18th June Road Ph. 4039
51. Safari Hotel, Opp. Municipal Garden.
52. Summan Lodge, 18th June Road Ph. 3892
53. Sunder Lodge, Caetino de Albuquerque Road Ph. 4325
54. Satkar Lodge, Ghankar Bldg.
55. Krishna Lodging and Boarding near Mahalaxmi Temple. Ph. 3179
56. Tourist House Family/Dormitory Wing, Rua de Qurem. Ph. 5031/4932
57. Udipi Lodging and Boarding, near Head Post Office.
58. Sunrise Lodge Opp. Sushila Bldg. 18th June Road.
59. Hotel Ajanta Opp. Old Bus Stand.
60. Karuna Guest House, Teleigo.
61. Kismet Lodge, Opp. Municipal Market.
62. Roshan Guest House, 3rd floor, Roshan Manzil Ormuz Road.

Hotels at Margao (35 km. From Panaji) :

1. Goa woodlands Hotel, Mingual Loyala Furtado Rd. Ph. 3121-25
2. Hotel La flor, Erasmo Canvalho Street Ph. 3402-6
3. Hotel Annapurna Lodging and Boarding, near Railway Gate. Ph. 2760
4. Mabai Hotel Opp. Municipal Garden. Ph. 3638/3654-55/3327
5. Hotel Green View, near Railway Station. Ph. 3546
6. Kokoda Tourist Lodge, Churchorem, Margao Main Road Ban Sen Kadoda.
7. Hotel Gold Star, Isidora Baptista Road. Ph. 3861-65
8. Carter Lodging, Station Road. Ph. 3888-3677.
9. Cavolina Hotel, near Cinelata.
10. Damodar lodging and Boarding, Station Road. Ph. 2394
11. Dilkash Cafe, Station Road. Ph. 2739
12. Durga Hotel, Khareband Road.

13. Dhond's Anand Bhavan, Station Road. Ph. 3427
14. Hotel Gokal, Behind, Grace Church. Ph. 3118
15. Germini Hotel, Station Road. Ph. 2208
16. Hotel Bambino, Fr. Miranda Road. Ph. 3134
17. Hotel Naaz, Khareband Road. Ph. 3208
18. Hotel National, Station Road.
19. Hotel Neptune, Rua Martires, near Hari Mandir. Ph. 2379
20. Longuinhe near India Air Lines Office. Ph. 2130
21. Laxmi Lodge, Station Road. Ph. 2679
22. Milan Lodging and Boarding, Station Road. Ph. 2715
23. Royal Hotel, near Bank of Baroda. Ph. 2203
24. Sunrit Hotel, near Railway Station. Ph. 3226-27
25. Seva Samiti. Ph. 2626
26. Swagat Lodging and Boarding, Gomes Road. Ph. 2268
27. Twiga Lodge, 413, Abida Faria Road.
28. Vishranti Lodge, near Railway Station. Ph. 3226
29. Goa Guest House, Jose Inacio Loyola Road. Ph. 2.57
30. Kiran Hall, Janta House. Ph. 2208/2546
31. Hotel Noor Jehan, near P.W.D. Don Basco Road Fatorda Ph. 3893
32. New Gujarat Lodge, near Cinelata. Ph. 3614-2850
33. Hotel Rayan, Bernard de Costa Road.
34. Hotel Rukrish, Francisco Luis Gomes Road near Taxi Stand. Ph. 3709

Hotels at Vasco-De-Gama (31 kms. from Panaji) :

1. Hotel Zuari. Ph. 2127-29
2. Chicalim Tourist Resort, Chicalin Ph. 2417-3192
3. Tej Jose-Mar Tourist Rest House, Opp. M.P.T. Institute.
4. Hotel Annapurna, Municipal Market. Ph. 3185
5. Maharaja Hotel, Rua Leopold, Flores Opp. H.P. Tank. Ph. 2269-2748-2559
6. Hotel Bigmarks, Next to Damodar Temple. Ph. 3165
7. Hotel Rebello, Vadem. Ph. 2620-2610
8. Hotel Maccel, Franciscoluis Gomes Road. Ph. 2646
9. Hotel Pravasi. Ph. 2389
10. Hotel Ricom. Ph. 2965
11. Manish Lodge, Opp. Tilak Maidan, F. Gomes Road. Ph. 2419

12. Meghdoot Lodge, Swatantra Path. Ph. 2785
13. Railway Retiring Rooms, S.C. Ph. 2398
14. Sultan Lodge, Opp. Municipal Market. Ph. 2507
15. Twiga Lodge, near St. Andrews Church.
16. Udipi Lodge, Opp. Bank of India, Shridhar Bldg.
17. Vandava Lodge, next to Khalap Mension, Korlim Niketan.
18. Indira Lodge, Opp. Bharat Petroleum Installation. Ph. 2484

Hotels and Ponda (30 kms. from Panaji) :

1. Hotel Pearl. Ph. 41-243
2. Hotel Padmani near Bus Stand.
3. Barne Lodge.
4. Geetashram Lodging and Boarding.
5. Navayug Lodging and Boarding. Ph. 175
6. Prashant Lodging and Boarding.
7. Tourist Cottages, Bondla, P.O. Usgao.

Hotels at Mapusa (13 kms. from Panaji) :

1. Hotels Bendez. Ph. 2607
2. Motel La Joy, Porvorim. Ph. 5533
3. Hotel Hilltop Alto Porrorim.
4. Hotel Safari, Opp. Mamlatdar Office.
5. Lodge Jankishankers, Kanekar Bldg. Ph. 2401
6. Sumant Lodge, Feira Baixa.
7. Sirsat Lodge. Ph. 2419
8. Hotel Poornima, Ansabhat. Ph. 2480
9. Norman Julian Hotel and Travel Service H. No. 495-521-522 Cotarbat Albuq.

Calangute (16 kms. from Panaji) :

1. Ancora Beach Resort, Santavado (Baga).
2. Benbosa Cottage, Information Bureau, Calangute Beach Road. Ph. 54
3. Cavala Beach Resort (Baga). Ph. 29
4. Calangute Beach Resort, Umtavado.
5. Hotel Riverside, Baga Beach.
6. Kismet Mahal Tourist Home, E-1/221, Gaurvaddo.
7. Penku's Lodging Umtavado Palmar Cottage, H. No. 1202, Umtavado.

8. Pinto Beach Cottages, H. No. 81/9. Dr. Sardesai Bus Stop, Candolim.
9. Royal Hotel.
10. Sea View Cottages, Baiso Sauntavado.
11. Oseas Tourist Home, House No. 1388, near St. John's Chapel, Umravado.
12. Holiday Beach Resort, Muradvado, Candolim Beach.
13. Meena Lodge, Cobrawado, Calangute Vivenda A. Beira Mar 368 Candolim.
14. Hotel Souza Lobo, Calangute Beach.
15. Xavier Tours Hotels International Baga Beach.
16. *Green Field Cottages, Morod, Porvaddo Calangute.*

Anjuna/Vagator (22 kms. from Panaji) :

1. Vagator Beach Resort, Fort Chapora. Ph. 41
2. Vales Happy Holiday Home, H. No. 361.
3. Punaw Guest House, Anjuna Beach.
4. Nobel and Rest, Opp. Chapal Chpora.

Benanlim (42 kms. from Panaji) :

1. 'O Palmar Benanlim Beach Cottages.
2. Palm Grove Cottages, H. No. Vaswado Benaulim.
3. L'Amour Beach Resort, Benaulim Beach Goa.
4. Carvan Tourist Nest, 1409, Opp. Bank of Baroda, Benaulim.

Dharamshalas/Agrashalas : *Rs. 3/- to 12/-* :

1. Agrashala of Shri Ram Nathi Devasthan, Ram Nathi, Bandivada, Ponda, Gova. Ph. 33
2. Agrashala of Shantadurga, Kavlem, Ponda. Ph. 57
3. Manguirish Saunsthan Agrashala, Mangueshi, Ponda. Ph. 31
4. Agrashala of Shri Mahalsa Temple, Mardol, Ponda.

Accommodation for Tourism Department :

1. Terekhol, Tourist Rest House, Terekhol. Ph 48
2. Lake Resort, Mayem Ph. 94
3. Tourist Home, Patto Bridge, Panaji. Ph. 4757/5583/5715
4. Tourist Dormitory, Britone, Handez, Goa.
5. Tourist Cottages, Farmagudi, Ponda. Ph. 177
6. Tourist Resort, Molem.
7. Youth Hostel, Miramar. Ph. 5433

8. Tourist Hostel : Vasco. Ph. 2673/3119
9. Tourist Hostel : Panaji. Ph. 3396
10. Tourist Resort/Cottages, Calangute. Ph. 24
11. Tourist Dormitory, Calangute.
12. Tourist Cottages, Colva, Ph. 2287
13. Tourist Hostel, Mapusa. Ph. 2794

Places of Interest

Panaji : The capital of Goa, Daman and Diu. A small and charming city on the left bank of silvery Mandovi river with modern houses, fine gardens and statues. Enchanting panorama unfolded from a top altinho.

Miramar : A lovely golden beach of soft sands girdled with palm trees facing the blue Arabian Sea.

Dona Paula Fine : 7 kms. An idyllic and picturesque picnic spot. Commands a fine/view of the Zuari estnary and Mormugao Harbour.

Old Goa : 10 kms. East of Panaji lies the site of city of old Goa. Founded by Adil Shah, in the first decade of 16th century, it was being developed by them with a view to shifting their capital from Bijapur. However, Afons de Albuquerque made a short work of its when he stormed and took over to house the centre of power of the portuguese colonies.

1. *Basilica of Bom Jesus* : Most popular and famous of all churches in Goa.
2. *Se Cathedral* : Most imposing of all churches at old Goa.
3. *Church of St. Francis of Assisi* : Entrance and the choir are in manueline style, the only fragment of its kind in the east.
4. *St. Cajetan Church* : Built in the style of St. Peter's Basilica in Rome.
5. *Church of Our Lady of Rosary* : One of the earliest built in Goa.
6. *Nunnery of St. Monica* : It is the only nunnery in Goa.
7. *St. Augustine Tower* : Close to the Nunnery is a lofty tower defying the torrential rains.
8. *Viceroy's Arch* : Every incoming Viceroy used to disembark at this place.

Reis Magos Church : 7 kms. from Panaji. It is one of the earliest churches built in Goa.

Shri Mangesh : 22 kms. from Panaji temple dedicated to Lord Shiva. Located on a hillock surrounded by rolling green hills.

Shri Mahalsa : At Mendol 1 km. from Shri Mangesh Temple. The deity worshipped is an attribute of Lord Vishnu.

Shri Gopal Ganpati : 26 kms. from Panaji. It is a good speciman of Indian temple architecture.

Shri Shantadurga : 33 kms. from Panaji. Built at Kavlem. Dedicated to Shantadurga.

Shri Kalikadevi : 14 kms. from Mapusa at Kausarpal. 8 years old.

Shri Datta Mandir : 37 kms. from Panaji. The deity is believed to have curved many people of unsound mind.

Shri Apta Koteswara : 37 kms. from Panaji. At Narve Bicholim favoured deity of Kadamba Kings.

Shri Shantadurga : 11 kms. from Mapusa. The temple has beautiful natural surroundings.

Shri Bhagwati : 28 kms. from Panaji. 500 years old.

Shri Shantadurga : (Kankalikarim) Fatropa (Quepem)

Shri Malikarjuna : 40 kms. from Margao, at Cana Cona. The temple has massive wooden pillars which indicate carvings. There are 60 deities around the temple.

Shri Damodar : 22 kms. from Margao, at Zanobhavali Sanguem. Situated in the picturesque surroundings on the bank of Kushavati river, popularly known as Panti.

Temple of Shri Mahadeva at Tambadisurla : 70 kms. from Panaji. The only specimen of Kadamba—Yadava, architecture available in Goa.

Bandla forest : 55 kms. from Panaji. A fast developing wild life sanctuary.

Margao : 35 kms. from Panaji. In the hinter-land of southern Goa is a thriving commercial metropols is linked by rail to the rest of India and Mormugao Harbour. It has fine Parks, Gardens as well as imposing modern Buildings.

Jama Masjid : 56 kms. from Margao, at Sangwur. Built in the last century. The Jama Masjid was completely renovated in 1959.

Colva Beach : 6 kms. from Margao. Here saved sea and sky blaud in enchanting natural harmony unsport by man.

Vasco-de-Gama : 31 kms. from Panaji. A modern well paid out city close to Mormugao.

Mormugao Harbour : 34 kms. from Panaji, 4 kms. from

Vasco-De-Gama one of the finest natural anchorages on the west coast of India and the hub of intense meritime activity. Passengers and cargo ships call here from all over the world.

Pilar : 11 kms. from Panaji important religious and educational centre of Christian Missionaries.

Calangute Beach : 16 kms. from Panaji. The queen of Goa Beaches and the most popular holiday resort in Goa for its scenic splendour.

Mapusa : 13 kms. capital of Bandez Taluka. It has beautiful layout with Gardens and a Church.

Mayem Lake : 35 kms. from Panaji. An ideal picnic spot.

Aguada fort : 18 kms. from Panaji, Arvalem water falls 39 kms. Bogmala Beach 29 kms, Dudh Sagar water falls 60 kms from Panaji.

Museum and Art Galleries : Archaeological Museum and Portrait Gallery.

Hindu Festival : Shimgotsav, Mahashivaratri, Ramnavami, Zatra, Chaitra Purnima, Gokulashtami, Ganesh Chaturthi; Deepawali, Navratree utsav.

Christian Festival : 6th January, 2nd Feb., 1st Sunday after easter, 1st fortnight of October.

Muslim Festival : Urs of Sheikh Abdullah.

For further details please contact :
Department of Tourist,
Govt. of Goa, Daman and Diu,
Panaji.

MADHYA PRADESH

Madhya Pradesh which is the central province is the heart of India. The biggest state in our country having area of 4,43,406 sq. kms. Bordering states are, Uttar Pradesh, Bihar, Orissa, Andhra Pradesh, Maharashtra, Gujarat and Rajasthan.

Madhya Pradesh consists largely of a plateau streaked with hill ranges of the Vindhyas and Satpuras with the Chhattisgarh plains to the east. The hills give rise to the main river systems—The Narmada and the Tapti running from east to west, and the Chambal, Sone, Betwa. Mahanadi and the Indravati west to east Intersected by these meandering rivers and dotted with hills and lakes, the state has a varied natural setting of great beauty.

Its cultural heritage is ancient and chequered. It has innumerable monuments exquisitely carved temples, Stupas, forts and places on hill tops. One third of the state is forested and offers a unique and exciting panorama of wildlife.

It has great importance in business and trade. Famous for brocades of Chanderi and Maheshwar, the raw kosa silk of Bastar and Rajgarh, the ball metal replicas of Bastar, the leather toys of Indore, Soap stone replicas of Jabalpur, Zari work and host of other products, main attraction for foreigners.

It has colourful fairs and festivals. Dussehra in Bastar, Shiv-Ratri in Khajuraho and Ujjain, Ram Navami in Chitrakoot, Bhagoriya in Jhabua and annual festival of dances at Khajuraho are events for tourist to remember.

GWALIOR

Gwalior is named after Gwalipa, a legendry saint of the 8th century. It is also sacred to the memory of the heroic queen, Rani of Jhansi, and freedom fighter Tantya Tope who led the revolt against the British in 1857. Gwalior fort, built by Raja Man Singh Tomar is one of the largest and the best in country. Best season for visit throughout the year.

How to Reach

Air : Daily Indian Air Lines flights connect Gwalior with Delhi, Bhopal, Indore and Bombay and with Jabalpur and Raipur five-days a week.

Rail : Gwalior is on the Central Railway's main Delhi-Bombay and Delhi-Madras lines. Among other major trains, the Taj Express connects Gwalior with Delhi and Agra thrice a week.

Road : Regular bus service connects with Agra, Mathura, Jaipur, Delhi, Lucknow, Bhopal, Chanderi, Indore, Jhansi, Khajuraho, Rewa, Ujjain and Shivpuri.

Distance between Gwalior and following cities :

Agra via Morena, Dholpur 118 kms.
Bhopal via Shivpuri, Guna, Biora 423 kms.
Bombay via Indore, Nasik 1086 kms.
Delhi via Agra 321 kms.
Sanchi via Shivpuri, Isagarh, Vidisha 381 kms.
Shivpuri via Morena 112 kms.
Khajuraho via Jhansi, Chhatarpur 275 kms.

Where to Stay

1. Motel Tansen (MP Tourism) Gandhi Road Ph. 21568
2. Hotel Usha Kiran, Palace Ph. 23453

3. Hotel President Ph. 24673
4. Hotel Safari Ph. 24638
5. Hotel Regal Ph. 22599
6. Hotel Gujri Mahal Ph. 23493
7. Hotel India Ph. 25983

Places of Interest

Chhatris : Cenotapha commemorating the kings and queens of the Scindia dynasty.

Man Singh Palace : Built between 1486-1517. It still has blue mamel painting along the outer walls.

Gujri Mahal : Built in the 15th century by Raja Man Singh for his favourite queen, Mrignayani, who was a Gujar by caste. At present, the palace houses an archeological museum.

Sas-Bahu-ka-Mandir : 11th century temple dedicated to Lord Vishnu.

Teli ka Mandir : Over 100 ft. in height, it is a Pratihar Vishnu temple of 9th century peculiar in plan and design. The form of the roof is Dravidian while the decorative details have Indo-Aryan.

Characteristics of Northern India.

Suraj Kund : Named after king Suraj Pal.

Rani of Jhansi Memorial : Dedicated to Rani Laxmi Bai of Jhansi, a leading figure in the 1857 war of independence.

Tombs of Tansen and Ghaus Mohammed : The tombs of Tansen, the famous musician and one of the nine gems at the court of the Mughal Emperor Akbar, and Mohammed Ghaus are examples of superb early Mughal architecture.

Jal Vihar Palace : Designed on the plan of an Italian Plazze, the palace combines three distinct styles of architecture, the Tuscan, the Italian and the Corinthian. It has an imposing audience hall with antique furniture and Chandeliers.

Tigra Dam : 23 kms. A picturesque setting for recreation.

DATIA

Situated on the Delhi Madras main line. Datia is mentioned in the Mahabharata as 'Daityavakra'. Among the historical monuments is the seven storey palace of Raja Bir Singh Deo built atop a hill. It is a unique example of Hindu architecture of 17th century. The other attractions are temple with Mughal frescoes and the Gopeshwar temple. Best season to visit throughout the year.

How to Reach

Air : Nearest air port is Gwalior 69 kms. Connected by regular flights with Delhi, Bhopal, Indore and Bombay.

Rail : Datia is a railway station on Delhi-Madras main line.

Road : Connected by regular bus service with Gwalior, Shivpuri, Jhansi, Lalitpur, Bhopal and Khajuraho.

Where to Stay

1. Circuit House, reservation through Executive Engineer, PWD, Datia.
2. Rest House, reservation through SDO (PWD) Datia.
3. Other Indian style hotels are also available.

Places of Interest

Palace : Built by Raja Bir Singh Ju Deo in 1614, entirely of stone and bricks. No Iron or wood has been used. Hanuman Mandir, Baura Vandeshwar Mandir, Govind Mandir.

Excursions

Sonagiri Temples : 11 kms. Jain temples of 10th century.

PAWAYA

68 km. from Gwalior on the confluence of Sindh and Parvati rivers. Pawaya was known as Padmavati in the ancient times and was the capital of the Nag kings in the 3rd century. It has been described by Bhava Bhuti in his celebrated drama, 'Malti Madhav'. The ruins of fort built by the Parmar kings in the early medieval times is another attraction. Dhoomeshwar Mahadeo Temple, example of Bundela architecture is at distance of 3 kms. The nearest railway station is Dabra 42 kms. on Jhansi-Gwalior section of Central Railway. Accommodation at Rest House, Dabra.

SHIVPURI

112 kms. from Gwalior on the Agra Bombay road is Shiv Puri town, the summer capital of the Scindias. Apart from Kothis, Palaces and Chhatris, Shiv Puri is famous for its 156 sq. kms. National Park, easily accessible throughout the year.

How to Reach

Air : Nearest air port Gwalior 112 kms. which is connected by daily flights with Delhi, Bhopal, Indore and

Bombay and by five-days a week flights with Raipur and Jabalpur.

Rail : Nearest rail head Gwalior on Delhi Madras and Delhi Bombay main line.

Road : Regular bus service connects Shiv Puri with Gwalior, Indore, Bhopal, Jhansi and Ujjain. Distance between Shiv Puri and other cities :

Bombay via Guna, Indore and Nasik 974 kms.
Delhi via Gwalior and Agra 433 kms.
Indore via Guna, Shajapur, Maksi 374 kms.
Jhansi via Karera Dinara 101 kms.

Where to Stay

1. Chinkara Motel (MP Tourism) Bombay Agra Road. Ph. 297.
2. Sakhya Sagar Boat Club, India National Park.
3. Circuit House. 4. Rest House.
5. Indian Style Hotels.

Places of Interest

Bhadiaya Kund : A shady picnic spot with a natural spring. The water is reputed to be rich in minerals with curative properties.

Chhatris : Set in a Mughal Garden are two cenotaphs of Maharani Skhya Raja Scindia and her son Madhav Rao Seindia. The cenotaph of the latter is a beautiful marble monument is laid with precious stones.

National Park : 156 sq. kms. in area. The Park has a variety of wild life which includes Panther, Bear, Sampher, Chital, Blue Bull and water migrants. Though the best season to visit the Park is from April to June, it is open throughout the year. The Park has two artificial lakes of which the Sakhya Sagar or Chandpatha, houses a boat club.

ORCHHA

Orchha is the medieval town ship situated on the banks of river Betwa 120 kms. from Gwalior on the Gwalior Khajuraho Rd. Once the flourishing capital city of Bundela Rajputs. Its palaces, temples and forts tell the story of its glory in the later medieval period. It came into prominence during the reign of the Rajput King Bir Singh Ju Deo in 17th century. Later, it was under the Mughal Emperors.

Best season October to March.

How to Reach

Air : Nearest Airport Gwalior and Khajuraho.

Rail : Nearest Rail head Jhansi 19 kms, on the Delhi Bombay and Delhi Madras main lines.

Road : Connected by regular bus service with Jhansi, Chhatarpur and Tikamgarh.

Where to Stay

Hotel Shah Mohd. (HP Tourism)

Places of Interest

Jahangir Mahal : The rectangular palace with eight minarets was constructed by Raja Bir Singh Ju Deo in the 17th century to commemorate the visit of emperor Jahangir to Orchha.

Chatur Bhuj Mandir : A rectangular temple on a high platform. It is situated half a km. from Jahangir Mahal. It has the image of Lord Vishnu.

Other Places

Janki Mandir, Laxmi Mandir, Raja Ram Mandir.

CHANDERI

The vast fort at Chanderi in Guna Distt. was built on a 200 meters high hill during the Mughal period. Its main Gate is known as the 'Khooni Darwaza' Chanderi is surrounded by hills, lakes, and forests and there are several monuments of Bundela Rajputs and Malwa Sultans.

How to Reach

Air : Nearest airport Gwalior 239 kms.

Rail : Lalitpur 37 kms. on Delhi Madras main line and Mungaoli 40 kms. on Kota Bina line are the nearest rail heads.

Road : Connected by bus with Gwalior, Guna, Shivpuri, Lalitpur and Mungaoli.

Distances from other Places :

239 kms. from Gwalior via Datia.

37 kms. from Lalitpur.

127 kms. from Shiv Puri via Isagarh, Lukwasa.

232 kms. from Khajuraho via Lalitpur, Tikamgarh.

237 kms. from Bhopal via Isagarh, Raisen.

560 kms. from Delhi via Datia, Gwalior, Agra.

40 kms. from Mungaoli.

Where to stay

1. Kila Kothi (Circuit House) Reservation, through Astt. Engineer (PWD) Mungaoli.
2. Rest House, -do-

Places of interest

Koshak Mahal : According to historical records Kosha Mahal was ordered to be built by Mahmud Khilji of Malwa. When he passed through Chanderi in 1445. The original plan of the Khilji ruler was to constant a seven storey palace though only two could be completed during his life time. The Mahal is divided into four equal parts and has architecture similar to Mandu.

Badal Mahal Gate : A gate without a Mahal. It was constructed to commemorate some important victory.

Jama Masjid : With imposing domes and long arcades, this is possibly the biggest mosque of the earstwhile Madhya Bharat State.

Shahzadi ka Rouza : The name is attributed to some unknown princess. The building is decorated on the exterior with ornamental arches and a band of Geometrical designs.

Parameshwar Tal : Built by Bundela Rajput Kings, the picturesque Parameshwar Tank is situated half a mile to the north-west of Chanderi Town. It has on its bank a well carved temples and centograph of three Rajput Kings.

Battisi Bavdi : Built by Sultan Ghiyasuddin Shah in 1485, the Battisi Bavdi derives its name from a flight of thirty two steps.

Handicrafts : Chanderi is still well known for its fine Muslim and brocade work. These products have already made their mark in the foreign markets. Chanderi Sarees are specially popular.

Buddhi Chanderi or Old Chanderi : The old Chanderi city has a number of Jain temples of 9th and 10th centuries. It attracts thousands of Jain pilgrims from all parts of the country every year.

Thubon : 15 kms. south west of Chanderi is the old village Thubon. The village has a number of Jain Temples of early medieval.

BHOPAL

Set around a lake, Bhopal, the capital of Madhya Pradesh, has surroundings known for their scenic beauty and archaeological wealth. The city it is believed, stands on the site of an old town founded by Raja Bhoj in 11th century. Dost Mohammad Khan laid the foundation of the present city in the first half of the 18th century.

Best season throughout the year.

How to reach there

Air : Indian Airlines operates daily services to Bhopal from Delhi, Gwalior, Indore and Bombay. From Raipur and Jabalpur five days a week.

Rail : Bhopal is on Delhi-Madras main line. Major Trains going from Bombay to Delhi via Itarsi and Jhansi also pass through Bhopal.

Road : Well connected by Bus with Indore, Mandu, Ujjain, Sanchi, Gwalior, Shivpuri, Jabalpur, Panchmarhi Khajuraho, Nagpur & Jaipur.

Distances between Bhopal and Other Cities

525 kms. : Agra via Guna, Shiv Puri, Gwalior.
786 kms. : Bombay via Indore, Dhulia, Nasik.
743 kms. : Delhi via Guna, Shivpuri, Gwalior.
186 kms. : Indore via Sehore, Ashta, Dewas.
540 kms. : Kanha via Sagar, Jabalpur, Mandla.
387 kms. : Khajuraho via Sagar, Chhatarpur.
290 kms. : Mandu via Indore, Dhar.
210 kms : Panchmarhi via Hoshangabad.
46 kms. : Sanchi via Dewanganj.
72 kms. : Raisen.
189 kms. : Ujjain via Dewas.
423 kms. : Gwalior, via Guna, Shiv Puri.

Where to stay

Tariff rates 50 to 250/-

1. Hotel Panchanan (MP Tourism) New Market Ph. 63047
2. Hotel Jehan Numa, Palace, Shamla Hills. Ph. 76080, 76190
3. Hotel Ramsons International, Hamidia Rd. Ph. 72298-99
4. Hotel President International, Berasia Rd. Ph. 75218
5. Hotel Imperial Sabre, Palace grounds. Ph. 73881
6. Hotel Rajdoot, Hamidia Rd. Ph. 72691-92
7. Motel Shiraz, near Board of Higher Secondary Education. Ph. 64513

8. Hotel Mayur, Berasia Rd.
9. Youth Hostel, (MP Tourism) T.T. Nagar, Tariff rate 20/- to 100/- Ph. 63671
10. Hotel Ranjit, Hamidia Rd. Ph. 73641
11. Pagoda Hotel, -do- Ph. 73949
12. Grand Hotel, Hamidia Rd. Ph. 74070
13. Hotel Samrat -do- Ph. 73621
14. Hotel Sangam, near Sangam Talkies Ph. 76061
15. Hotel Gulshan Hamidia Rd. Ph. 73506
16. Hotel Manjit -do- Ph. 74664
17. Ashoka Hotel -do- Ph. 74968
18. Hotel Shalimar Deluxe -do- Ph. 72563
19. Capital Hotel, opp. Bharat Talkies Ph. 72676
20. Hotel Meghdoot, Hamidia Rd. Ph. 72661
21. Hotel Rainbow -do- Ph. 76305

Places of interest

Taj-ul-Masjid : One of the longest mosques in India built by Shehjehan Begam who left it unfurnished. The mosque consists of an impressive main hall with inter-arched roof and wide courtyard.

Jama Masjid : Built in 1837 by Qudasia Begum. The tall, dark minarets of the mosque are crowned with glittering golden spikes. A queen of King Upayaditya Paramure (1059-80 A.D.) grandson of Raja Bhoj is said to have founded a temple here known as Sabha Mandali.

Moti Masjid : Patterned on Delhi's Jama Masjid, the mosque was built by Sikandar Jahan, daughter of Qudasia Begum, in 1860.

Sadar Manzil : A former Durbar Hall or Audience Hall of the rulers of Bhopal.

Bharat Bhawan : The city's newest centre for performing and visual arts. Bharat Bhawan is a national institute designed to promote consciousness about various aspects of our culture.

Van Vihar : Declared into a National Park, Van vihar houses a variety of wild animals.

Gandhi Bhawan : Situated on Shamla Hills, the Bhawan houses an exhibition of Gandhiji's photographs and a Gandhi Museum.

Laxmi Narain Temple : This beautiful temple on the Area Hills has a Museum attached to it.

Shamla Hills and Idgah Hills : A panoramic view of the

city with minarets and mosques can be seen from here at sunset. It presents a beautiful sight during dark and evening against the back drop of the glittering city lights and rippling water of the two lakes.

Upper Lake and Lower Lake : The upper Lake is a larger sheet of water, 6 sq. kms. in area. An overbridge divides the lake from the lower lake. At night, the place is like a fairy land when myriad lights from the houses along the lake are reflected in its placid waters.

Excursions

Bhojpur : 28 kms. from Bhopal famous for its equisity by Shiva Temple built in the 11th century by Raja Bhoj. Also known as the Som Nath of Northern India, the temple consists of many Shiva images and shrines engraved on the walls. The main Shivaling is carved out of a single stone.

Bhimbetka : 40 kms. from Bhopal, this village is surrounded by the northern fringe of the Vindhya mountains near the legendary river Betwa. This range is covered by huge rocks and deep forests. Recent discoveries of 600 caves and rock shelters belonging to neolithic age reveal that the whole area has been populated since time immortal. The walls and ceilings of most of the caves have paintings of the stone age and depict. Mythological scenes, men riding horses and elephants, war-scenes, processions and animals. Red and white dominate the paintings but occasionally green and yellow have also been used.

Delawadi : 62 kms. from Bhopal and situated in the midet of a lovely forest glade. Delawadi is a picturesque picnic spot, rich in scenic splendour and natural beauty. A small well furnished forest Rest Houses provides accommodation.

Hathai Kheda : 10 kms. on Raisen Road, an ideal fishing and angling spot.

Islamnagar : 11 kms. on Bhopal Berasia Road famous for its palace and garden which stands on hillock. It was built by Dost Mohammed Khan, the founder of the present city of Bhopal.

Samardha : 26 kms. on Raisen Road. situated amidst enchanting forest glades.

Kerwan : 17 kms. a dam and a beautiful picnic spot.

RAISEN

45 kms. from Bhopal, ancient fort of Raisen on Bhopal

Khajuraho Road. The fort was built in early 6th century. The fort is situated on a high hill and had 84 lakes and ponds out of which only 15 remain. The fort was under the famous Hindu king Rai Puran Mal before it was seized by Sher Shah and brought under the Afghan control.

How to reach there

Connected by Bus with Bhopal, Indore, Ujjain, Sanchi, Jabalpur and Khajuraho.

Where to stay

1. Circuit House (Reservation through Collector Raisen)
2. Rest House -do- SDO (PWD) Raisen.

SANCHI

Sanchi has all kinds of Buddhist Stupas, Chaityas, Temples and Monasteries. The history of the town goes back as early as 3rd century B.C. when Buddhism was at its peak during the reign of Emperor Ashoka. Best season throughout the year.

How to reach there

Air : Nearest Air port Bhopal : 46 kms. via Dewanganj and 72 kms. via Raisen. Daily service from Delhi to Bhopal, Gwalior, Indore, Bombay. Five days a week from Raipur and Jabalpur.

Rail : Itself Railway station on Jhansi Itarsi Section of Central Railway.

Road : Connected by road with Bhopal, Indore, Sagar, Gwalior and Vidisha.

Where to stay

1. Traveller's Lodge, ITDC Tel : 23
2. Circuit House
3. Rest House
4. Buddhist Guest House.

Places of interest

Great Stupa No. 1 : 36.5 meters in diameter and 16.4 meters in height, this magnificent commemorative structure is the oldest stone structure in the country. It surmounts a high circular dome with a railing around its base.

Toranas or Gateways : The relief on the toranas depict Jataka tales of the Buddhas precious incarnations and main events in his life in symbolic forms like footprints, the Bodhi tree, the wheel of law, and Stupa motifs.

Stupa No. 2 : Situated about half a km. from the great stupa. This stupa dates back to the 2nd century B.C. and stands on the edge of a hill. It is surrounded by a well preserved balustrade.

Stupa No. 3 : Situated near the great stupa. This stupa was built during 150-140 B.C. It has a hemispherical dome surrounded by an umbrella.

Ashoka Pillar : The fragments on the Ashoka column depict an inscription in Brahmi characters ordaining Buddhists to avoid schirms. An outstanding feature of the pillar is its lustrous polish dating back to the 3rd century.

Buddhist Vihara : The re-enshrinement of the relics of the two disciples of Buddha in the new vihara at Sanchi was one of the greatest Buddhist events in the present century. The relics have been enshrined in glass gaskets on a platform in the inner sanctum of the new temple.

Monasteries : Emperor Ashoka built many monasteries which served as residential quarters for his wife and nuns.

PANCHMARHI

Situated at an altitude of 1067 meters. Panchmarhi is a large plateau ringed by hills on the evergreen Satpura range. The landscape is characterised by rugged hills, forests and ravins. One of its main attractions is its scenic beauty at dark when the red sandstone scrap reflects its colour into a variety of delicate shades of purple and violet.

Best season-October to June.

How to reach there

Air : Nearest Airports : Bhopal 210 km. Nagpur-262 km.

Rail : Piparia 47 Railway Station on Bombay-Howrah main line via Allahabad.

Road : Connected by regular Bus service with Bhopal, Hoshangabad, Nagpur, Piparia and Chhindwana.

Distance from the following cities

683 kms. from Allahabad via Jabalpur, Rewa.
368 kms. from Indore via Harda, Hoshangabad.
421 kms. from Ujjain via Harda, Indore.

Where to stay

1. Satpura Retreat (MP Tourism) Ph. 97
2. Amaltas -do- Ph. 98
3. Panchvati Holiday Homes -do-

4. Panchvati Huts -do-
5. Holiday Homes -do- Ph. 99
6. Nandanvan
7. Old Hotel Block
8. New Hotel Block
9. There are number of Dharamshalas.

Places of interest

Apsara Vihar : (Fairy pool) 5 kms. this pool formed by a water falls is suitable for swimming and is an ideal picnic spot.

Chauragarh : 15 kms. this rugged hill 1312 meters high, enjoys considerable religious importance. By the path to its summit are numerous tridents, symbol of Shiva deposited by pilgrims over centuries.

Dhupgarh : 10 kms. the highest point in Satpura ranges (134 meters) this is the most frequently climbed hill in the periphery of Panchmarhi and commands a magnificent view of the surrounding ranges.

Jata Shanker : 15 kms. The river Jambu tekes its source here, and it has an idol of Shiva within a cave.

Mahadev : 12 kms. the Mahadev caves around a pool at the foot of the Mahadev hill, have an image of Shiva. On the occasion of Shivratri, an annual fair is held here.

Pandav caves : 4 km. there are the famous caves from which Panchmarhi takes its name according to popular belief, the Pandav brothers spent a part of their exile here.

INDORE

Indore, planned and built by Rani Ahlyabai lies on the banks of the rivers Saraswati and derives its name from the 18th century Indreshwar Temple.

How to reach there

Air : Connected with Bhopal, Gwalior, Delhi and Bombay.

Rail : On the Western Railway and is connected with major cities of India.

Road : Connected by Bus with Bombay, Ahmedabad, Aurangabad, Bhopal, Gwalior, Mandu, Maheshwar, Onkareshwar, Sanchi, Ujjain and Vidisha.

Distance Between Indore and following cities

398 kms. from Ahmedabad via Jhabua, Nadia.
186 kms. from Bhopal via Dewas, Ashta.
600 kms. from Bombay via Nasik, Dhulia.
91 kms. from Maheshwar via Mhow, Dhamnod.
99 kms. from Mandu via Dhar.
89 kms from Mandu via Mhow, Manpur, Gujri.
77 kms. from Omkareshwar via Barhawa.

Where to stay

1. Tourist Reception Centre (MP Tourism) Ph. 38888
2. Hotel Shri Maya Ph. 34151
3. Hotel Sheeba Ph. 7720
4. Hotel Samrat Ph. 30751
5. Hotel Central Ph. 32041
6. Hotel Lantern Ph. 30371.

Hotels tariff rate Rs. 10/- to 100/-

1. Hotel Ashoka	Ph. 37391
2. Hotel Shalimar	Ph. 5581
3. Hotel Sheesh Mahal	Ph. 36581
4. Hotel Neelam	Ph. 37161
5. Hotel Mayur	Ph. 36757
6. Hotel Chanderlok	Ph. 36196
7. Hotel Standard	Ph. 21892
8. Janta Hotel	Ph. 37695
9. Friends Lodge	Ph. 31951
10. Aram Lodge	Ph. 31970
11. Gujarat Lodge	Ph. 30201.

Places of interest

Bada Ganpati : A colossal statue of Lord Ganesh installed in the main street in Malharganj.

Chhatri Bagh : Containing majestic cenotaphs of the Holkars. Madhav Rao Holker's cenotaph is richly decorated with frescoes.

Juna Rajwada : An old palace in the heart of the city now housing Govt. Office.

Kanch Mandir or Hukumchand's Temple : Shrine of Digamber Jains. Its walls, roof and floor are lavishly in laid with mother of pearls, glass and multi-coloured beads.

Museum and Art Galleries : Kendriya Sangrahalaya, with galleries of sculpture, painting and natural history specimens, is a must for every tourist.

UJJAIN

One of the oldest and holiest city in India, on the banks of river Shipra, 53 km. from Indore. It was governed by Ashoka and later during the reign of the Guptas and the legendary. Vikramaditya was a great centre of learning, the poet Kalidasa being one of its illustrious sons. It is one of the Venus of the Mammoth Kumbha Mela, held once in twelve years.

Best season July to March.

How to reach

Air : Nearest Airport Indore, connected by regular flights with Delhi, Gwalior, Bhopal and Bombay.

Rail : Itself Railway Station on the Bhopal Nagda sector of Western Railway.

Road : Connected by regular Bus service with Indore, Bhopal, Ratlam, Gwalior, Mandu, Dhar, Kota and Onkareshwar.

Where to stay

1. Shipra Motel (MP Tourism) Ph. 4862
2. Grand Hotel Ph. 42
3. Savera Hotel Ph. 403
4. Adarsh Gupta Lodge
5. Hotel Chinar
6. Vikram Hotel.

Places of interest

Mahakal Temple : The temple is dedicated to Lord Shiva one of the twelve Jyotirlingas is enshrined here.

Jantar Mantar : An oldest observatory on the outskirts of the city.

Gopal Mandir : Famous for the beautiful silver image of Lord Krishna.

Bharathari caves : 6.4 km. from the city. These caves are dedicated to the sage Bharathari.

Sandipani Ashram : 3.2 km. from the city is the Sandipani Ashram. Where Krishna. Sudama, and Balram received education from Sandipani.

Ghats on the Shipra : Streams of pilgrims gather at the Shipra Ghats to take a dip in the holy water.

DHAR

64 kms. from Indore on Indore Ahmedabad road is Dhar, the capital of Parmar Kings amongst whom Bhoj was the most prominent. During the Muslim rule, Dhar was under the Sultans of Delhi. In the monuments, one can see the combi-

nation of Hindu, Afghan and Mughal architecture. Bhoj Shala Laat Masjid, Fort and lakes are the main tourist attraction.

How to reach there

Dhar is connected by regular bus service with Indore, Mandu, Ujjain, Ratlam, Ahmedabad and Baroda.

Where to stay

Circuit House, reservation through collector Dhar.
Rest House, reservation through SDO (PWD) Dhar.

Omkareshwar : Situated at the confluence of Narmada and Kaveri with temples of medieval Brahamini style of architecture Omkareshwar has one of the twelve Jyotirlingas at the temples of Shri Omkar Mandhata Amidst an extremely picturesque setting "Best season throughout the year".

How to reach there

Air : Indore 77 km. nearest Airport.

Rail : Nearest Rail head Omkareshwar road 12 km on Ratlam Khandwa section of western Railway.

Road : Regular Bus service from Omkareshwar to Indore, Ujjain, Khandwa, Barwaha, Sohawd and Omkareshwar Road.

Where to stay

1. Holkar Guest House.
2. Forest Rest House.
3. Dharamshalas.

Places of interest

Siddhanath Temple : The temple with a frieze of elephants carved on a stone stale at the outer perimeter, is a unique example of early medieval Brahminic architecture.

Shri Omkar Mandhata : Built on an island one mile along and half a mile wide formed by the bifurcation of Narmada, the temple is made up of soft stone and has verandahs with huge pillars which are several carved in squares.

Polygons and Circles : It has a frieze of stone figures at the top, supporting the ornately carved stone roof.

24 Avtars : Jain as well as Hindu temples, called 24 Avtars, have remarkable architecture and style.

Excursions

Dahayadi Kund : 19 kms. spot whose Narmada bifurcates.

Satmatrika Temple : 6 km. 10th century temples.

Kajal Rani Cave : A picturesque picnic spot.

BAWAN GAJA

10 km. from Barwani, Tehsil H Qrs. of Khargone Distt. the Bawan gaja temples are 170 kms. from Indore. The 72 ft high Jain statue has been hewn in the rock. It belongs to early 15th century and is an important Jain Pilgrim centre.

How to reach there

Nearest airport Indore 170 kms. Regular Bus Service is available for Bawangaja from Barwani and Khargone.

Where to stay

Rest House Barwani (Reservation through Sub Divisional Officer PWD, Barwani.)

MANDU

For centuries a pleasure resort of many (Hindu and Muslim rulers, Mandu, the city of joy, still possesses an atmosphere of romance and mystery. Situated at the edge of the Vindhya hill ranges, it is haunted by the memories of a long lost country life in the Kingdom of Malwa and the name of Rupamati and Baz Bahadur.

How to reach there

Air : Nearest Airport Indore 99 kms.

Rail : Nearest Railway Stations Mhow 58 kms., Indore 99 kms., and Ratlam 124 kms. Direct Buses are available from here for Mandu.

Road : Connected by Bus with Dhar, Mhow, Ratlam, Indore, Ujjain, Bhopal.

Distance between Mandu and the following Cities are

575 kms. from Bombay via Dhamnod, Dhulia, Nasik.

903 kms. from Delhi via Dhar, Indore, Guna, Gwalior.

283 kms. from Bhopal via Dhar, Indore, Dewas.

149 kms. from Ujjain via Dhar, Indore.

66 kms. from Maheshwar via Dhamnod.

127 kms. from Omkeshwar via Dhamnod.

Where to stay

1. Tourist Bunglow (MP Tourism). Ph. 35
2. Tourist Huts, (MP. Tourism).
3. Traveller's Lodge (ITDC). Ph. 21
4. Taveli Mahal Rest House.
5. Dharamshalas.

Places of interest

Hoshang Shah's Tomb : The exquisite tomb was originally built by the great warrior himself but was completed by his son. The first marble structure in the country, the tomb is famous for its carvings and unique conception. Emperor Shah Jahan sent his master builders to study it before starting on the Taj Mahal at Agra.

Jami Masjid : The Jami Masjid, pattered on the great mosque at Damascus, is perhaps the finest example of Afghan Architecture in India.

Asharfi Mahal : Facing the Jami Masjid is the Asharfi Mahal or the palace of Gold Coins. It was here that the tower of victory was constructed by Mahmood Khilji.

Neel Kanth Temple : Located at the edge of a deep gorge, the temple commands beautiful view of Mandu.

Jahaz Mahal : The elegent double storey structure situated in between two lakes with airy kiosks and overhanging balconies, it gives the impression of a fantastic pleasure craft ready to stream off.

Hindola Mahal : Hindola Mahal or Swinging Palace gets its name from the slopping side walls which look like a swing.

Baz Bahadur's Palace : The palace was built by Baz Bahadur the last Afghan ruler of Mandu. It is a unique example of Afghan architecture

Rupmati's Pavilion : Build by Baz Bahadur for his consort, Rupmati, the pavilion is situated on the southern erect of a hill overlooking the Nimar valley. At sunset or on a full moon night, the pavilion provides a magnificent view of the winding silver streak of the Narmada River on the plains below.

JABALPUR

Jabalpur was once the pleasure resort of the Gond kings. King Madan Shah, the most famous, built Madan Mahal in the twelfth century when the Gond Empire was its Zenith. Jabalpur was later the capital of the Kalchuri kings and the Marathas until the British seized it in 1817. Thereafter it has been an important cantonment and administrative centre. Best season throughout the year.

How to reach there

Air : Indian Air Lines five days a week flight connects Jabalpur with Delhi, Bhopal, Raipur and Gwalior.

Rail : Jabalpur is an important Railway station on the

Bombay Howrah via Allahabad main line. It is connected with major cities of the country.

Road : Connected by regular Bus service with Varanasi, Allahabad, Khajuraho, Bhopal, Nagpur, Indore, Satna and Raipur.

Distance between Jabalpur and the following cities :

Agra via Sagar, Lalitpur and Jhansi	604 kms.
Bhopal via Damoh, Sagar	368 kms.
Bombay via Nagpur, Amravati, Dhulia	1132 kms.
Delhi via Sagar, Jhansi and Gwalior	807 kms.
Gwalior via Sagar, Jhansi	486 kms.
Khajuraho via Damoh, Panna	272 kms.
Varanasi via Maihar, Rewa, Mirzapur	423 kms.
Kanhvia, Mandala	173 kms.
Bandhangarh via Katni, Umaria	194 kms.

Where to stay

1. Ashok Hotel, Wright town — Ph. 22267
2. Jacksons Hotel, Civil line — Ph. 21321-21323

Tariff Rate Rs. 20/- to 60/-

3. Hotel Rahil, Opp. Jyoti Talkies — Ph. 25570
4. Hotel Samrat, Russel's Crossing — Ph. 23183
5. Hotel Ambassador, -do- — Ph. 21771
6. Hotel Anand, Nandra Bridge — Ph. 233118
7. Hotel Swayam, -do- — Ph. 23377
8. Hotel Raj Hans, -do- — Ph. 24954
9. P.W.D. Circuit House — Ph. 25724
10. Rest House — Ph. 20350

Places of interest

Madan Mahal Fort : The fort was built by the Gond king Raja Madan Shah in 1116 on the top of a rocky eminence. The fort commands a panoramic view of the city.

Pisan Hari Jain Temple : 7 kms. appx. from Jabalpur, near the Medical College, are the Jain Temples atop a hill. They are believed to be 150 years old. The temples got their name from the woman who started them with money earned from milling flour.

Tilwara Ghat : 9 kms. this Ghat on the bank of Narmada is an ideal picnic spot. The Gandhi memorial here was built in 1935 to commemorate the All India Congress Session here in that year.

Mala Devi Mandir : 7 kms. this 12th century temple situated near Garha, has a beautiful image of Mala Devi or Laxmi.

Gwari Ghat : 11 kms. Another beautiful picnic spot on the banks of Narmada.

Sangram Sagar and Bajna Math : 6 kms. the Sangram Sagar tank and Bajna Math temple, now in ruins, are medieval constructions. They are built by the famous Gond king Sangram Shah between 1480-1540.

Marble Rocks (*Bheda Ghat*) : 23 kms. from Jabalpur, connected by an excellent road are the Marble Rocks rising on either side of a mile long gorge through which the Narmada flows. The gleaming Jagged cliffs of limestone are more than a hundred feet high. Boating amidst the gorge in moon light is a unique experience. Best season to visit throughout the year.

How to reach there

Air : Jabalpur 23 km. nearest Air port.

Rail : Jabalpur on the Bombay Howrah line via Allahabad. Main line is the main Rail head.

Road : Frequent Buses, tempos and taxis are available from Jabalpur.

Where to stay

1. Rest House.
2. Dharamshalas.

After marble rocks visitors should see: Chonsath Yogini Temple: built on a hillock is the 10th century temple of chounsath yogini, dedicated to goddess Durga.

Dhuandhar : At the far end of the marble gorge, the Narmada singes down in a water fall known as Dhuandhar or smoke cascade.

KANHA NATIONAL PARK

One of the Asia's finest parks, Kanha is the home of a large variety of animals like tiger, panther, sambher, cheetal, gour, black buck, barking deer etc. It is the last preserve of Barasingha. It has dense forests with bamboos on the slopes and the stately Sal groves interspersed with rolling meadows in the valleys. Best season November to June. Park remains closed from 1st July to 3 st October due to rains. Entry fee Re. 1 per adult, child 50 paisa. Photography chargeable. Guides are available on payment.

How to reach there

Air : Jabalpur 173 km. Nagpur 266 km. Air ports.

Rail : Most convenient Rail head.

Road : Connected by regular Bus service with Jabalpur.

Where to stay

1. Log Hut, Kisli (MP Tourism)
2. Youth Hostel Kisli (MP Tourism)
3. Tourist Bunglow, Mukki (MP Tourism)
4. Tourist Huts, Khatia (MP Tourism)
5. Kanha Safari Lodge, Mukki (ITDC)

BANDHAVGARH

The Bandhavgarh National Park lies in the heart of the Vindhyan mountain range in Central India. Besides its enchanting landscape formed by the Sal forest in the valleys and majestic tree clad hills in the back drop, it is famous for a wide variety of wild life and archaeological remains of the Kalchuri period. The park once is hilly and is dominated by the majestic Bandhavgarh fort, built in the 14th century. The fort and the adjacent hills have a long number of caves belonging to the pre-historic period of Indian history. Some of the caves have inscriptions in oriental scripts.

How to reach there

Air : Nearest Airport Khajuraho 210 km. and Jabalpur 194 km.

Rail : Nearest Rail head Umaria 30 km. on the Katni Bilaspur Section of South-Eastern Railway.

Road : Directly connected by Bus with Satna, Rewa, Shehdol and Umaria.

Where to stay

1. White Tiger Forest Lodge (MP Tourism)
2. Forest Rest House.

Note : The Park remains closed form 1st July to 31st October due to rains.

BHORAMDEO

18 kms. from Kawardha on the Raipur 116 kms. Jabalpur 220 kms. road on the banks of the river Sankari among that Satpura hills and their scenic valleys, the Bhoramdeo temples have a special attraction for lovers of history and archaeology. The temples were built by the celebrated King Ram Chandra of the Nag dynasty who married princess Ambika Devi of Haihaya dynasty. The Temples are superb example of contemporary architecture and have much historical, religious and archaeological importance. In an area of 5 km. in the palaces

of Manwa and Madan Manjari, are the erotic sculptures similar to those in Khajuraho temples.

How to reach there

Raipur is the nearest Airport.

Buses plying on Raipur-Jabalpur road halt at kawargha (18 kms.) from here. Private buses are available for Bhoramdeo.

Where to stay

Rest House Kawardha. Reservation through such Divisional Officer PWD. Kawardha.

BURHANPUR

The Later-medieval fort and palace at Burhanpur were built by Meeran Adil Shah Farooqi. The fort was known for its exquisite persian bath houses with coloured tiles and glass work. They are a fine example of Iranian architecture.

How to reach there

Burhanpur is a major Railway station on Itarsi-Bhusawal section of the Central Railway. It is also connected by Bus with major cities of the state and the bordering state of Maharashtra.

Where to stay

Rest House : Reservation through SDO (PWD) Burhanpur.

ASIRGARH

Asirgarh fort has immense historical and archaeological importance because it served a barrier to invaders, from the North, from entering Gujarat, Deccan and Marathwada. The fort was built by Usa and Ahir and is situated atop a hill with a palace. Just below the fort is a fine Shiva temple constructed in the early 10th century.

How to reach there

Burhanpur 20 kms. is the nearest Rail head on Itarsi-Bhusawal section of Central Railway. Regular Bus service is available from Burhanpur to Asirgarh.

Where to stay

1. Indian style hotels are available.
2. Rest House at Burhanpur. 20 kms. Reservation through Sub-Divisional Officer, PWD, Burhanpur.

AMARKANTAK

A great pilgrim centre for Hindus, is the source of the rivers ; Narmada and Sone. Situated at an altitude of 106 , Metres in the Vindhyas.

Places of Interest

Bhrigu Kamandal : 7 kms, there is an ancient Kamandal or water pitcher which is always full of water.

Dhuni Pani : 7 kms. a hot spring in a thick forest.

Dugdh Dhara : 7 kms. the water falls from a height of about 5oft., in a milk white cascade.

Kapildhara : 6.5 kms. a beautiful picnic spot.

Mai Ki Bagiya : 1.8 kms. lovely garden with a temple.

Narmada Udgam Mandir : 1 km. A temple built at the source of the Narmada, the holiest spot in Amarkantak.

Sanmuda : 2 kms source of the river Sone.

How to Reach There

Air : Nearest Airport is Jabalpur 246 kms. and connected by are with Raipur, Bhopal, Gwalior and Delhi.

Rail : Rail eads are Aunppur 48 kms and Pendra Road 17 kms on the Katni Bilaspur Section of South Eastern Railway.

Road : Connected by regular Bus service with Shahadol, Umaria, Jabalpur, Rewa, Bilaspur, Anuppur and Pendra Rd. Distance from Amarkantak to Jabalpur via Shahpura Dandori 246 kms. Khajuraho via Maihar, Shahdol 445 kms. Rewa via Shahdol 265 kms, Varanasi via Shahadol, Rewa and Mirzapur 265 kms. Bandhavgarh via Shahadol and Umaria 211 kms.

Where to Stay

1. Circuit House, Reservation through collector Shahadol.
2. Rest House, Reservation through Subdivisional Officer PWD Anuppur.
3. There are a number of Dharmshalas.

KHAJURAHO

The temples of Khajuraho represent some of the most exquisite specimens of Hindu architecture and sculpture in medieval India. Built between 950 and 1050 only 32 temples out of 85 now survive.

Best season, throughout the year.

How to Reach There

Air : A daily Boeing 737 service links Khajuraho with Delhi, Varanasi and Kathmandu.

Rail : The nearest Rail head is Harpalpur 94 kms. Jhansi 170 kms. for visitors from Delhi and Madras. Satna 117 kms. on the Bombay, Allahabad line of Central Railway for visitors from Bombay, Calcutta and Varanasi.

Road : Connected by regular Bus service with Jhansi, Satna, Bhopal. Herpalpur and Jabalpur.

Distance between Khajuraho and the following cities

478 kms. from Agra via Chhatarpur, Jhansi, Gwalior.
289 kms. from Allahabad via Panna, Rewa.
387 kms. from Bhopal via Chhatarpur, Sagar, Raisen.
596 kms. from Delhi via Chhatarpur, Jhansi, Gwalior, Agra.
275 kms. from Gwalior via Chhatarpur, Jhansi.
359 kms. from Varanasi via Rewa, Mirzapur.

Where to Stay

1. Hotel Payal (MP Tourism) Tel. 76
2. Hotel Rahil (MP Tourism) Tel. 62
3. Tourist Bunglow (MP Tourism) Tel. 74
4. Tourist Village (MP Tourism)
5. Hotel Chandela Tel. 54
6. Hotel Jass Oberoi Tel. 66
7. Hotel Khujuraho Ashok

Places of Interest

The temples of Khajuraho can be devided into the Geographical groups.

Chousath Yogini Temple : Oblong in shape and standing on a five metre High masonary terrace. Here only entirely granite Chousath (Sixty-Four) Yogini (female ascetic attending Kali) temple is the earliest surviving shrine at Khajuraho and is date back to 900 A.D. The temple is dedicated to the goddess Kali, whose image is no longer there.

Kandariya Mahadeo Temple : To the north of Chousath Yogini Temple lies the 31 metre high Kandariya Mahadeo Temple, the largest and the most typical temple at Khajuraho. At the entrance is a richly carved torana or archway decorated with different figures, musicians playing different instruments, lovers in fond embrace, winged gods or goddesses. The ceiling and pillars of the assembly halls and that of the main hall are rich in superb carvings.

Devi Jagdamba Temple : Situated to the north of Kandaria Mahadeo temple Devi Jagdamba temple was long regarded wrongly as dedicated to Kali.

Chitra Gupta Temple : The temple enshrine the image of Sun god Surya driving his Chariot drawn by seven horses There are interesting carving of the outerside walls portraying hunting scenes, rural processions, dances by beautiful damsels and fight between mad elephants. An eleven headed Vishnu can also been seen in the central niche its ten heads representing the ten incarnations.

Parvati Temple : The temple is believed to have been originally dedicated to lord Vishnu. The original deity of the temple has been replaced by a statue of Goddess Ganga standing on a crocodile. The name Parvati seems to be a misnomer.

Lakshmana Temple : Also known as Ramchandra or Chaturbhuj, the temple is dedicated to Lord Vishnu. The main sanctum is note-worthy for its highly decorated entrance.

Mathan Geswara Temple : To the south of Lakshmana Temple is the matangeswara temple which is still a place of worship. A colossol 25 metre high lingam installed in the sanctum is the object of veneration.

(b) Eastern Group

Brahma Temple : Originally dedicated to Lord Vishnu, the temple is built of granite and sandstone.

Vamana Temple : The Vamana Temple is dedicated to Vamana, a dwarf incarnation of Vishnu. The temple is noted for the two bands of sculptures on outside walls depicting apsaras or celestial maidens in an infinite variety of erotic attitudes.

Ghantai Temple : To the south-east of the Khajuraho Village, the Ghantai Temple through in ruins still retains the evidence of the great artistic skill of its builders.

Parsvanath Temple : The Parsvanath Temple is the largest and the first of the Jain temple of Khajuraho. The sanctum contains an ornamental throne with a carved bull, the emblem of the first Jain Tirthankara Adinatha

(c) Southern Group

Situated about 5 kms. fram the Khajuraho, the southern group consists of two temples. Dulhadeo temple is dedicted to Lord

Shiva and has some fine sculptures on its main wall showing women sporting around trees. The chaturbhuj temple dedicated to Lord Vishnu, has a colossal exquisitely carved image of Lord Vishnu.

Excursions

Beni Sagar Dam : 7 kms. picnic spot.

Dhubela museum : 64 kms. located on the bank of a lake, the museum houses a wide variety of Shakti cult sculptures. There are different sections on garments, weapons and paintings.

Punna National Park : 32 kms. this recently constituted national park houses a wide variety of wild animals.

Pandav falls : 35 kms on Panna Road. A scenic spot.

Raj Garh Palace : 25 kms. a picturesque 150 year old palace.

Raneh falls : 20 kms a beautiful picnic spot on river ken.

Rangam Lake : 25 kms. picnic spot Angling facilities available.

CHITRAKOOT

Legend is this that on the sacred soil of Chitrakoot, Brahma. Vishnu and Mahesh took their incarnations. When Rama came to Chitrakoot, he took shelter in its peaceful forests, and came into intimate contact with the sage Atri and Sati Anusuya. The great poet Tulsidas also came here many centuries later in search of spiritual peace. The famous poet, Abdul Rahim Khankhna, one of the nine Jewels of Akbar's court took refuge in Chitrakoot after he became a victim of Jahangir's wrath. Full of natural beauti and murmurring streams, the place attracts lowers of nature as well as religious Tourists. Best season to visit throughout the year.

How to Reach There

Air : Nearest Air Port Khajuraho connected by daily flights with Delhi, Agra and Varanasi.

Rail : Nearest Rail head Karvi on Jhansi-Manikpur section of Central Railway.

Road : Regular Buses connect Chitrakoot with Jhansi, Mahoba, Karwi, Harpalpur, Satna, Rewa and Varanasi.

Where to Stay

Tourism Bunga ow (M.P. Tourism).
Dharamshalas are also available.

Places of Interest

Kamodgiri, Bharat Milap Gupta Godvari, Ramghat Janki Kund. Sphatik Shila, Sati Anusuya Asharam, Bharat Koop and Hinumandhara.

KARNATAKA

BANGALORE

Capital of Karnataka. Well designed and planned, neat and clean city. Connected with Air, Rail and Road with major cities of India. Accomodation at hotels.

Places of Interest :

Tippu Palace : Situated near fort, this palce was begun by Tippu Sultan's father, Hyder Ali and completed by Tippu himself, in 1791. It resembles the Daria Daulat palace at Srirangapatna, Tippu's capital and was used as a summer palace.

Bull Temple : Built in the Dravidian style of architecture it was a monolithic figure of a bull 15 feet high and 20 ft. long. History reveals that it was built by Kompegowda, the founder of the Bangalore city.

Lal Bagh : This beautiful garden was laid out over 200 years ago by Hyder Ali and Tippu Sultan covering an area of about 240 acres and containing over 1000 varieties of trees and plants, many of which are rare. There is a famous glass house, a venue of many a momentous occasion in the past, where flower-shows are held during August and February.

Museum : Visvesaraia technological museum, archaeological museum and Venkatappa Art Gallery.

Vidhan Saudha : An example of modern art and building architecture.

Excursions :

Sravanabelgola : 18 kms, Gomteswara stands here in timeless penance. Sculpted out of a single rock, Gomata is Bahubali, the Jain Prince. He has stood there for a thousand years and is given the periodical abhisheka once in twelve years.

Belur : Belur which was the 12th century capital of the prosperous Hoysala Kingdom in an intricate story in stone. Each piece of sculpture bespeaks a legend, stone becomes supple yeilding, exuberant feminine forms dancing and playing in the Channakeshava temple.

Halebidu : 16 kms to the east lies Halebidu on obscure village but once the capital of the eleventh century Hoysala kings. When you see Halebidu you do so with a sense of shock. Both the Hoysaleswara and Kedareswara temples have been ravaged and plundered by conquering Mohammedan armies and delicate sculpture has been mutilated and deformed. But beauty has defied the best efforts of the conquerors.

MYSORE

Mysore is Verily the jewel of Karnataka. It is the quintessence of Karnataka's cultural heritage. Its lovingly maintained gardens and quaint bunglows, its sacred aura of gods and goddesses, its regal past and its tradition of Dussehara—all these are part of the special lure of Mysore.

The centre of the city is occupied by the historic fort within which is the New Palace. Superb architecture, eloquent stone carvings in the Hoysala style, the turrets and domes, the vast surroundings, the fairy land setting, the ancient fortifications, these conjure up visions of a truly, regal and magnificent past. A visit to the Palace is a must.

How to Reach There :

Mysore is connected with major cities of India by Air, Rail and Road.

Where to Stay :

1. Lalita Mahal Palace Hotel, Ph. 23650
2. Metropole, Station Road, Ph. 20681
3. Hotel Krishnaraja Sagar, Brindaban Garden 22 (Belgola)
4. Hotel Rajendra Vilas, Chamundi Hills, Ph. 22050
5. Hotel Ritz, Bangalore, Nilgiri Rd., Ph. 226 1
6. Hotel Highway, New Bannimantappa Extn. 21117
7. Hotel Dasa Prakesh, Gandhi Square, Ph. 22887
8. Hotel Brindaban, Bangalore-Nilgiri Rd., Ph. 23426/24550
9. K.S.T.D.C. Tourist Hotel, Station Rd., Ph. 23652
10. Chamundi Guest House, Jhansi Laxmi Rd., Ph. 21152

Places of Interest :

Srirangapatana : Of 10 kms. Quiet Island town which was once the capital of Hyder Ali and his son Tippu-Sultan, Tiger of Mysore. Srirangapatana now reminds us of many fierce battles and brave patriotic deeds.

Ranganatha Swamy Temple : The presiding deity of the Ranganatha Swamy Temple is lord Rangnatha who in sleeping posture on the bed of the seven headed serpent 'Adishesha' blesses the visitors.

Gumbaz : The great Gumbaz was built by Tippu Sultan for Hyder Ali and his mother Fathima Begum. Summer Palace, called Dariya Daulat meaning the flowing river of wealth, is a fine example of saracenic architecture.

Philomena's Church : The magnificent St. Philomena's Church has the distinction of being the biggest in South India.

Chamundi Hill : It is in 13 kms and 1095 meters in height. It overlooks Mysore city. A fine Road leads to the top of the hill but the energetic visitor can make use of the 1000 stone steps built by Dodda Deva Raja in the 17th century.

Art Gallery : Well known for its rare collection of paintings.

Mysore Palace : Built in Indo-Sarcenic style, is a treasurer house of exquisite works of art and princely possessions. The stained glass of the ceilings, the wall paintings, the exquisitely carved silver door in the Ambavilas Hall and last but not least, the 200 kg. Golden throne is laid with precious stones and all these cast a lasting impression on the memory.

Krishnaraja Sagar Dam - Brindavan Gardens : Laid between the dam is a truly splendid sight. Every evening the gardens came alive in a burst of dazzling colour and illumination. Cascading silverling fountains light up in varying hues and the whole place becomes a visual experience which lingers on in every once's memory.

Bandipur Wild Life Sanctuary : It is 80 kms from Mysore enroute to Ooty, is the inner sanctum of a much wider wild life park known as Venugopal wild life national park.

Ranganathithu : Soon after the K.R. Sagar, turning from the highway in Ranganathithu, one of the most remarkable bird sancturies.

BIJAPUR

Foundation, of this historic city was laid by the Chalukyan Kings of Kalyana in the llth century. They called it 'Viajya Puram' city of victory. The city came under Muslim influence.

How to Reach There :

Bijapur is linked by Rail and Road with all important cities in South India. It is 613 kms from Bangalore via Hubli.

Where to Stay :

1. Adil Shahi, Ph. 934
2. Travellers Lodge, Ph. 401
3. K.S.R.T.C. Guest House near Sainik school, Ph. 448
4. APMC Guest House, India Rd., Ph. 713
5. Inspection Bungalow, Station Rd., Ph. 153
6. Tourist Bungalow, Station Rd., Ph. 153

Places of Interest :

Gol Gumbaz : Dominating the Landscape of Bijapur is this imposing dome, the tomb of the 7th king Muhammad Adil Shah.

Ibrahim Rauza : This exquisite Buldg. contains the tomb of Ibrahim Adil Shah II. The structure is said to have inspired the Taj Mahal of Agra.

Bara Kaman : One of the major attractions is the unfinished mausoleum of Ali Adil Shah II. Its twelve graceful arches give it the name Bara Kaman.

Asav Mahal : A must for the devout Muslims, for it has two hairs from the prophet Muhammad's beard.

Taj Bawdi : The great tank commemorates Ibrahim II's first wife, Taj Sultana.

Gagan Mahal : Built in the second half of the 16th century by Ali Adil Shah. Here the Shah held the Darbar at which he received petitions and pleas from his subjects.

Malik-i-Maidan : On the walls of the city, is situated proudly to this day, the legendary cannon of the Adil Shah.

Jama Masjid : This mosque built between 1557 and 1686, best seems in the early morning when sunlight streams across the gardens bringing out all the details of running ornaments round its arch.

Mehtar Mahal: An excellent example of Indo-Saracenic Style of architecture.

Old Mosque: It was formerly a Jain Temple, at the end of the 15th century it was converted for Muslim Worship.

Makka Masjid : Behind the blank wall within the citadel completely and enclosed by arcaded court is a replica of the Masjid of Mecca.

Asar-i-Sharif : A palace built as a court house in 1646. It has teak pillars and wood-work.

Lambachari : Longest Jum owned by the Adil Shah. It is houred on solitary tower inside the City.

AIHOLE

Aihole is today a tiny village that conceals Visual wealth accumulated for two centuries of Indian History between the fifth and seventh centuries A.D. when it was the capital of the mighty Chalukyan Kings.

How to Reach There :

Rail : Nearest Railway station Bagalkot 46 Kms on the Hubli Sholapur line.

Road : Connected by Road with all important places ; 32 Kms from Pattadakkal and 46 Kms from Badami.

Where to Stay :

1. Tourist Bungalow

Note:—Tourists are advised to stay at Bagalkot and visit Aihole during the day time.

Places of Interest :

1. Lad Khen Temple : Mussive building
2. Konti Gudi Temple
3. Durg Temple

BADAMI

In this town of lake and sandstone hills, an ideal locale for sculpture and architecture once flourishing capital of the great Chalukyas and now the centre of Taluk administration. You can explore the thrilling forms the human hands have hewn out of hard rocks. There are four rock-cut temples which vie with one another in architectural in genuity and sculpture excellence.

You can begin with the nalegiti Shivalaya perhaps the oldest of the temples in the Badami complex. Then see the Bhutanath temple on the western fringe of the Lake, but make it at sunset when it looks like a dream follow it up with the Shiva at the Lakulisa temple. And then the incredible Rock face to the South-west of Bhutanath, carved with the relief image of Vishnu, Shiva Mahishasura Mardini, Varaha, Ganapati and Narsimha. On the South side of the rock Rests Lord Vihnu on a bed of the coiled and serpent Sesha.

To the south east of the Lake, crawl through a tunnel to cavern where you are sure to meet the fascinating image of Koshtaraya—the King who got cured of his Leprosy at Badami and commemorated it with this half Buddhist, half Jaina image.

How to Reach There :

Rail : On the Hubli-Sholapur line, well connected by Rail with all the important places. It is 5 Km from town.

Road : Hubli 128 Kms
Bijapur 163 Kms
Aihole 50 Kms

Pattadakkal 29 Kms.
Bagalkot 41 Kms.

Where to Stay :

1. Inspection Bungalow
2. Tourist Bungalow

PATTADAKKAL

The most important monument here, the Lokeshwari or Virupasha temple, is a memorable ancient feat. Its sculpture glory lies in the vivid way it narrates in stone the great episodes from the immortal Hindu epics of Ramayana and Mahabharata.

But at the Mallikarjuna temple you will find the stone telling you different tales.

Do not miss the two elephants in the old Jain temple.

How to Reach There :

Rail : Nearest Railway station Badami 29 Kms.

Road : Connected by Road with all the important places. Aihole is 79 Kms from here.

Where to Stay :

No tourist stays here. You can stay at Badami or Bagalkot. Visit at day time.

HAMPI

Known centuries ago as Vijayanagar, the city of victory. Hampi eloquently recalls one of the most illustrious chapters in Indian History.

400 kms from Bangalore, Hampi bears eloquent testimony to the fabulous civilisation of the Vijayanagar era. The tall Uddana Veer Bhadra Temple stands alongside the ruins of a big hiriya-Satara. Nearby a canal flows from an ancient time constructed by the Vijayanagar Kings for improving the water supply of the city. The formidable underground Shiva temple and huge stone linga are situated on the route to city.

To the north stands the many-pillared temple of Krishna.

Closer towards Hampi, on top of the hill looks Ganesha received Hindu deity carved out of a single rock.

Down in the valley are spread the ruins of what was once the Hampi Bazaar.

To the east of the Bazar is the Kodanda Rama temple on the river bank. Further down is the Achyuta temple dedicated to god Sri Thiruvengalanathan.

Where to Stay :

1. Hampi Power House, Guest House, Ph. 272
2. Hampi Power House Camp, Ph. 272
3. Inspection Bungalow, Kamalpur, Ph. 754

The Thungabhadra Dam :

Six kms from Hospet is the 49 meters high Tung Bhadra Dam. Its 378 kms reservoir spells prosperity for both Karnataka and Andhra Pradesh.

Where to Stay :

1. Vaikuntha and Kailasa Guest House, Ph. 54
2. K.S.T.D.C. Tourist Lodge, Ph. 270
3. Inspection Bungalow
4. Indira Bhavan and Lake View Guest House, Munirabad, Ph. 35/36

BIDAR

Some believe that Nala and Damayanti lived at Bidar. The story of their love was enacted here. But modern research has shattered this claim to antiquity by maintaining that Bidar was Vidarbha and not Bidar.

The golden age of Hindu India starting with the Mauryan Dynasty had ended with the Chalukyas and Pallavas in the South. The invasion into India by Mohammed of Ghazani, Mohammed of Ghauri and by Changez Khan had paved the way for the establishment of Muslim ruler in the North. The slave dynasty followed each other of short intervals at Delhi and it was during the reign of the Tughlak that Bidar was annexed and a Governor appointed there.

Bidar can be reached by Road and Rail from Hyderabad or Gulbarga. The 133 kms of tarred road from Hydrabad makes a pleasant drive, except in the summer months of April and May. An equally good road leads to Bidar from Gulbarga, 56 kms away. Direct express buses ply between Gulbarga and Bidar providing connections to the incoming and outward bound trains at Gulbarga. Bidar can also be reached by Air as it has a full-fledged Air trip maintained by the air force for their training establishment, but at present no scheduled commercial flights are planned and the nearest Airport is at Hyderabad.

Where to Stay :

On the Road from Hyderabad convenient traveller's bungalows are available enroute at Pattanchruvu, Sadashivapet, Zaheerabad and Mirzapur. On the Gulbarga road well equipped traveller's bungalows are situated at Homnabad, Mangalaqi and Mirzapur. At Bidar itself accommodation can be secured at the Hubshi Kot Guest House and the Orient House to the Executive Engineer at Bidar or at the PWD Travellers' Bungalow or the forest Deptt's lodge. Accommodation is also available in KSTDC Hotel Barid Shahi, at Kalyani or at Sastapur 5 km away on the Bombay-Hyderabad National High Way.

Places of Interest :

1. The Inner Fort
2. The Sharaza Darwaza
3. The Gumbad Darwaza
4. The Rangin Mahal
5 The Royal Kitchen
6. The Royal Baths
7. The Zanani Masjid or the Saha Khambah Masjid
8. The Tarakash Mahal
9. The Gagan Mahal
10. The Dewan-e-Am
11. The Takhat Mahal
12. Royal Pavillion
13. The Hazar Kothari
14. The Naubat Khana
15. The Behmani Tombs ut Ashtur
16. Smaller Tombs at Ashtur
17. The Baridi Tombs
18. The Chaubara
19. The Madarsa of Mahmud Gawan
20. The Habshi Kot
21. Dargha of Hazrat Shah Abul Faid
22. Tombs of Hazrat Shah Ali
23. Grave of Mahamud Gawan
24 The Nanak Thera
25. Rock Temple at Narasinha Zarni
26. Kalyani
27. Umapur
28. Jalsangvi

ANDHRA PRADESH

Andhra Pradesh is a land of Krishna and Godavari rivers, with rich cultural heritage of literature, art, music, dance and drama. It abounds in magnificent monuments which breathe history, lakes and beaches which exude charm and beauty, wild life sanctuaries that brings to our eye the majestic animal kingdom, great ancient temples, mosques and churches and modern temples like Nagarjuna Sagar Project.

HYDERABAD

The state's capital is a major attraction for tourists, which could be a starting point. One of the few twin cities of the world. Hyderabad can aptly be described as the Budapest of India. Hussain Sagar separates the twin cities of Hyderabad and Secundrabad. Situated at a height of about ‹ 10 meters above the sea level. It enjoys pleasant climate almost throughout the year

The city houses in its bosom, monuments of majesty, lakes of excellent beauty, mosques, marvellous minarets and hills. The most famous of them is Charminar an imposing structure built by the Golcunda ruler and founder of the city Mohammed Quli Qutab Shah in 1591, having handsome paintings, statues, wood carvings, rare pieces of furniture from west Asia, Japan, China etc. The magnificent statue in marble of the veiled Rebacca is exampled. The Mecca Masjid, one of the impressive mosques in the south is located in Hyderabad. Lofty colomiades and door arches are made of single piece o. granite. It was completed by Aurangzeb in 1687. The city has many lovely lakes, Himayat Sagar, Osman Sagar, Hussain Sagar and the Mir Alam Tank.

The massive Golcunda fort and the tombs of Qutab Shahi kings with their characteristic style are of great historical impottance.

Mir Alam Tank constructed by French Engineer, is today's Nehru Zoological Park set up in 1959. The Zoo has a mini traica and children's corner with facilities for joy rides on camels and elephants. The lion safari park and pre-historic park are the star attractions here.

Hyderabad is connected by Rail and Air with the rest of India. Bus service is also available in and outside the city.

Where to Stay :

Hotels :

1. Annapurna, Nampally, Station Rd.
2. Asrani, M.G. Road, Secundrabad
3. Deccan Continental, Minister Rd., Secundrabad
4. Park Lake, 115, Parklane, Secundrabad
5. Perey's, Sardar Patel Rd. do-
6. Blue Moon, Raj Bhavan Rd., Begumpet

7. Emerald, Chirag ali lane, Abid Rd.
8. Hyd. Inn, Lake Hill Road
9. Nagarjuna, Bashir Bagh
10. Ritz, Hill Fort Palace
11. Rock Castle, Jubilee Hills
12. Sarovar, Secretariat Road
13. Siddharth, Bank Street
14. Welcome Hotel Banjara, Banjara Hills
15. Ashoka, Lakdi ka pul
16. Brindavan, Station Rd.
17. Dwarka, Lakdi ka pul
18. Firdaus, Lake Hill Rd.
19. Hardwar, Eslamia Bazar
20. Jaya International, Abid Rd.
21. Krishna, Lakdi ka pul
22. Rajdhani, Sidamba Bazar
23. Royal, Nampally
24. Taj Mahal, King Kothi Rd.
25. Taj Mahal, 88, Sarojini Devi Rd., Secundrabad
26. Tourist, Kachiguda
27. Venkateswara, Lakdi ka pul

Other Accommodations :

1. Youth Hostel, Behind Boats Club, Secundrabad
2. Guest House, Lake View, Somaji Guda
3. Dilkhusha, Raj Bhavan Rd.
4. Green Lands, Begumpet
5. Ananda Nilayam -do-

Dharamshala :

1. Dharamshala, Grain Bazar, Secundrabad
2. Municipal Sarai. Nampally
3. Ram Pratap, -do-

Restaurants :

Non-Vegetarian : *Hyderabad* :

1. Blue Diamond
2. Johu
3. Kwality
4. Espresso
5. Manju
6. Savoy
7. 3 Aces

Vegetarian :

1. Brindaban
2. Dwarka
3. Kamat
4. Madhura
5. Neo Mysore cafe
6. Orient
7. Royal
8. Swagat
9. Taj Mahal
10. Tourist

Non-Vegetarian : *Secundrabad* :

1. Elpha
2. Kwality
3. Lido
4. Monty's Nanking
5. New Peking Chinese Garden Restaurant

Vegetarian :

1. Taj Mahal
2. Anand Bhavan
3. Sri Laxmi Bhavan

Arts and Crafts :

Silver work of Hyderabad is very popular. It is called Bidri work. Wood-work is also famous.

Places of Interest :

Salarjung Museum Hyderabad : A unique treasurer house of exquisite art pieces. The exhibits include a rich collection of Jade Jewellery, paintings, statues, wood-carvings, furniture, Emperor Jehangir's wine cup, Nurjehan's dagger, Tippu-Sultan's chair, and Aurangjeb's sword. The museum is closed on Fridays and entry is permitted by tickets.

Gandhi Bhavan and Museum : Cultural programmes are organised in the auditorium apart from reading room facilities.

Golcunda fort : It was the capital of Kutb Shahi kings. It was famous for its diamond mines.

Naubat Pahar : It was used for reading of proclaimations after beating drums during the Kutb Shahi regime.

Nehru Zoological Park : Biggest in India and offers a magnificent view of more than 1100 animals and birds.

Osman Sagar : In 25 kms area Beautiful lake covering an area of 46 kms popularly known as Gandhipet. It is also a beautiful picnic spot.

Himayat Sagar : 22.5 kms area Himayat Sagar is a lovely picnic spot.

Lion Safari Park : First of its kind in India and in South-East Asia.

Osmania University : Distance 8 km built by late Nizam of Hydrabad.

Charminar : Built in 1591 A.D. in the middle of city. It has graceful minarets.

Mecca Masjid : Situated near Charminar. It has a capacity of 10,000 worshippers a time.

VIJAYWADA

A Commercial city, dedicated to Lord Shiva. Surrounded by many hillocks, of which two are famous · Kanakdurga and Indrakilla. Accommodation at Govt Guest House, and Inspection Bungalow Vijaywada is connected by Rail and Road with Hyderabad and other important towns of Andhra Pradesh.

NAGARJUNA SAGAR

Situated on the right bank of the Krishna river. Nagarjuna Sagar dam has made it modern temple of India. Regular bus service from Hyderabad to Nagarjuna Sagar Dam. Nearest Airport is Hyderabad. Road distance between Nagarjuna Sagar and the following cities are :

Hyderabad 149 kms
Macherla Rly. Stn. 29 kms
Madras 566 kms
Vijaywada 181 kms
Warangal 237 kms

Where to Stay :

1. Vijay Vihar Hill Colony
2. River View Right Bank
3. Project House, Hill Colony
4. Tourist Annexe -do-
5. Youth Hostel -do-

VISHAKHAPATNAM

Formerly it was called Vizagapatham. It is an important harbour and shipyard. Most important commercial town in South India. It is also a famous pilgrimage centre.

How to Reach There :

Air : It is connected with Hyderabad, Bhubneshwar, Calcutta and Vijaywada by Indian Airlines Service.

Rail : It is also connected by Rail and nearest Rail head is Waltair.

Road : Connected with all important towns of South India by Road.

Where to Stay :

Hotels : 1. Sun-n-Sea, Apsara, Vikram

Other accommodations : Railway Retiring Rooms, Andhra University Guest House, Youth Hostel.

WARANGAL

140 kms from Hyderabad. In the past this city was surrounded by two walls. The ruins of the walls can be seen now. It was the capital of Andhra Kings. Following places are worth seeing at Warangal :

1. Ramappa Temple
2. Ramappa Lake
3. Pakhal Lake is situated at a distance of 40 kms from Warangal.

Where to Stay :

1. Ekasila
2. Shanker
3. Natraj
4. Ganesh Bhavan
5. Anand Lodge
6. Annapurna Lodge
7. Laxmi Lodging
8. PWD Travellers' Bungalow
9. Municipal Travellers' Bungalow
10. Two Dharamshalas are also available.

SRI SAILAM

232 kms from Hyderabad, this temple dedicated to lord Siva, is situted in Rishabgiri hills on the southern bank of river Krishna in Kurnool district. The place is famous as Sri Parvati. This temple is believed to be in existence even before the Vedic age, since a mention of 'Sriparvata' is made in Mahabharata, the great Hindu epic The presiding deity lord Mallikarjuna Swamy Swayamodbhava (selfborn) in the form of Linga, is the second of twelve 'Jyotirlingas in India. Sri Bhramaramba Devi, the goddess is one of the daughter Mahashakti, mentioned in Puranas. The river Krishna here is called as 'Patal Ganga'.

How to Reach There :

Air : Nearest Air port is Hyderabad.

Rail : Nearest Rail head is Markapur Rd. on Guntur-Hubli meter gauge Railway line.

Road : Well connected by A.P. State Road Transport Corpn. and Devasthanam buses with Hyderabad Mehbubnagar, Nalgonda, Devaskonda, Vijaywada, Guntur, Kurnool, Ongale, Mahanadi, Mantralayam, Anantpur, Tirupati and Chitradurg.

Distance between Sri Sailam and other cities :

Dornal 49 kms.
Markapur 85 kms.
Atmakur 113 kms.
Nandyal via Atmakur and Dornal 158 kms.
Nagarjuna Sagar via Macherlo 180 kms.
Kurnool via Almdun-Dronal 180 kms.
Guntur via Narsanopel, Virukonda Dornal : 216 kms.
Hyderabad via Amangal, Dindi, Mannanur 232 kms.
Vijaywada via Guntur 260 kms.
Anantapur via Murnool 410 kms.
Tirupati via Cuddapet, Allagadda, Nandyal 423 kms.

Reservation authority Executive Sri Sailam Devasthanam, Sri Sailam : Ph: 59/60

Where to Stay :

1. Devasthanam Cottage
2. Devasthanam Choultries Officer
3. Saila Vihar Tourist House
4. Karnataka Guest House
5. Zila Parishad Guest House
6. Tirumala Tirupati Devasthanam Choultry
7. All India Arya Vysya Choultry
8. Akhil Bharat Arya Vysya Choultry
9. Veera Saiva Choultry
10. Veera Saiva Saravanta Basawesware Choultry
11. Kerivena Brahma Choultry
12. Srowth Saiva Choultry
13. Sri Jagadguru Vasaga Panditharadhya Matham Choultry
14. Thi Viswa Brahmin Choultry
15. Sri Jagadguru Kanchi Kamakoti Peetham Matham
16. Sri Jagadguru Sringeri Peetham Matham

Places of Interest :

1. Sri Bhramarambha Mallikarjuna Swamy Temple
2. Silkharam: Highest peak 2835 ft. of Sri Sailam
3. Shakshi Ganpathi
4. Patala Ganga
5. Hatakeshwaram
6. Dam site

Festivals :

1. Mahashivaratri
2. Ugadi

TIRUPATI TIRUMALA

Situated on the top of Tirumala in Chittoor district. Tirupati is one of the most important pilgrimage centre in India. It attracts millions of devotees from different parts of country. There are a number of sacred tanks and water falls on the hill. They are known as Kapilateertham, Akasha Ganga and Papanasam. Opening timings of temples : 4 am to 1 pm and 3 pm to 9 pm.

How to Reach There :

Air : Nearest air port Madras

Rail : Nearest Railway Station Madras

Road : Regular Buses connect with Madras, Bangalore, Hyderabad, Chittur and Vijayawada etc.

Where to Stay :

There are a number of hotels and Devasthanam.

BHADRACHALAM

Situated on the left bank of river Godavari. It is famous throughout India. The Puranic and historic facts, relate that here lord Rama, long after he had shed his mortal coil, manifested himself to save his devotee Bhadra Maharishi, whom he promised Moksha. That is why the village is named after Bhadragiri or Bhadrachalam.

How to Reach There :

Air : Nearest Airport Vijayawada 207 kms.

Rail : Bhadrachalam road is 40.23 kms from the pilgrim town and connected with regular Bus service. Dornakal junction on Vijaywada Kazipet line is the convenient Rail head for change over to reach Bhadrachalam Railway station.

Road : Bhadrachalam is connected by S.R.T.C. buses with the following places :

40 Kms from Bhaprachalam Rd.
207 Kms from Vijay Wada via Khammam.
250 Kms from Rajahmundry, via Kothagudem, Zongardai guden.
255 Kms from Warangal, via Kothagudem, Yellandu.
399 Kms from Visakhapatnam, via Gudem, Chintapalli.
672 Kms from Madras, via Vijaywada.
615 Kms from Tirupati, via Vijaywada.

Where to Stay :

Tourist Rest Houses :

1. Paransala Ph: 21
2. Panchvati

Dharamshalas under the control of Devasthanam

1. Alluri Nilayam Cottage, Ph. 5
2. Yadgiri Gutta Guest House
3. Chandramouli Sadan
4. Kurnool Srinivasa sadan, Ph. 67
5. T.T.D. Satram
6. Yatrika Sadan
7. Nagireddy Sadan
8. Kumara swamy Cottage
9. Vemulavada Satram
10. Puchu Pentiah cottage
11. Agarwal Cottage
12. Amba Satram Hall

Hotels :

1. Srinivasa palace, Ph. 99
2. Murthy Hotel
3. Ajanta Hotel
4. Padmaja Hotel

Excursions :

Ushanagundam :

6 Kms from temple. It is said that Lakshmana Swamy have brought here hot water for Sita to bath.

Mothi Gadda :

32 Kms on Paransab Kd. Sivaratri is celebrated here.

Paransala :

35 Kms on Venkatapuram Road. It is said that Sita was separated from Rama here.

TAMILNADU

Tamilnadu is a window of the modern South. It has tall palms, taller gopuram, carved temples, legends and of silver-lined beaches. Tamilnadu is a land that has seen the rise and fall of many ancient kingdoms.

MADRAS

Capital of Tamilnadu is the fourth largest city in India. It is the major city and gateway of South India.

How to Reach :

Air : Indian Air lines service

Rail: Connected by Rail

Road :

Bangalore	360 kms	Kanya Kumari	704 kms
Bombay	1355 kms	Madurai	460 kms
Calcutta	1616 kms	Pondicherry	160 kms
Cochin	694 kms	Trichirapalli	320 kms
Coimbtore	488 kms	Thanjavur	351 kms
Delhi	2278 kms	Salem	330 kms
Hyderabad	696 kms	Tirupati	160 kms

Where to Stay :

Western Style Hotels :	**Phone**
1. Hotel Atlantik, Egmore, Madras	810562
2. Hotel Holiday Inn, Aya Gate	444676
3. Hotel Admiralty, Myton Rd.	71121
4. Hotel Blue Diamond, High Rd.	
5. Hotel Chola Sheraton, Cathedral Rd.	82091
6. Hotel Cannemara, Binny Rd.	810051
7. Hotel Imperial, Gandhi Irwin Rd.	847076
8. Hotel Madras International, Anna Malai	811811
9. Hotel New Victoria, Kennet Lane	847738
10. Hotel Ranjit, High Rd.	810521
11. Hotel Sudarshan International, Egmore	812061
12. Hotel Savera, Dr. Radha Krishnan Rd.	810031
13. Hotel Taj Coromandal, High Rd.	848888
14. Tourist Hotel, Adyar Bridge Rd.	416001
15 Queen's Hotel, Village Rd.	82176

Indian Style Hotels :	
1. Hotel Ashoka, Pantheon Rd.	841977
2. Hotel Dasaprakash, High Rd.	661111
3. Hotel Kanchi, C. in C. Rd.	83101
4. Hotel Maris, Dr. Radhakrishnan Rd.	810541
5. Hotel New Wood Lands, -do-	83111
6. Hotel Palmgrove, High Rd.	811881
7. Hotel President, Dr. Radhakrishnan Rd.	842211
8. Hotel Silver Stars, High Rd.	664414
9. Hotel Shri Lekha, Anna Malai	840582

10. Hotel Swagath, R.H. Rd. 848422
11. Tourist Home, Egmore 844079
12. Hotel Guru, -do- 87939
13. Woodlands Hotel, Rogapeth 82151

Other Accommodations :

1. Youth Hostel, Indira Nagar, 42882
2. Railway Retiring Room, Central/Egmore 30337/843927
3. YMCA, Espalanade 23941
4. YWCA, Guest House, High Rd. 39920
5. Lahary Transit Hotel

Places of Interest :

1. Fort St. George
2. St. Mary's Church
3. Fort Museum
4. War Memorial
5. Marina Beach
6. Anna Square
7. Aquarium
8. Light House
9. Kapaleeswarar Temple
10. Parathasarthy Temple
11. Southern Cathedral Basilica
12. Theosophical Society
13. Elliots Beach
14. Kalakshetra
15. Gandhi, Rajaji, Kamaraj Memorial
16. Chinamalai
17. Parangimalai
18. Valluvarkottam
19. Govt. Estate
20. High Court
21. Ripon Bldgs.
22. Museum & Art Galleries
23. Garden and Parks

Excursions :

1. Mamallapuram 60 Kms
2. Crocodile Bank 55 Kms
3. Kovalam 40 Kms

4. Thiru Porur 40 Kms
5. Thine Kazha Kundram
6. Vedanthangal 86 Kms
7. Uthiramerur
8. Kancheepuram
9. Thiruthani

KANCHEEPURAM

The city of thousand temples. It is one of the seven sacred cities of India. A former capital of the Pallavas. It is famous for its exquisitely woven silk sarees. Places to see include Ekambareswarar Temple, Varadarajaswamy Temple, Vaikunth Peruma Temple, Kailasnath's Temple, Kamakshi Man Temple and the homes of bulk fabric weavers. 70 kms. from Madras. Nearest airport—Madras. Regular bus services available. Accommodation at Travellers Lodge run by TTDC.

MUDUMALAI

60 Kms from OOTY. Famous Wild Life Sanctuary. Coimbtore is the nearest Airport. Nearest rail head is Udhagamandalam. Regular Bus Service. Accommodation at rest house, lodge, huts and rented accommodations.

CHIDAMBARAM

A famous pilgrimage centre with its main temple dedicated to Lord Nataraja. Annamalai University is here. Pilchavaram is a place of rare scenic beauty 20 kms away. Nearest Airport Tiruchirapalli 160 Kms. and Madras is 227 kms. Express trains and buses connect these cities.

POOMPUHAR

Situated at the confluence of the river Cavery in Thanjavur District, this was ancient port of the Cholas. Visiting places are:— Art gallery, Elanji Manram, Pavai, Manram, Nedungal Manram and the beach. Nearest Airport is Tiruchirappali 160 Kms Nearest Railway Station is Manram 90 Kms. Frequent Bus service is available. Accommodation is at tourist Bungalow—Ph.-39.

VEDAN THANGAL

A major Wild Sanctuary. This bird watcher's paradise is only 83 Kms from Madras on the road to Tiruchi. The best season is from October to March. Regular Bus service is available from Madras and Chengalpattu. Accommodation either at Madras or Mamallapuram or at the Forest Deptt's Rest House.

TIRUCHIRAPPALLI

Most famous is the Rock Fort, abruptly rising to over

83 Meters. Other notable temples are—Srirangam, Sri Ranganathaswamy temple, Siva temple at Tiruvanaikaval.

Excursions :

Narthmalai
Kudimianmalai
Kodunbalur
Jain caves Sittannavasal

Tiruchi has its own Airport served by Air Lanka and Indian Airlines. Tiruchi is 320 Kms from Madras on the National Highway. Important Rail junction, Southern railway. Daily express buses connect it. Accommodation at T.T.D.C's Tourist. Bungalow, TTDC's Traveller's Lodge, Hotels etc.

COURTALLAM

Health Resort, water falls, popular Excursions to:—

1. Tiruchandur Mungam a temple 99 Kms
2. Tirunelveli, 50 Kms
3. Krishna Puram, 60 Kms
4. Tenkasi 5 Kms
5. Mundanthurai, Tiger Sanctuary 75 Kms

Madurai 100 Kms is the nearest Airport, Tenkasi 5 Kms the nearest Rail head Regular Bus service available. Accommodation at Township Guest Houses, Hotels etc.

HOGENAKAL

Health Resort, waterfalls Bush green woods. Bangalore is the nearest Airport 130 Kms. Madras is 350 Kms. Accommodation at T.T.D.C. Tourist Bungalow.

YERCAUD

Year round Tourist attraction, altitude 1500 Meters. Visiting places are—Lake, Anna Park, Orchidorium, Killiyur falls, Pagoda Paint, Bear's cave and the Servârayan temple. Accommodation at TTDC. Tourist Bunglow, Guest Houses and other Hotels. Tiruchi is the nearest Airport 188 Kms, nearest Rail head is Salem Junction 35 Kms. Yercaud Express is the most convenient train. Regular Bus service from Salem.

MADURAI

It was planned in the pattern of a Lotus flower, with the famous Meenakshi Sundareswarar Temple as its centre. The town is situated on the banks of river Vaigai. Legend attributes, the foundation of the temple and town to a Pandiyan King Kulasekara. On the occasion of naming the town, Lord Siva appeared and drops of nectar from his Locks Bellon the Town so it is called (Mathuram) Madurai, the nectar city. It is one of the most ancient cities of India.

Places of Interest :

Sri Menakshi Sundareswarar Temple

Rectangular in shape, the temple is about 847 feet in length and about 792 feet in breadth. South Tower of the temple is tallest to a height of 160 feet.

Thirumalai Nayak Palace

This palace is about one Km. South East of the Srimeenakshi Temple

Mariamman Teppa Kulam

This tank, known as Vomdiyur Teppakulam is at the east end of the city. It is almost equal in area to that of the Sri Meenakshi Temple. The float festival is held here every year.

The Koodal Alagar Temple :

To the west of city is this ancient Vaishnavite temple with beautiful sculptures. The Lord here is in three poses : sitting, standing and reclining.

Roya Gopuram, Pudu Mandapam and Gandhi Museum are the other places of interest.

Excursions :

Thirupparan Kudram :

8 Kms South of Madurai Junction. The temple here is dedicated to Lord Subramanya and is one of the six abodes of the Lord. Its inner most shrine is cut out of a solid rock.

Alagar Koil :

21 Kms north-east of Madurai. The famous Vishnu Temple called Alagar Koil is at the Southern end of the hill called Alagar Malai.

Kodai Kanal :

A very popular hill station Kodai is located at an altitude of 2133 meters in the western Ghats. It is 120 Kms from Madurai and 83 Kms from Kodai Road Railway Station.

Vigai Dam :

69 Kms from Madurai on the way to the Periyar Wild Life Sanctuary. A fine picnic spot.

Palani :

122 Kms, a famous pilgrim centre of the South and one of the six abodes of Lord Subramanya. At the top of the Hill, connected with Rail or Bus.

Suruli water falls :

128 Kms from Madurai on the way to Thekkadi. A picnic spot.

Gourtallam :

160 Kms from Madurai famous for water falls. Season June to September.

How to Reach :

Air : Madurai has an Airport connecting Madras and Trivendrum.

Rail : Madurai is connected by Rail.to Madras, Trvivandrum, Tıruchirapalli, Rameshwaram etc.

Road : Buses, taxis etc. are available.

Where to Stay :

Western Style Hotels :

1.	Hotel Tamil Nadu, Alagar Koil Rd.	Ph. 27139
2.	Hotel Temil Nadu, West Velist.	21435
3.	Traveller's Lodge, Alagar Koil Rd.	23676
4.	Pondyan Hotel, Alagar Koil Rd.	26671

Indian Style Hotels :

There are many Indian Style Hotels.

KODAI KANAL

Charming Hill Station. Situated amidst the Sylvan grandeur of the Southern east of the upper Palani Hills, in western Ghats and unspoilt by modern civilization, lovely 'Kodai' is 120 Kms. from Madurai. Kodai Kanal will mesmerise any visitor with her wooded slopes, mighty rocks, enchanting water falls and beautiful lakes. Having more Sun shine than other hill resorts. Kodai Kanal is one of the most popular health resort in India.

Places of Interest :

1. Byrant Park.
2. Pillar rocks 7.24 Kms
3. Coaker's walk 1 Kms
4. Green Valley view 6 Kms
5. Golf club 6 Kms
6. Silver Cascade 8 Kms
7. Perumal Peak 20 Kms
8. Bear Shola falls 1-5 Kms
9. Kuruji Andavar Temple 3.2 Kms

How to Reach Kodai Kanal :

Air : Nearest Airport Madurai 120 Kms

Rail : Nearest Rail head is Kodai Road Railway station 80 Kms from Kodai Kanal

Road : Kodai Kanal is connected by Road with all important towns

Where to Stay :

Western Style Hotels :

1. Hotel Tamilnadu, Feru Hill Rd. Ph. 481
2. Carlton Hotel 252

Indian Style Hotels :

There are number of decent hotels to stay.

Other Accommodations :

1. Township new Rest House, Ph. 298
2. Bus stand Rest House
3. Kamaraja Puram Rest House
4. Housing Board Rest House

UDHAGAMANDALAM

Chief of Hill Stations of Tamilnadu, called as Ooty the queen of hill stations, located at a height of 2286 meters.

Places of Interest :

1. Botanical Garden
2. Lake
3. Dodabetta
4. Mukenti Peak
5. Pykara Dam

How to Reach There :

Air : Coimbtore 80 kms is the nearest Airport. Connected by Indian Air Lines with Madras, Bangalore and Cochin

Rail : Connected by mountain Railway with Coimbtore via Mettupalayam

Road : Connected with important towns

Where to Stay ;

Western Style Hotels :

1. Hotel Tamilnadu Ph. 2543/2544
2. Hotel Savoy 2572
3. Tamil Zhagani 2497/2498/2499
4. Hampton Manor Hotel, Coonoor 244
5. Ritz Hotel, Coonoor 242/465

Indian Style Hotels :

1. Hotel Dasaprakash
2. Hotel Woodlands 2551

Other Accommodations :

1. Tamilnadu Cooperative Guest House Ph. 2638
2. Y.W.C.A. Anandgiri 2218
3. Railway Retiring Room 2246

MAMALLAPURAM

60 kms South of Madras. Situated on the shore of Bay of Bengal, Marvellous monuments. Major Holiday Centre in South India.

How to Reach There :

Air : Meenambkkam Airport, Madras is the nearest Airport

Rail : Chengalpattu on the Madras-Tiruchi Section

Road : Good motoring road

Where to Stay :

Western Style Hotels :

1. Temple Bay Ph. 51
2. T N.T.D.C. Beach Resort 35/68
3. Ideal Beach Resort 40

Indian Style :

There are a number of Indian Style Hotels to stay

Places of Interest :

1. *Caves* : Nine rock-cut cave temples. Krishna Mandapam cave is notable.
2. *Bas Relief* : The world's largest stone bas relief is another pride of Mamallapuram.
3. *Arjuna's Penance Theory* : The emaciated figure standing on one leg is Arjuna in the penance posture, praying Lord Siva for powerful weapon to destroy enemies. Lord Siva granting him his boon.
4. *The Descent of the Ganga Theory* : Rama praying to the gods to give the Ganga to the earth.
5. *The Shore Temples* : The oldest temple, contains two rock-cut Shrines, one Siva temple and one Vishnu temple.
6. *Five Raths* : To the south of the hillock holding the cave temple are the fine monolithic temples known as Pancha Pandavaraths.

THANJAVUR

This District is called as the 'Rice Bowl' of Tamilnadu. It is also known for its exquisite handicrafts, castings etc.

How to Reach There :

Air : Nearest Airport Tiruchirapalli is 60 kms and is connected by Indian Air lines with Colombo and Madras.

Rail : Connected by Rail with Tiruchi, Madurai, Negone and Madras.

Road : Good Road system connected Tiruchirapalli, Pondicherry, Nagercoil, Courtallam, Madurai, Vellore and Sharcottai.

Where to Stay :

Western Style Hotels :

1. Hotel Tamilnadu, Gandhiji Rd. Ph. 601
2. Travellers' Lodge, Vallam Rd. 365

Other Accommodations :

1. Indian style Hotels are available
2. Railway retiring rooms
3. Municipal Rest House
4. Rajah's Rest House, Gandhiji Rd.
5. Municipal Rest House, Central Bus Stand
6. -do- Opp. Bus Stand
7. -do- Gandhiji Road

Places of Interest :

Sri Brihadeswarar Temple : Built by the great Chola king Raja Rajal, is an example of Chola architecture.

The Palace The palace near the temple is a vast building of masonary. It is a grand pile of buildings with huge corridors and spacious halls.

Art Gallery : It contains a number of granite and bronze statues of Chola period.

Library : In another section of the palace is the Saraswathy Mahal Library. Hall of music, Schwartz Church and the tank area, also visiting place.

KANYA KUMARI

Kanya Kumari occupies unique place among the tourist centres of India. It is the lands end, where waters of the Arabian sea, the Indian Ocean and the Bay of Bengal meet. It is one of the important pilgrim centres of India.

How to Reach There :

Air . Trivandrum is the nearest Airport 86 kms.

Rail : Kanya Kumari is a Railway terminus on the Trivandrum Kanya Kumari section of the Sourthern Railway.

Road : Connected by Road with all the important places.

Where to Stay :

Western Style Hotels :

1. Hotel Tamilnadu	Ph. 22

Indian Style Hotels :

1. Hotel Tamilnadu	57

Other Accommodations :

1. Kerala House	29
2. Devasthanam	23
3. Kalaimagal Illam	
4. Malaimagal Illam	
5. Township Lodge	79
6. P.W.D. Rooms	
7. Railway retiring rooms	
8. Vivekananda Puram	
9. New Guest House	
10. Lodge Vivekananda	
11. Lodge Vivekananda Annexe	50

Places of Interest :

The Kumari Amman Temple : Dedicated to the virgin-goddess Kanya Kumari, who eternally protects the country legend has it that the goddess Parvathy in one of her incarnation as Devi Kanya did penance to obtain the hand of Lord Siva. The temple is a symbol of unity and sanctity.

Gandhi Memorial : A mandapam has been rected near the temple in memory of Mahatama Gandhi. The memorial has been built on the spot where the urn containing his ashes was kept for public view before immersion.

Vivekananda Memorial : There are two rocks projecting out of the ocean, south east of Kumari Amman temple. These rocks provide an ideal vantage point for visitors desiring to view the land's end of India. It was one of these rocks that Swami Vivekananda sat in long and deep meditation. On this rock stands the 'Vivekananda Rock Memorial' built in 1970. Ferry services are available to this memorial from 7 am to 5 pm.

Sunrise and Sunset : Every day people gather here to watch the sunrise and sunset but to watch the sunset and the moonrise on full moon day is an experience.

Exc ursions :

Suchindrum : 13 kms from Kanya Kumari by road on the way to Trivendrum. The Thanumalayan temple here is a repository of art treasures belonging to many kingdoms.

Nagarcoil : The Nagoraja temple situated here is unique in many respects. The images of Lord Siva and Anantha-krishna (Vishnu) are also enshrined. The images of the Jain Theerthankarars, Mahavira and Parswanatha are found in the pillars of the temple. 19 kms from Kanya Kumari on the way to Trivendrum.

Udayagiri Fort : This fort was popularly known as foundry for casting guns. 34 kms from Kanya Kumari, 14 kms from Nagarcoil 54 kms from Trivendrum. Accommodation at PWD Rest House.

Triuchendur : 90 kms from Kanya Kumari on the way to Rameshwaram. Situated on the sea shore. It attracts pilgrims. Abodes of Lord Subramanya.

RAMESHWARAM

Rama sanctified this place by worshipping Lord Siva after the war against Ravana. It is sacred place for Saivites and Vaishnavites.

How to Reach There :

Air : Nearest Air port Madurai 173 kms

Rail : Connected by Rail

Road : Connected upto Mandapam then by Rail

Where to Stay :

Western Style Hotels :

Hotel Tamilnadu Ph. 77

Indian Style Hotels :

There are some ordinary hotels

Other Accommodations :

1. Temple Trust Rooms and Cottages Ph. 41/92
2. Railway Retiring Rooms

Places of Interest :

1. The temple
2. Agniteertham

Excursions :

1. The Gandhamadhana Parvatham : 5 kms from Main Temple
2. Dhanushkoti 21 kms
3. Coral-reef
4. Kurusadai Island 20 Kms from Rameshwaram via Mandapam
5. Mandapam : 19 kms from Rameshwaram

PONDICHERRY

Pondicherry hailed as a land of everlasting enchantment, is today a living monument of French culture in India. About 160 Kms, south of Madras, edging the coast, it reposes in the eternal embrance of the foam flecked waves, holding out hope and happiness to all alike. The 'virgin' town at once possesses the mysteries of the orient and the glamours of the accident.

Pondicherry Town, founded by the French in the seventeenth century, has developed into a city, beautiful in its fashion, reflecting the charms of a centimental city. Oval-shaped and clean with uniquely aligned street, it is a model of skilful town planning with parallel streets running criss-cross, mutually cutting each other at right angles and an esplanade about three Kms in length skirting the town.

People speaking fifty-five different languages of the world line here adding a new character and dimension to its vibrant cosmopolitanism.

Any visitor during, his brief sojourn here would certainly be impressed by some of the unique features of this land carry home fragrant memories of a sweet mixture of 'Bouquet de France' and 'Monorangithem'.

Raj Nivas :

Situated at the eastern and of rue Jawahar Lal Nehru is Raj Nivas. The official residence of the Lt. Governor. A four monolithic sculpture adorn the Garden in front.

The Government Park :

Just opposite to Raj Nivas is a well laid greenery beautifully designed with flower paths. Lawns and fountains and monument at the centre. It is a popular evening resort for the young and the old alike. There is a childern's corner on the Southern end of the Park.

Midway on the road stands majestically the Gandhi Statue, 14 feet tall, surrounded by eight exquisitely huge monolithic pillars facing the sprawling Gandhi square. Facing the sea to the right is the "Hotel de ville". Town Hall to its left, you will find the war memorial.

A couple of hundred meters away to the South is the new pier—a 284 meters long concrete structure with a beautiful road stead projecting into the sea. From there, the coast all the way down to Ariya Kuppam estuary provides ideal niches for sun and sea bath.

Sri Aurobindo Ashram :

The Ashram runs a number of institutions which aim at giving shape to the ideal of "Life Divine" on earth. Notable among them are Sri Aurobindo International centre of Education, Sri Aurobindo Society, the world union etc. Veritably has it been described as a vast human Laboratory seeking to discover the secrets of 'Integral Yoga' Sri Aurobindo Ashram has more than 1500 inmates.

Places of Interest :

In and around Pondicherry are some of the most celebrated temples and churches of South India.

Monakula Vinayagar Temple : It is situated in rued Orleans. Devotees who throng in hundreds, especially on Fridays, believe that the reigning deity favours them with scucess in all new ventures.

Bahour Temples : 26 kms from Pondicherry is the Srimodanathar temple of Bahour. The basement of this 10th century temple carries inscriptions of Pallava-Chola days. Some beautiful granite statues expounding the mudra of Bharatha-Natyam adorn the walls of the temple.

Thiruvandar Temple : This ancient temple dedicated to Lord Siva lies about 8 kms away from Villianur on the road to Villupuram. Some of the sculpturs in the temple date back to the seventh century.

Thiru Bhuvanai Temple : The temple of Varadraja Perumal at Thirubhuvanai is situated at about 23 kms west of Pondicherry. The 12th century insccription of the temple reveals the existence of a cottage of Saukrit here.

Villianur Car Festival : This temple built in the 12th century and dedicated to Lord Thirukameshwarar carry the inscriptions of 'Koperunchingan'. The annual car festival of the temple takes place some times in May-June every year and attracts thousands of pilgrims.

Masimegan Festival : In the full moon day of the 'Magam' asterism in the Tamil month of Masi (February-March) thousands of people in good faith go to the sea-shore in the early morning hours to have a holy dip in the sea for ablution of their sins.

Veerampattinam Car Festival: Chengazhunir Amman Temple at the coastal village of Veerampattinam about seven kms to the South of Pondicherry is popular for the annual car festival that takes place on the fifth Friday in the Tamil month of Adi or in the following month of Avani (August).

Eglice De Secre Coeur De Jesus: This church in south Boulevard is dedicated to the sacred heart of Jesus. It is noted for its gothic architecture. The stained glass panes therein depict some events from the life of Jesus Christ.

Eglise De Notre Dame De La Conception: A church originally built by the Jesuites in 1691. It was finally completed in its present shape in 1765.

Eglise De Notre Dame Des Anges: In typical Roman style this church in rue Dumas was built in 1856 by Louis Guerre. A large size oil portrait of our Lay of Assumption presented by Emperor Napoleon III is still preserved here.

Eglise De Notre Dam De Lourdes William: This was constructed in 1876 on the model of the Basilica at lourdes in southern France. This statue of 'Our Lady' was brought from France and was installed in 1877. The Festival of 'Our Lady of Lourdes' celebrated in the month of June every year attracts people of all religion. This is perhaps the only catholic church in India with a 'Teppakulam' within its precincts in the traditional pattern of Hindu temples.

Mascarade Festival: Mascarade or the Mask festival celebrated some time during March-April in Pondicherry reflects one more facet of the French sense of humour. With fantastic mask and fancy costumes, revellers ground the streets in joyous merriment including in a kind of gimmic dance to the accompaniment of bleating accordion and trumpets.

Pondicherry Museum: Here you will find on display the findings of Arikamedu, Princess Chola Bronzes and sculptures, Glimpses of the French Heritage, specimens of modern and traditional handicrafts, paintings. Armouries, wood carvings etc.

Botanical Gardên: Conceived and established by C. S. Perrotet in 1826, it is situated at the junction of west Boulevard and Lal Bahadur Street. It preserves a large variety of exotic species of plants collected from all over India and abroad.

Aquarium: This modern aquarium is maintained by the Fisheries department. It gives an idea of the piscicultural methods and coastal fishing of Pondicherry. There are also a few rare ornamental fish varieties here.

Where to Stay :

1. Govt. Tourist Home, Uppaland Rd., Ph. 6376-78
2. Govt. Tourist Home, Indra Nagar, 6145
3. Youth Hostel (1 km from Pondicherry)

Excursions :

Karaikal : 163 kms to the south of Pondicherry. Lying on the east coast this region has an area of 158 sq. kms. This place is connected by Road and Rail. Right from the ancient times, Karaikal is considered to be a pilgrimage centre.

Karaikal Ammayar Temple : Situated in the heart of town it holds an annual Mangani festival which is well attended 'Melas'.

Thirunallar : Situated about five kms away from Karaikal, it has a famous temple dedicated to lord Saniswara Bhagwan, probably the only one of its kind in the whole of India. Once in two and a half years, the great 'Sani Peyarchi' festival is celebrated and it is attended by nearly five lakhs of pilgrims from all over India.

Mahe : Mahe region with an area of 10.4 sq. kms is situated on the Malabar coast at a distance of about 8 kms from Tellicherry in Kerala State. The distance from Pondicherry to Mahe by Road or Rail varies from 664 kms to 832 kms. depending on the route taken. The feast of St. Theresa is an important festival attended even by non-christians from all parts of Kerala. The festival falls in the middle of October.

Yanam : Yanam, a narrow stretch of land in the east Godavari district of Andhra Pradesh, consists of a town and six villages covering a total area of 20.7 kms. The coringha river divides the regions into two parts. I is served by the Kakinada Railway Station and by the Bus route on the Kakinada Rajahmundry road.

Note : For further Information and accommodation please contact, The Director of information, Publicity and Tourism, Pondicherry : Ph: 4398/4278/4575.

KERALA

(*Area* : 38863 kms. Population 25403217 (1981)

Language : Malyalam, Capital Trivandrum.

Kerala the land of the *cheras*, protected by natural

barriers on the east, has evolved largely unaffected by the strife wrought of countless foreign incursions in the rest of India. According to Legend, the land was a gift of Parasurama, one of the ten *Avtars* of Lord Vishnu. It is believed that he threw his battle axe into the sea, to atone for his sin of slaying generations of *Kshatriyas* and the sea receded, thus creating the Land-man, Kerala.

Kerala is the land of a highly articulate and literate people. A land whose rockets take off Palm fringed beaches and sophisticated equipment is assembled in thatcheu huts. Where you can get in from anywhere in the world, to bark on a golden beach or float on a fisherman's Catamaran on a clear blue sea. Kerala is famous the world over for its Verdant Scenery and insulied beaches, its colourful dames and herbal massage, its halectable carilince and romantic history.

The best thing to wear light tropical clothing throughout the year Kerala enjoys the 'Sunshine and blue skies' Kind of weather. Days are usually warm but nights are pleasant. Monsoon comes to Kerala twice in a year—May-June, and October-November.

TRIVANDRUM

Trivandrum or Thirn-anantha-puram gets its name from the reitz of the Sree Anantha Padamanabhaswamy temple and literally means "the town of Anantha", the serpent that forms the couch for Vishnu.

The city and its environs have retained their tranquil beauty. Kovalam, the world famous beach, Ponmudi, a mini hill station, Varkala, a pilgrim centre of great scenic beauty, are all within a short motoring distance from Trivandrum.

Trivandrum is air-linked to all the major Indian cities. International flights operate from Trivandrum to Colombo and Male. There are also direct flights from here to several cities in the middle East. Trivandrum is connected with the rest of the country by an extensive Rail and Road net work.

Distance to	*By Road* kms	*By Rail* kms
Bangalore	712	851
Bombay	1613	2063
Cochin	219	221
Delhi	—	3057
Hyderabad	1773	—
Kanyakumari	85	87
Kodai Road	416	374

Kottayam	154	161
Kozhikode	445	414
Madras	784	920
Madurai	307	330
Mangalore	633	635
Mysore	643	911
Palghat	379	373
Ponmudi	61	—
Quilon	71	65
Thakkady	271	—
Trichur	300	296
Varkala	54	41

Transport

Apart from State govt's bus service, Taxis and auto-rikshaws are available for local visits.

Where to Stay

Hotels

1. Hotel Belair, Vellayasi Ph. 3402/3487
2. Hotel Geeth, near Pulimoodu jn. Ph. 63267
3. Hotel Jas, Thy caud Ph. 64881
4. Hotel Luciya, East fort Ph. : 3441/3442
5. Hotel Moscot, Moscot jn. Ph. 68990
6. Hotel Pankaj, statue Ph. 66557
7. Hotel Wood Lands, Thy caud Ph. 67129
8. Youth Hostel, Veli Ph. 2364
9. Y.M.C.A. Pulimoodu jn. Ph. 68059
10. Y.W.C.A. M.G. Rd. Ph. 62690

Places of Interest

Shree Padmanabha Temple : At east fort is an ancient Vishnu Temple from which the city gets its name. This temple is full of indicate stone carvings and beautiful mandapams. The temple is open only to Hindu worshipors and at specific times.

The Museum, Zoo and Gardens : Disigned by a British architect at the turn of the century are centrally located. The Museum houses a rich collection of bronzes, stone carvings, ancient musical instruments and jewellery. The Trivandrum Zoo, set in undulating terrain, provides a pretty setting for its exotic animals and birds. Timings 9 A.M. to 6 P.M., Wednesday and Monday closed.

Shankhu mukhans Beach : Close to the Trivandrum Air port is a pleasant place to spend an evening at and watch the sunset.

Excursions

Nayyar Dam : 29 kms. from Trivandrum is a beautiful spot with land scaped gardens with swimming pool. A small guest house caters to tourists. Cruises on the lake and treks in the surrounding forest are also organised.

Padmanabhapuram Palace : 53 kms from Trivandrum on a deviation from Thuckalay along the Trivandrum-Kanyakumari route, is a unique wooden palace which once belonged to the legendary Maharaja Marthand Varma. Its murals and architecture are fascinating examples of art and craftsmanship. Padmanabhapuram was also the capital of Travancore until it was shifted to Trivandrum.

Suchindram Temple (in Tamilnadu) : 74 kms along the Trivandrum-Kanyakumari route is a pilgrim spot known for its temple with indicate stone carvings.

Kanyakumari (in Tamilnadu) : 85 kms from Trivandrum is the Land's End of India. Kanyakumari is famous for its temples dedicated to Devi Kanyakumari. The Memorial dedicated to Swami Vivekananda, built on a rock island just offshore, also attracts many visitors. Sunrise and Sunset over the wide expanse of sea can be spectacular. Gandhi Mandapam is another interesting place to visit.

Kovalam : 18 kms from Trivandrum. New Trivandrum is the internationally renowned beach resort Kovalam, one of the most picturesque stretches of sandy beach anywhere. A high rocky promotory julting into the sea has created a beautiful day of clear waters that is ideal for swimming, surfing skiing. Beach facilities include Ayurvedic Massage, yoga and water sports.

Where to Stay

1. Ashok Beach Resort (ITDC) Ph. : 3331/3031.
2. Hotel Samudra (KTDC) Ph. 3605

Ponmudi : 61 kms from Trivandrum/Kovalam. A hill station restling among the mist shrouded green hills of Kerala, at an altitude of about 1000 metres above sea level. Ponmudi is refreshingly cool and unspoilt. Nature trecks in the area are of particular interest.

Regular bus services connect Ponmudi with Trivandrum. Accommodation in cottages, rooms, dormitory at the Ponmudi Tourist Complex. Ph. 30 (Vithuna Exchange).

Varkala : 54 kms from Trivandrum. Varkala, a sea side town and pilgrim centre is famous for its Janardana Temple that is believed to the more than 2000 years old. High cliffs border the beach. The clear water springs gushing out from these cliffs are well known. The beach is called Papanasame. There is a nature cure centre near the beach. To the east of the town is the Sivagiri Hill, where shree Narayana Guru, the philosopher Social reformer and Saint established a centre of spiritual and social reform. A Temple dedicated to Sarada the Goddess of Learning, the building where the Guru lived and his Samadhi are centres of pilgirimage. Accommodation at the government Guest House.

Quilon : 71 kms. from Trivandrum. This sea side commercial centre and port had been visited by Phoenecians, Arabs, Persians, Greeks, Romans and the Chinese in the early days. The town has been associated with the origin of the Malayalam Era Kollavarsham, which began in 825 AD Chinnakkada, one of the busiest centre of the town, the light house at Thangassery, the Thirumullavaram beach and the model park at the Kochipila moodu beach use three places of interest. Accommodation at Govt. Guest House, Hotel Karthika, Hotel Parsanthi.

Alleppey : 156 kms from Trivandrum, 63 kms from Cochin. Alleppey town is a varitable maze of bridges and canals, the presence of which has given it the appelation Venice of the East. A major tourist attraction in Alleppey is the Nehru Trophy Boat Race organised on the second Saturday of August every year. The Snakeboats, unique to Kerala, vie with one another to win the coveted trophy. This colourful water carnival attracts thousands of spectators from all over the country, and many from abroad. Alleppey is also famous for the manufacture of Coiryarn, Coir mats and matlings. A boat journey through the canals and lake, is a delightful experience. Situated in the heat of Alleppey is the Mullackal Bhagavathy Temple, where the famous chirappu festival is celebrated in November-December.

Aranmula : 10 kms from Chengannur on the Trivandrum Kottayam route On the bank of the river Pampa is Araumula holy place with temple dedicted to Parthasarathi or Lord Krishna represented as the charioteer of Arjuna. The annual commemoration of the installation of the deity falls on the last day of the week-long celebration of *Onam* festival. The snakeboat race is held annually on this auspicious day. The thrill of show lies in the majesty with which numerous snake-boats move forward along the calm waters of the Pampa, with a thousand voices. singing in unison.

Sabarimala : 100 kms from Trivandrum Sastha temple in the wilderness. Main festival in December-January. 5 kms treck from Pumpa river.

Kottayam : 154 kms from Trivandrum, 68 kms from Cochin. Kottayam is a prominent commercial centre, especially for cash crops like rubber, tea, paper and cardamom on the foothills of the Western Ghats. Accommodation in Hotel Aida, Hotel Anjali, and Hotel Ambassador.

Kumarakom : 10 kms from Kottayam, Kumarakom is a typical Kerala village on the eastern bank of the Vembanad lake. A fast developing tourist complex, Kumarakom and the nearby islands area roosting place for migratory birds. A striking feature of the Baker mansion on the premises are the *Punkhas*—huge manually-operated cloth fans on wooden frames, suspended from the ceiling. *Accommodation* : Kumarakom Tourist Complex (KTDC) Ph. 58.

Peermade : 75 kms from Kottayam. Hill station. Plantation country, perfect half on the way to Periyar wild life sanctuary *Accommodation* : Guest House of the Tourism Deptt.

Thekkady : 271 kms from Trivandrum. Thekkady is known for the famous Periyar wildlife sanctuary. Covering 777 sq. kms of Lush, tropical forest. It is the natural habitat of a great variety of wild life.

Thekkady is connected by roads with Trivandrum, Cochin, Kottayam and Madurai. The nearest Railway junction is Kottayam on the Ernakulam—Trivandrum line.

Where to Stay

1. Periyar House
2. Aranya Niwas

Idukki : 121 kms from Kottayam, the name Idduki is derived from the word Idukku meaning a narrow gorge. The famous arch dam is constructed across the river

Periyar, between two huge granite hills called Kuravan and Kurathi. According to a Tribal legend, Kuravan and Kurathi were a tribal couple who were cursed by Srre Rama and became rocks. Idukki with its many streams, lush wooded valleys and hills, is a beautiful place to visit any time of the year.

Munnar : 152 kms from Kottayam 224 kms from Cochin. Munnar is a small hill station at an altitude of 1600 to 1800 meters above sea level. The town is situated at the confluence of three mountain streams and hence the name Munnar meaning '3 rivers'. The heart land of the plantation country. Some of the largest tea estates are seen around Munnar. Beyond the estates are rich forests. At the Eravikulam National Park near here 'Nilgiri Talir' a rare species of mountain goat, roam about safely. Facilities to play golf. Devikulum is also nearby.

COCHIN (Ernakulam)

Cochin, the commercial huk of Kerala, is a town of great historical importance. Cochin, having one of the finest natural harbours, is called the 'queen of the Arabian Sea'. Cochin port with modern facilities was declared a major port in 1936. The harbour is the nucleus around which Cochin has grown. Cochin is linked by Air to all the major cities. There is also an extensive rail and road network connecting Cochin with various cities and Town in India.

Where to Stay

1. Bharat Tourist House, Denbar Hall Rd., Ph. 33501
2. Bolghatty Palace Hotel, Bolghatty Island, Ph. 35003
3. Hotel Casino, Willington Island Ph : 6821.
4. Hotel Dwarka, M. G. Road, Ph. 32706
5. Hotel Grand, M.G. Road, Ph. 33211
6. Hotel International, M. G. Road, Ph. 33911
7. Hotel Sealord, Shanmugham Road, Ph. 32682
8. Hotel Woodlands, M.G. Road, Ph. 31372
9. Malabar Hotel, Willingdon Island, Ph. 6811
10. Y.M.C.A., Ph. 25288
11. Y.W.C.A., Ph. 355588

Places of Interest

Bolghatty Island : This is a small palm fringed island which is easily accessible from the main places. The main attraction here is the Bolghatty Palace built by the Dutch in 1744, now a hotel under K.T.D.C. The palace has a golf course on its grounds.

Willingdon Island : This is a man made island built from the soil dredged while deepening the Cochin Port. The Southern Naval Command has its headquarters here. The Seaport, Airport, Railway terminus, important offices of the port, and the customers House are all located on this Island.

Cochin Museum : The Archaeological Museum at Cochin has many antiques belonging to the 19th century. Models of Temples and sculptures of various deities from different parts of Kerala are exhibited here. Closed on Mondays and Govt. holidays.

Jewish Synagogue : Situated at Mattancherry, about 8 kms from Ernakulam, this magnificent structure was built in 1568.

Dutch Palace : This palace is also situated at Mattancherry. It was built by Portuguese and presented to the Maharaja of Cochin in 1568. So the name 'Dutch Palace' is really a misnomer. At the centre of the building is a large coronation hall. These are three temples of the deities Vishnu, Siva and Pazhayanoor Bhagwati in the premises of the Dutch Palace. Scenes from Ramayana can be seen in this palace.

Fort Cochin and St. Francis Church. The unique and distinctive European architectural patterns of the buildings here distinguish Fort Cochin from the other towns of Kerala. The chief attractions of this palace are the St. Francis Church and the Santa Cruz Church. The St. Francis Church was the first church to be built in India by the Portuguese. Vasco-De-Gama was burried here, but his body was removed later.

Gundu Island : This is the smallest island in the back water of Cochin.

Vallar padam : This is an island near Bolghatty where there is a beautiful Church dedicated to St. Mary. New and important pilgrim centre.

Excursions

Kodungallor : 32 kms from Cochin, known to the Greeks as Musiris, was an important part in ancient times until a natural phenomenon closed the harbour entrance from the sea while simultaneously opening up the access to Cochin nearby. St. Thomas the Apostle is believed to have landed here in 52 A.D. The oldest Mosque in

India, an ancient Portuguese fort, the renowned Bhagvathi temple are all situated here.

Kali Temple : 13 kms from Perumbavoor is a rock-cut temple, originally of the Jains. A flight of 120 steps leads to the statue of Mahavira carved out of natural rock. The temple though Jain in character is attended for rituals and rites by Hindu now.

Kodanad : 52 kms from Ernakulam. Wild elephants were until recently trapped in large pits made at selected points in the forests and lead to cages of the Kodanad elephant training centre on the bank of river Periyar.

Kalady : 45 kms from Cochin. Situated on the bank of river Periyar. Kalady is a pilgrim centre. It is the birth place of Sree Sankara, the great Indian Philosopher of the 8th century. There are two shrines in memory of Sree Sankara, one dedicated to him as Dakshinamurthy and the other to the goddess sharda. There is an ancient Shree Krishna Temple which was the family temple of Sree Sankara. Sree Rama Krishna Temple is also there. There is also a Memorial Tower.

Malayattur : 8 kms from Kalady. Malayattur is believed to have been visited by St. Thomas for meditation while on his travels through Kerala. The makrs on Kurisumala, the hill near by church, are said to be foot prints of the Apostle. It is a great pilgrim centre. The major festival is Malayattur Perumal on the Sunday after Easter.

Trichur : 74 kms from Cochin. The name 'Trichur' is derived from the word *Trisivaperur* meaning the "Town with the name of Lord Siva". Trichur was once the capital of the old Cochin state before it was shifted to Ernakulam.

Guruvayoor : 29 kms from Trichur. Guruvayoor with its temple dedicated to Sree Krishna is one of the most popular pilgrim centres of India. The installation and consecration of the idol is believed to have been done by the celestial Guru of the preceptor 'Devas' alongwith vayu, the 'God of the air'. Hence the place is called Guruvayoor. The Ekadasi, Mandalam and Visakham are the important festivals here. Accommodation at K.T.D.C. Tourist Bungalow 'Panchajanya' and Private Hotles.

KOZHIKODE (Calicut)

Kozhikode has been still one of the most important

commercial centres of Kerala. Kozhikode is connected to the major cities of an extensive Rail and Road network. The nearest Airports are Cochin and Mangalore.

Where to Stay

1. Alakapuri Guest House, Jail Road, Palayam, Ph. 73361
2. Kalpaka Tourist House, Town Hall Road, Ph. 76171
3. Govt. Guest House, West Hill, Ph. 73002
4. Hotel Maharani, Taluk Road, Ph. 76161
5 Hotel Sea Queen, Beach Road, Ph. 60201
6. Y M.C.A., Ph. 72520
7. Y.W.C.A., Ph. 77007

Places of Interest

Beach : The Lions Park on the beach is a popular retreat for the people of the city.

Kallai : 6 kms from Kozhikode, is the centre of the Timber Industry. The Timber Yard here is reputed to have been the second largest in the world.

Pazhassiraja Museum : This museum is located at East Hill, 5 kms from Kozhikode.

Excursions :

Beypore : Beypore is one of the important ports of ancient Kerala situated 11 kms from Kozhikode.

Badagara : 48 kms from Kozhikode, flourishing centre for Trade and Commerce.

Kappad : 16 kms from Kozhikode. The historic Beach of Kappad is locally known as *Kappa Kadavu.* This is the place where Vasco-De-Gama landed in India 1498.

Kondotti : On the way to Malappuram is a pilgrim centre of the Muslims. The Valia Nercha festival at the Pazhayangadi Mosque draws huge crowds. The Mosque is believed to be five centuries old. A Muslim saint Mohammed Shah is interred here.

Lakkidi : A place of great scenic beauty with picturesque hills, streams and luxuriant vegetation. 3 kms from here is the placid Pookote Lake, a picnic spot.

Wynad : The famous Jain Temple at Valpetta indicated that Wynad was once a stronghold of Jains.

Note : For further Details and booking of accommodation

Tourist Bungalows' visitors should contact the following Tourist offices of Kerala Govt. :

1. Deptt. of Tourism, Park View, Trivandrum, Ph. 61132
2. Tourist Information office, Govt. of Kerala, 28, Commander-in-Chief Rd., Madras-600105.

BIHAR

Bihar is a land where history whispers. It has the first recorded capital of India, It also boasts of having established the first republic of the world. It is the land where Buddha attained enlightenment, and Lord Mahavir Jain was born. Here the 10th and last Guru of Sikh religion Guru Gobind Singh was also born. It is the place where Emperor Ashoka was born, who was a great ruler and who made himself immortal by spreading the message of peace. Not only history but also its land and people, flora and fauna, fairs and festivals, art and architecture, industrial complexes and "Modern Temples" all invite tourists to visit Bihar.

PATNA

Patna is a city of great historic and cultural importance. The ancient name of the city is Patliputra. It is said that it was built by the son or grandson of Ajatasatru. Lord Buddha, while passing through it, when the city was being built, had prophesied that it would grow into a great and wealthy city. Among the great kings and emperors who ruled from here, the most famous are Chandragupta Maurya and Ashoka. It was from Patliputra that Ashoka issued his world famous edicts.

Patna has a large number of historical buildings and public institutions. The relics of the ancient city of Patliputra are excavated at Kumhrar which is the site of the ancient Mauryan Royal palace. Golghar, Patna Museum, Khudabins Khan oriental library, Hari Mandir, Martyrs' Memorial are other places of Tourist interest in Patna.

Patna is connected by Indian Airlines services with Delhi, Lucknow, Ranchi, Calcutta and Kathmandu. It is also connected with Kathmandu by Royal Nepal Airlines service. It is on the main line of the Eastern Railway and is also connected with Gaya by a branch line. There is a regular steamer service also which connects Patna with northern districts of the state.

Where to Stay

Western Style of Hotels

1. Hotel Maurya, South Gandhi Maidan, Patna-1 Ph. 22061-9
2. Hotel Patliputra, Beer Chand Patel Path, Patna-1 Ph. 26270-8
3. Hotel Satkar International, Groser Road, Patna-1 Ph. 25270
4. Hotel Republic, Exhibition Rd., Patna-1. Ph. 22021
5. Hotel Chanakya, Beer Chand Patel Path, R-Block, Patna. Ph. 23144-23142

Other Hotels

1. Tourist Bhavan Beer Chand Patel Path
2. Hotel President, Sinha Library Road
3. Apsara Hotel, Kadamkuan
4. Palace Hotel, South Gandhi Maidan
5. Hotel Rajasthan, Frazer Road
6. Hotel Anupam Kadamkuan
7. Marwari Hotel, Fraser Road
8. Hotel Lalita, R.R. Diwakar Path
9. Daichi Hotel, New Dak Bungalow Road
10. Hotel Tulsi, Ashok Rajpath
11. Hotel Rajdhani, New Dak Bungalow Road
12. India Hotel, East Gandhi Maidan
13. Railway Retiring Rooms, Railway junction

Places of Interest

Ruins of Patliputra at Kumhrar : 7 kms from Patna. A part of the renowned ancient capital of Patliputra. It remains open to visitors from 9 A.M. to 5-30 P.M. Mondays closed. Entry by tickets.

Patna museum : It is the principal Museum of Bihar and it houses some of the rarest piece of art treasures.

Golghar : This is shaped huge and impressive beehive structure and is 27 meters high with walls of 3.6 metres thick at the base. It is used as State granary. One gets a panaromic view of the city and Ganga.

Harmandir : It consecrates the birth-place of the tenth and the last Sikh Guru, Guru Gobind Singh. It is located in the heart of old Patna city and is open all the times.

Martyr's Memorial : Life size statues of seven brave young man who sacrificed their lives in the struggle for independence in 1942.

Quila House : Site of the fort of Sher Shah. It houses a rich private collection.

Sadaqat Ashram : The retreat where Dr. Rajendra Prasad, the first President of Indian Republic lived after retirement.

Khudabux Oriental Library : It is one of the national library of India and has rare collection of manuscripts and paintings.

Biological Park : It has a collection of both animals and plants. Entry by tickets.

Pathan ki Masjid : It was built by Parwaz Shah, son of Jahangir in 1621. It is also known as Sangi Masjid.

Gaya : 174 kms via Rajgir from Patna. Gaya is a very important place of Hindu Pilgrimage. Hindu Pilgrimage go there to offer oblation for salvation of their dead ancestors. The famous Vishnupad Temple attracts a very large number of Hindu Pilgrims from different parts of the country. Gaya is on the Grand chord line of the Eastern Railway. It is also connected with Patna by branch lines.

Places of Interest

Vishnupad Temple : The present Temple was constructed by Maharani Ahilya Bai of Indore in 1787.

Gaya Museum : Centrally Located.

Where to Stay

There are Railway Retiring Rooms and a good number of medium class Hotels and Dharamshalas.

BODH GAYA

188 kms from Patna via Rajgir and Gaya. Bodh Gaya is the most important and sacred pilgrimage centre of the Buddhist world. It was here that Lord Buddha attained the Supreme enlightenment and dedicated himself for the good of the humanity. Bodh Gaya 515 kms from Gaya. Buses, Taxis and Rikshaws are available at Gaya for going to Bodh Gaya.

Place of Interest

Mahabuddha Temple : Lord Buddha had attained enlightenment here under the Bodhi Tree. The present Temple was construted in the 2nd century AD.

There are other places to be seen:—

1. Tibetan Monastary
2. Thai Temple
3. Japanese Temple
4. Burmese Temple
5. Chinese Temple
6. Archaeological Museum

Where to Stay

There are two Tourist Bungalows of the State department of Tourism. Traveller Lodge of ITDC and one PWD inspection Bungalow.

RAJGIR

This place was the first recorded capital of India. It was flourishing city in the 6th century B.C. when Lord Buddha was roaming throughout the country to preach Buddhism. It is a winter health resort.

A Branch broadgauge railway line connects Rajgir with Bakhtiarpur, which is on the main line of the Eastern Railway. By road, it is 102 kms from Patna and 65 kms from Gaya.

Places of Interest

Hot-springs : There are a number of hot springs in Rajgir. The water of the springs is very good for health and a large number of tourists come to Rajgir in winter for taking both in the hot springs.

Shanti Stupa : The stupa has been constructed on the top of a hill by the Japanese Buddhists.

Aerial Ropeway Chainlift : It goes upto Shanti-Stupa from the foot of the hill and provides a hilarious drive to tourists.

Vultures Peak : It was a favourite abode of Lord Buddha. Here he used to give his sermons. Its rocks are shaped like vultures and hence its name.

Cyclopean Walls : Ruins of the ancient walls which provided protection to the ancient city of Rajgir.

Swarna Bhandar Cave : A rock cut cave Mavihar Math—A serpent Temple.

Saptaparni Cave : A cave on the top of Vaibhara Hill, where the first Buddhist council was held after the demise of Lord Buddha.

Old Fort : Remnants of the ancient fort of Rajgiri.

Where to Stay

1. Tourist Bungalow I, Ph. 39
2. Tourist Bungalow II, Ph. 26
3. P.W.D Rest House
4. M.O. Rest House
5. Distt. Board Rest House
6. Distt. Board New Inspection Bungalow.

Dharamshala

1. Digamber Jain Dharamashala
2. Swetamber Jain Dharamashala
3. Sanatan Dharamashala
4. Bowmer Temple Dharamashala
5. Japanese Temple Dharamashala

NALANDA

Nalanda is on the branch line between Bakhtiarpur and Rajgir. By road it is 90 kms from Patna and 15 kms from Rajgir.

Nalanda's famous international Monastic university was established in the 5th century, and is continued to flourish until the end of 12th century.

Where to Stay

P.W.D. Rest House. Since Rajgir is only 15 kms from here people prefer to stay there.

PAWAPURI

It is 80 kms from Patna on Patna Ranchi Rd. Vardhaman Mahavira, the greatest propounder of Jainism, came to Pawapuri in the fag end of his eventful and benevolent life. Pawapuri was the last point of his incessant journey and here he gave his last sermon. Disciples and admirers of the Lord came to pawapuri, took the ashes and the dust as blessings of the Master. The result was that a tank came into being. In the centre of the lotus Tank, a beautiful temple of white marbles has been constructed to consecrate cremation or Nirvana of

Vardhamana Mahavira. On Dewali day Pawapuri becomes the Venue of a big congregation at which prominent Jains from all over India assemble here.

Places of Interest :

Jal·nandhar : This is the place where Vardhamana Mahavira, attained Nirvana. The white marble temple here in the midst of a large lotus Lake has a singular atmosphere of peace and serverity.

Samosaran : This temple makes the holy site where Mahavira is believed to have delivered his last sermon.

Naya Mandir : A newely built Digamber Jain Temple.

Where to Stay : A large number of Jain Dharam shalas are here.

SASARAM

Sasaram is on the G.T. Road, 100 kms from Patna.

The Mausoleum of the great Pathan ruler of India Sher-Shah Suri is at Sasaram. Shershah was enthroned as emperor in 1542. Sher Shah was a great Military leader and an able administrator, but he is best remembered for the architectural mounments which were erected under his orders of which the first is his Mausoleum, built during his life time of Sasaram. He also built a long road connected East to West.

Where to Stay : A Youth Hotel of Deptt. of Tourism and Rest Houses of P. W. D. Irrigation Deptt. & Distt. Board.

VAISHALI

55 kms from Patna across the Ganga. It has beeen identified as the birth place of Mahabir, the 24th Tirthankar of Jainism. It was also the capital of the powerful confederacy of the Lichhavis. It was thrice Visited by Buddha. It was a stronghold of Buddhism. It was at Vaishali that Buddha pemitted the order of nuns against his own wish at the instance of Anand and his foster Mother. Maha Prajapati who became the first Buddhist nun at Vaishali.

Vaishali came into prominence 2500 years ago.

Where to Stay

1. Tourist Bungalow
2. P.W.D. Inspection Bungalow

Places of Interest

Ashokan Pillar : The lion pillar at Kolhua erected by

Emperor Ashoka. It is made of highly polished sand stone surmounted by a ball shaped capital supporting a life size figure of lion.

Buddha stupa I : The stupa is now in a dilapidated condition. Beneath it was deposited portion of the sacred centres of the Buddha in a stone casket.

Buddha stupa II : Excavations at this site in 1958 led to the Discovery of another casket containing the ashes of the Buddha.

Raja Vishal Ka garh : It is a huge ruin with a circumference of about one and a half kilometre. It is nearly 8 feet high with an about 140 feet wide most around it. It is said to be the ancient Parliament House, where the 7707 representations of the Vijian Federal Assembly gathered to legislate and discuss the problem of the day.

Coronation Tomb : It is a Abhisheka Pushkarini, popularly known as Kharama Pokhar. Its water was considered to be holy and used for the purpose of appointing the Rulers of Vaishali at the time of oath-taking ceremoney.

Lotus Tank : It is 2 kms in length from East to West and is believed to be the picnic spot of the Lichhavis.

Bawan Pokhar Temple : It is an old Temple at Basarh located on the northern bank of Tank known as Bawan Pokhar, enshrining beautiful images of several Hindu Gods, built in the Pala period.

Hari Katora Temple : It is another Hindu Temple at Basarh containing an image of Lord Kartikeya.

Jain Temple : It is a newly constructed Jain Temple at Basarh having an old image of Jain Tirthankara belonging to the Pala period.

Chaumukhi Mahadeva : At Kamman Chhapra there is an image of four-faced Lord Shiva belonging to the 4th century A.D.

Miranji Ki Dargah : There is a ruined brick stupa with some Muslim tombs on its top. The most important among them is called Miranji ki Dargah which contains relics of Sheikh Mohammed Quazim a famous local saint of 5th century A.D.

RANCHI

Ranchi is picturesquely situated in the valley of Chhotanagpur at an altitude of 2140 feet above the sea level. It is a popular hill station. Health and Holiday resort in Summer season. It is also well known for its scenic attraction such as water falls, forests, barren rocks and verdant hillocks.

Ranchi is connected by Air with Calcutta, Patna, Varanasi, Lucknow, Allahabad and Delhi. On broadgauge connected with Howrah, Patna, Rourkela and Jamshedpur.

Where to Stay

1. S.E. Railway Hotel, near Railway Station Ranchi
2. Hotel Arya, Lalpur Chowk
3. Hotel Yuvraj, Doranda Ranchi

Places of Interest

Ranchi Hill: Shiva Temple is a very attractive spot in the centre of the town 2 kms from main road.

Tagore Hill: 4 kms from main road. Rama Krishna Ashram is situated near the foot of the hill.

Kanke Dam: 4 kms from Ranchi on kanke road. The dam has great scenic beauty and is popular picnic spot.

Ranchi Lake: It is the biggest lake in Ranchi. The lake is situated in the heart of the town near the foot of the Ranchi Hill.

Hatia Dam: 12 kms from the city. The lighting arrangements of the Dam makes it more beautiful during the evening and night.

Jagannath Temple: This is a Hindu Temple built in 17th century, resting on hillock, 10 kms from Ranchi Town. Rath yatra or Car festival, similar to that of Puri, is held every year in the month of June-July.

NETRAHAT

155 kms from Ranchi. Bus service from Gumbla, Ranchi and Daltonganj to Netrahat. Nearest Airport is Ranchi.

Netrahat is situated at a height of 3700 ft. above sea level. It is a beautiful hill station and is called "Queen of Chhotanagpur". Here summer is cool. In Rainy season one sees the beauty of clouds. Winter is pleasant. The Sunrise and Sunset views from here are very fascinating and rose in Eastern India.

Places of Interest

Magnolia Point: 10 kms from Netrahat. Ideal site for Sunset view.

Upper Ghagri water falls: 6 kms from Netrahat. Popular picnic spot.

Lower Ghagri water falls 10 kms beautiful scenery and popular picnic spot with thick evergreen forest.

View Tower : Near forest Bungalow from where scenic beauty of Netrahat can be seen.

Where to Stay

1. Tourist Bungalow
2. Forest Rest House
3. Palaman Bungalow
4. P.H.E.D. Rest House
5. P.W.D. Inspection Bungalow
6. Revenue Bungalow
7. Rest House-cum-Panchayat center
8. Youth Hotel

HAZARI BAGH

Hazari Bagh is a most popular health resort on a plateau at an altitude of 2019 ft. above sea level. One of the beautiful towns in Bihar surrounded by picturesque hills and forests on all the sides. Hazari Bagh with its soothing climate pleasant scenery, and excellent roads has been very popular with visitors especially in the raining and the autumn. It is situated on National high way no. 16. Nearest Railway station Hazari Bagh Road, 66 kms from here.

Places of Interest

Cavary Hill : The hill stands just on the outskirt of the Town from the top of the hill one can have a panoramic view of the town. Very popular picnic spot. Hazari Bagh Lake and Hazari Bagh National Park are also worth-seeing places.

Where to Stay

1. Tourist Lodge
2. Tourist Information centre, Ph. 236
3. Circuit House, Ph. 317
4. P.W.D. Inspection Bungalow
5. P.H.E.D. Inspection Bungalow
6. Rest House
7. D.V.C. Rest House
8. D.V.C. Inspection Bungalow
9. D.V.C. Dormitory
10. Tourist Lodge, National Park

11. Tourist Cottage
12. Forest Rest House Kanari Hazari Bagh

JAMSHEDPUR

Jamshedpur is known as Steel Town of India. Its surroundings are very picturesque and retains old beauty of hill station. The Town is also an industrial centre. It is connected by Road and Rail with different parts of India. Its Railway station is Tatanagar on South-Eastern Railway.

Places of Interest

1. Tata Iron and Steel Co.
2. Indian Tube Company
3. Tata Locomative and Engineering Company
4. Tinplate Company of India
5. Dimua Lake
6. Rivers meet
7. Jubilee Park
8. Dohna Hill Top

Where to Stay

Government Rest House and Hotels

DHANBAD

Dhanbad is a great industrial centre of India for coalfields and other natural resources. Dhanbad is connected with Road and Rail.

Places of Interest

Jharia : Rich Coalfields

Top Chancki Lake : The lake is situated in the picturesque back ground of hill at a distance of 37 kms from Dhanbad. Popular picnic spot.

Sindri : 25 kms from Dhanbad

Where to Stay

1. Sivoy Hotel
2. Rest House
3. Other medium class Hotels

BAIDYANATHADHAM (DEOGHAR)

Baidyanathdham is situated in the district of Santhal Paraganas. The temple of Baidyanath Dham is one of the most sacred temples of India. Hindu pilgrims visit this place in a very large number throughout the year. It is also a health resort.

Baidyanath Dham station is the Railway terminus. Jasidih which is on the main line of Eastern Railway is the changing junction from where a line branches off to Baidyanath Dham at a distance of 2 kms only.

Places of Interest

1. Baidyanath Temple
2. Naulakha Mandir
3. Leela Mandir
4. Satsangh
5. Tapovan—6 kms South-East
6. Trikut—16 kms East
7. Basukinath Temple—43 kms
8. Ram Krishna Mission Vidyapith

Where to Stay

Tourist Bungalow of the Tourist Department

Bhimbandh : 65 kms from Mangy is Bhimbandh. It is situated in lush green valley surrounded by hills from three sides. Here two streams, one hot and the other cold flow and meet together into a pool in the dense forest. There is also a watch tower in the forest, which provides a panoramic view of the whole valley. It is a very picturesque place situated in the beautiful hills and forests and is also rich in scenic beauties as well as wild life.

Bhimbandh is connected with Maughy by road. The nearest Railway station is Jamui.

Where to Stay :

1. Forest Rest House
2. Rest House Irrigation Deptt.

Buxar : A Place where epic fight between Lord Rama and Taraka was fought and where Lord Rama and Lakshman were confessed higher knowledge by sage Vishwamitra. The Temple of Ahalya at a village Ahirauli has a religious back ground. Ahilya was the wife of sage Gautam Muni. Choritarban area of Buxar Town was taken to be the training ground of Sri Ramchandra.

Other Places of Interest :

1. *Ram Rekha Ghat,* footprint of Lord Rama on a stone
2. *Battle field* of Buxar 6 kms
3. *Chausa* 12 kms from Buxar

Buxar is situated on the main line of Eastern Railway.

Jagdishpur : Birth place of Babu Kunwar Singh, a leader of Mutiny of 1557. 35 kms from Arrah good number of buses connects with Bihaa, Arrah and Piro.

Maner : 27 kms to the West of Patna. Maner has two dargahs known as the Basi and Chhoti Dargahs. It is a large village of historical antiquities. A beautiful picnic spot. Accommodation at inspection Bungalow

WEST BENGAL

The State of West Bengal in Eastern India is a land of infinite variety and charm. It is a complete tourist region with the lively and many splendoured metropolitan city of Calcutta and charming resorts on the sea due to the mountains.

CALCUTTA

Calcutta is the capital of the State of West Bengal and the Gate Way of Eastern India. Thickly populated and full of life, the city is rich in its heritage—cultural. economic and political. Calcutta is the most convenient base for Tourists visiting places in Eastern India.

How to Reach There

Air : Indian Airlines operate Air services from Calcutta to Delhi, Bombay, Madras, Patna, Ranchi, Varanasi, Gorakhpur, Lucknow, Nagpur, Raipur, Gauhati, Dibrugarh, Silchar, Imphal, Jorhat, Tezpur, Bagdogra, Bhubneshwar, Hyderabad, Visakhapatnam, Agartala, Port Blair, and also to Kathmandu, Dacca, Chittagong

Rail : Calcutta is connected by Rail with all major cities of India : Himgiri Express, Ispat Express, Howrah-Guntur East Coast Express. Toofan Express, Howrah Bombay Express, Howrah Amritsar Express, Howrah New Bongaigaon Express, Gitanjali Express. Mithila Express, Rajdhani Express, Howrah Tata Steel Express, Coromandal Express, Howrah Punjab Express, Howrah Bombay Mail, and other many more trains.

Road : Connected by Road with all major cities of India.

Delhi—1495 kms
Bombay—2060 kms
Madras—1734 kms
Varanasi- 676 kms
Puri—555 kms
Ranchi—448 kms
Gauhati 1164 kms
Darjeeling—731 kms

Sea : The shipping Corporation of India operates steamer service from Calcutta to Port Blair.

Where to Stay

Western Style Hotels :

1. Air port Ashok, Calcutta Airport, Ph. : 57-4440
57-5111
2. Carlton Hotel, 2 Chowringhe Place, Ph. : 23-3009
23-8553
3. Fairlawn Hotel. 13A Sudder street Ph. : 24-4460
4. Great Eastern Hotel, Old Court House Street
Ph. : 23-2311
5. Hotel Hindustan International, Acharya J.C. Bose Road Ph. : 44-2394
6. Hotel Ruth Deen, London Street, Ph. : 44-3884
44-5210
7. Lytton Hotel, Sudder Street, Phone : 23-3937 23-2760
8. Majestic Hotel, Madan Street, Ph. : 27-1089
9. Minerva Hotel, Ganesh Chandra Avenue, Ph. 26-4505
10. New-Kenil worth Hotel, little Ressull Street.
Ph. : 44-2647
11. Oberai Grand, Jawaharlal Nehru Rd. Ph. : 23-0181
12. Park Hotel, 17 Park Street Ph. : 24-8301

Other Hotels

13. Asis Hotel, Rash Behari Avenue Ph. : 46-6669
14. Ashoka Hotel, Acharya J.C. Bose Road, Ph. : 35-9311
15. Avtar Hotel, Shakespear Sazani Ph. : 43-1931
16. Bhim Sain Hotel, Rishi Bankim Chandra Road, Howrah Ph. : 66-3866
17. Broadway Hotel, Ganesh Chandra Avenue Ph. : 26-3930
18. Everest Lodge, Sri Arvindo Rd. Howrah, Ph. 66- 922
19. Florence Hotel, Hazaria Road, Ph. : 48-2248
20. Gujarat Guest House, Lindsag Street Ph. : 24-0620
21. Hotel Diploment, Sudder Street Ph. : 24-2145
22. Hotel Embassy. 27, Princept Street Ph. : 23-4582
23. Hotel Holiday House, 16 -do- Ph. : 23-8707
24. Hotel Homely Raj, Manohar Pukur Road
Ph. : 43-4344
25. Hotel Natraj 5 Debson lane, Howrah, Ph. : 66-3018

26. Hotel Paradise, 5 Dharam talla Street Ph. : 23-2834
27. Hotel Saket, Mukhram Kanorie Road Howrah Ph. : 66-:404
28. Hotel Shalimar 3, S.N. Banerjee Road Ph. : 23-7193
29. Hotel Trimurti, 24, Roy Street Ph. : 47-3171
30. Hotel White Hall, 5/2, Sudder Street Ph. : 24-?311
31. Lindsag Guest House, 8-B, Lindsag Street Ph. 244640
32. Modern Lodge, 1, Stuart lane, Ph. : 24-4060
33. Paragon Hotel, 2, Stuart lane, Ph. : —
34. Pusparag Hotel, 28, Acharya Prafulla Chandra Road, Ph. : 35-3954
35. Rajasthan Guest House, 19 Zakaria Street, Ph. : 34-8153
36. Shilton Hotel, 5A, Sudder Street, Ph. : 24-3613
37. Time Star 2, Tottee lane, Ph. : 24-4610
38. Highway Youth Hotel, Alampur, Bally Road Junction.
39. Youth Hotel, AR Foundation, 10, Jaynarayan Baba-Anand Dutta Lane Howrah, Ph. : 67-2869

Other Accommodations :

1. Automobile Association of Eastern India, 13, Promotherh Barus Sarani, Ph. : 47-5131
2. Calcutta Air Port Rest House Ph. : 57-2611
3. International Guest House, Gole Park, Ph. : 46-3431
4. International Scholars House, -do- Ph. : 46-3431
5. International Student House, Park Street Ph. : 44-1207
6. Railway Retiring Rooms, Howrah
7. Salvation Army Red Shield Guest House, 2, Sudder Street Ph. : 24-2895
8. T.M.C.A. 25, J.L. Nehru Road Ph. : 23-3504
9. Y.M.C.A. 1, Middleton Road Ph. : 24-0260
10. Y.W.C.A. 42, S.N. Banerjee Road Ph. : 24-3814

Dharamshalas :

1. Bava Sikh Sangat, 172 M.G. Road Ph. : 33-5227
2. Shamdeo Gopiram Bhotika Dharamshala, 150 M.G. Road Ph. : 33-2728
3. Babulal Agarwala's Dharamshala 169A, M.G. Road Ph. : 33-1123

4. Estate Ram Krishna Das Harikishan Das Saraoji Trustee 165/167 M.G. Road, Ph. : 34-3974
5. Digamber Jain Bhavan Dharmshala, 10A, Chitpur Road Ph. : 34-2663
6. Haryana Charitable Society, 10 Vivekananda Road, Ph. : 34-6837
7. Seth Jamunalal Tibrawal Bhavan, 164 Chitranjan Avenue Ph. : 34-3135

Places of Interest

1. Benoy-Badal-Dinesh-Bagh (Dalhousie Square)
2. Eden Garden
3. Shahid Minar
4. Indian Museum
5. Victoria Memorial Hall and Museum
6. Academy of Fine Arts
7. Birla Planetorium
8. Nehru Children's Museum
9. Netaji Museum
10. Kali Temple at Kalighat
11. Zoological Garden
12. National Library
13. Rabindra Sarobar
14. Birla Academy of Art and Culture Museum
15. Birla Industrial and Technological Museum
16. Nakhoda Mosque
17. Asutosh Museum of Indian Art
18. Marble Palace
19. Rabindra Bharti Museum
20. Jain Temple
21. Howrah Bridge (Rabindra Setu)
22. Botanical Gardens
23. Dakshineshwar Temple
24. Belur Math

Excursions

1. Darjeeling
2. Diamond Harbour, 48 kms from Calcutta
3. Bakkhali, 132 kms from Calcutta
4. Digha, 187 kms from Calcutta

5. Durgapur, 184 kms from Calcutta by Road
6. Murshidabad 220 kms from Calcutta by Road
7. Shanti Niketan, 210 kms from Calcutta by Road
8. Vishnupur 152 kms from Calcutta by Road
9. Tarakeshwar, 58 kms from Calcutta

MALDA

Malda has many medieval historical relics. Then early Gour which came into prominence as a Kingdom during the reign of Sasanka was once the capital of ancient Bengal for several centuries. As the power of the Guptas waned, that of Sasanka increased and ultimately he established himself as an independent king in eastern India. Soon after the death of King Sasanka, there were successive political upheavals and thereafter another dynasty, the Palas, came into power. The Palas in turn gave way to the Sen Dynasty. Ballal Sen being the most famous Hindu King of Bengal, in the 12th Century A.D. and it is during their reign that Gour became known all over India as a seat of learning, art and culture. During the reign of Lakshman Sen, Gour was invaded by Bhakhtiar Khilji, during early thirteenth century A.D. and after the conquest of Bengal by him, the fortunes of Gour were Temporarily eclipsed. The city was plundered by Sher Shah during his war with Mohmmad Shah, the last independent Sultan of Bengal. Most of the monuments in Gour today are the remains of the Muslim period, and a number of them are constructed with materials taken from Hindu temples. The city of Gour was once completely fortified by a high earthen rampart, the top of the wall being covered with buildings.

How to Reach There

Malda is 335 kms from Calcutta on the National Highway No. 34, regular Bus services are available between Calcutta and Malda. There are two ways to reach Malda by train—via Tinpahar, Rajmahal, Manik Chak and via Gorakka and Khajuria Ghat.

Where to Stay

1. Tourist Lodge
2. Inspection Bungalow
3. There are so many private Hotels

Places of Interest

1. The Baroduan or the great Golden Mosque, the largest monument in Gour

2. The Dakhil Darwajah, the main gate way to the fort
3. The Chiko Mosque.
4. The Tameltals at Ramvali, Shri Chaitanya the great religious reformer of Bengal
5. The latian Mosque
6. The Eklakhi Mausoleum, the most elegent monument in Pandua
7. The Adina Mosque
8. Museum
9. Bari Dargah in Pandua 20 kms from Malda
10. The Qutab Shahi Mosque in Pandua

MURSHIDABAD

At one time the capital of Bengal, Murshidabad formerly known as Makhsusabad, is named after Nawab Munshid Kulikhan, a Dewan of Bengal, Bihar and Orissa under Emperor Aurangzeb. Murshidabad is intimately related to events that ultimately changed the history of India. Nawab Sirujiddawalla lost the Battle of Plasseg against Clive, the orchited of the British Empire in India and gradually, power passed on to the hands of the British. Murshidabad is only 219 kms from Calcutta and is connected by both train and road.

How to Reach There

Regular Bus service is available from Calcutta. By train the distance between Calcutta and Murshidabad is only 197 kms.

Where to Stay

1. Tourist Lodge of Berhampur 10 kms from Murshidabad
2. There are some Indian style Hotels

Places of Interest

1. Nizamurt Kila : The Hazarduari Palaces, a house of thousand gates
2. The Jafraganj Deoshi, known as Tailor's gate
3. The Kat-gola, the golden house of a rich Jain merchant
4. The palace of Jagat Sett
5. The Katra Mosque, model of mosque of Macca
6. Moti Jheel, the pearl Lake

7. Moti Jhil Palace
8. Khusbagh
9. Baranagar Temple
10. Top Khans
11. Cossimbazar Palace
12. Maharaja Nanda Kumar's Palace

SHANTINIKETAN

Better known as Tagore's Santiniketan the world over, the place derives its name from two Bengali words: Santi means 'peace' and Niketan means abode. Santi Niketan thus denotes the 'Abode of peace'.

Rabindra Nath Tagore's father Maharsi Debendra Nath Tagore conceived it as on Ashrama, when he broke his journey there for a short period on his way to Raipur, then a prosperous village.

Rabindranath Tagore shared his father's liking for the place and converted the Asharam in 1901 into an experimental open air school then known as Brahamcharyasrama with only five students on the roll. Santiniketan proved a great success and has become the seat of Viswa Bharati, an international University. Students and Scholors from all over the world came to Viswa Bharti.

How to Reach There

145 kms from Howrah by Rail via Bolpur on the Eastern Railway. From Calcutta, Santiniketan may be reached by Road via Panagarh. 160 kms cycle Rikshaws are available at Bolpur Railway Station for going to Santiniketan and other places nearby. Tourist Taxi may be available at Santiniketan Tourist Lodge.

Where to Stay

Tourist Lodge and Tourist Cottages provide comfortable accommodation at Shantiniketan.

Places of Interest

1. Uttarayan complex where the poet lived
2. Udaydas, Konarka, Shyamali, Piwascha and Udichi. Rabindra Bhavan and museum.
3. Kala Bhawan, Sangeet Bhavan, Vidya Bhavan, Shiksha Bhavan, Vinay Bhavan, China Bhavan and Hindu Bhavan.

Excursions

1. *Deer Park* : 3 kms from Shantiniketan.

2. *Bakreshwar* : 52 kms from Santiniketan by Road, famous for hot springs with mineral waters.
3. *Messanjore* : 78 kms from Santiniketan by Road, massive Dam, on the Mayurakshi river with beautiful scenery.
4. *Kendubilwa* : 42 kms from Santiniketan Birth place of poet Jaydev, the noted author of Geet Govind.
5. *Nanoor* : 23 kms from Santiniketan connected by Bus. Birth place of the Vaisnava poet Chandi Das.
6. *Fullara* : 40 kms from Santiniketan. A fair is held here on 'Maghi Purnima.'
7. *Nelhati* : 104 kms from Santiniketan, famous for 'Lalateswari' temple.

Tarapitha : 80 kms from Santiniketan. Important place for Hindu Pilgrimage. A Temple of Tara Devi is located here.

Kankali Tala : 8 kms from Santiniketan. A placc of Hindu Pilgrimage. A fair is held on the last day of the month of Chaitra (April).

SUNDERBAN

Along the extreme southern beaches of West Bangal, the state resembles a coconut—palm leaf seen in the big closeup. The land is split by numerous rivers and water. channels, all emptying into the blue water of the Bay of Bengal Rivers broaden out to proportions that match the sea. This is the area known as Sunderban, the biggest estuarine forest in the world. There are no roads to this watery wilderness. The water ways are the only pathways into the heart of the forest. Sunderban is actually composed of 54 tiny islands. There are some 40 different species of trees and shrubs in Sunderban.

The forest is the natural habitat of the world famous Royal Bengal Tiger, Jungle cat, Fishing cat, Cheetal or oxis Deer, Wild pig, rhesus monkey, mongoose, other and the large estuarine crocodiles in the world.

Among birds there are herons; egrets, storks, cormorants, fishing eagles, white bellied sea eagle and sea gulls etc.

Among raptiles you may see king cobras, python, chequered kellbacks, lizards and monitors including the salvator lizard etc.

How to Reach There :

Sunderban is accessible only by riverine water ways. Embarkation points can be reached by Sunderban trains to canning ; Raidighi, Basanti, Namkhana and Najat due connected by regular and frequent bus service from Calcutta. Outwards by the Madhukar, Luxury Launch of the Tourist Bureau. You can also go by private boats or Launches to be found on here. The best and safest way to go is on the connected Trips of the Tourist Bureau, Govt. of West Bengal. Best time to visit is September to mid March.

Where to Stay :

Tourist lodge at Sajnakhali

Places of Interest :

1. *Sajnakhali Bird Sanctuary* : On the banks of the immensel wide rivers Matla and Gumdi, 11 to 12 kms wide in places.
2. *Kalas Dwip :* A densely wooded island where the river Matla meets the sea is yet another biotope. You sail down the rivers Matla and Bidya.
3. *Bhaghatpur Crocodile Project :* Home of the biggest estuarine crocodile in the world.
4. *Project Tiger :* Covering an area of 2585 Sq. Meters, world's largest Tiger colony. The persent tiger population is 264.

Other Places :

Lothian Island and Holiday Island. full of wild life at the point where the rivers enter the sea. Jambudwip and Ganga Sagar at Sagar island where millions throng on Makar Samkranti day.

For further Details please contact Deptt. of Toursim, Govt. of West Bengal, Writen Bldg. Calcutta-700001.

KALIMPONG

Located 51 kms in the East of Darjeeling at an altitude of 1250 Meters above the sea level offers excellent possibilities of a quiet holiday amidst gently rolling hills and deep valleys the mighty Himalayas in the back ground. Best season : March to mid June and September to December.

How to Reach There :

Air : Nearest Airport is Bagdorgra 80 kms Indian Airlines operate regular services between Calcutta-Bagdogra, Calcutta-Delhi, Lucknow, Patna, Bagdogra, Gauhati.

Rail : Nearst Railway Station New Jalpaiguri, Siliguri Junction, direct connection with Calcutta.

New Delhi/Delhi : Tinsukia Mail, Assam Mail

Bombay : Bombay Mail, Kamrup Express, Geetanjali Express.

Madras : Howrah Mail, Kamrup Express, Coromandel Express.

Gauhati : Assa m Mail, A. T. Mail, Lucknow Express.

Road Route ;

1. Gauhati 512 kms.

2. Delhi, Mathura, Agra, Kanpur, Allahabad, Varanasi, Sasaram, Arrah, Patus, Bakhtiarpur, Mokameh, Barauni, Begusarai, Purnea, Dalkhola, Kishanganj, Siliguri—1312 kms.

3. Bombay—Nasik, Dhule, Jalgaon, Nagpur, Jabalpur, Rewa, Allahabad, Varanasi, Sasaram, Arrah, Patna, Bakhtiarpur, Mokamah, Barauni, Purnea, Dalkhoda, Kishanganj, Siliguri 2138 kms.

4. Kathmandu—Naraynaghat, Hatauta, Dhalkewar, Itahri, Kakanbhita, Siliguri-721 kms.

5. Calcutta — Kishanganj, Berhampur, Malda, Raiganj, Dalkhoda, Kishanganj, Siliguri, 651 kms.

State Transport Bus Service is available.

Where to Stay :

1.	Tourist lodge, B.T.D.C.	Ph. : 384
2.	Tourist lodge Annex, Tashiding	
3.	Hill top Tourist lodge	
4.	Shangrills Tourist lodge	Ph. : 230

Hotels :

1.	Himalayan Hotel	Ph. : 248
2.	Park Guest House	Ph. : 304
3.	Crown lodge	Ph. : 546
4.	Hotel Sunnydale	Ph. : 371
5.	Lodge Magal Lyang	Ph. : 333
6.	Sherpa Lodge	Ph. : 572
7.	Gomphu's Hotel	Ph. : 418
8.	Lodge Coosy Nook	Ph. : 306
9.	Punjal Hotel	
10.	Hotal Madhuban	Ph. : 589

DHARAMSHALA

1. Rati Ram Bansi Lal Dharamshala, Below Motor Stand.

Places of Interest :

On the way to Kalimpong from Darjeeling there is a

view point, from where a magnificent view of the confluence of the Rangeet and the Teesta Rivers can be had.

Dr. Graham's Homes: School for Destitute children 3 kms from town.

Durpai Dora : A vantage point in Kalimpong from where the breathtaking birds eye view of the plains can be seen.

Swiss Welfare Dairy : 4 kms from the town. A small co-operative Dairy.

Kalimpong Arts & Crafts Centre : Within a walking Distance from Motor Stand. Famous for Kalimpong Handi-crafts.

Tibetan Monastery : The Tharpa choiling Monastery at Tirpai Hill.

Flower Nur Series ; Kalimpong is famous for Nur Series.

Kalimpong Market : Market is interesting.

Excursions :

1. *Takdah orchid Centre* : 44 kms from Kalimpong
2. *Rissisum* : 20 kms from Kalimpong
3. *Lav* : 33 kms from Kalimpong
4. *Lolay Gaon* : 56 kms from Kalimpong. Panoramic view of Kanchan Junga.

MIRIK

Newest Hills Station in India. Altitude 1767 meters. 49 kms from Darjeeling, 52 kms from Siliguri. A 1.25 kms long lake is fed by perennial streams. A floating formation in the middle of the lake a joy for ever and very often you may find the glory of Kanchanjunga reflected in the lake waters. A 3.5 kms Zig Zag foot walk takes you along the lake. You are sure to enjoy a boat ride in the lake.

How to Reach There

Air : Nearest Air port Bagdogra 55 kms from Mirik.

Rail : Nearest Rail heads are Ghoom 41 kms Darjeeling 49 kms and Siliguri 52 kms.

Road : Connected with Darjeeling, Siliguri and Kenseong on the following routes.

(1) *Mirik*. Hilay, Bhanjang, Pashupati Fatak, Siwmansa, Sukhiapokhari, Ghoom, Darjeeling 49 kms.

(2) *Mirik*. Soureni, Phugari TE, Gaybaree TE, Dudey, Garidhara, Kheprail, Siliguri 52 kms.

(3) *Mirik*. Garidhara, Longview TE, Makai bari TE, Kurseong 46 kms Jeepable Way.

Where to Stay

1. Tourist Hotel
2. Tourist Cottage
3. Tourist Tents
4. Varthan Hotel
5. Mrigaya Hotel
6. Bengal Hotel
7. Chandrama Lodging centre
8. Lodging Park Hotel
9. Zila Parishad Dak Bungalow
10. P.W.D. Inspection Bungalow

Places of Interest

1. *The Lake* : 1.25 kms long lake. Most attractive spot. Boating is available.
2. *Rameetay Dara* : Fabullous, view of plains and mountains. Beautiful view of Sunrise and Sunset.
3. *Deosi Dara* : For stupendous landscape view
4. *Raidhap* : Ideal picnic spot
5. *Tea Estates*
6. *Orange Orchards*
7. *Cardamom grove*
8. *Debisthan* : famous Hindu Temple
9. *Carpet Weaving Tourist Centre*

DARJEELING

Situated at an altitude of 2134 meters above the sea level. The name of the town is a compution of 'Dorje ling' which means 'The place of Dorje' the mystic thunderbolt of the lamaist religion. The town lies on the spur projecting northwards from the Ghoom Sanchal Ridge. Its commanding position enables one to get an unparalleled view of the majestic Himalayan panorama with the snowy peak of Kanchanjunga towering above it. Darjeeling Truely deserves the title "Queen of the Hill Stations". The best way to get there is to take Indian Airlines Jet service from Calcutta to Bagdogra. From Bagdogra is an exciting Drive of 80 kms over road through dense green forest and terraced the gardens, to Darjeeling.

With some time to hand it is better for one to make it to Darjeeling by a thrilling Rail journey to the 'Toy Train'. The sporting point of this Toy Train is New Jalpaiguri Railway station near Siliguri 8 kms from Bagdogra Airport.

Darjeeling is famous for its colourful people. The culture

of the hill people of Darjeeling is unequally expressed in the exquisite and unimitable artistic handicrafts anc their traditional colourful designs. Darjeeling is a plant lovers' paradise. Darjeeling is famous for wild-life sanctuary. Darjeeling is the house of six Hundred varieties of beautiful birds.

Tista, a broad mountain torrent with numerous shallowers and rapids dominates the river system rises in a glacier in North Sikkim 2370 meters above the sea level. The great Rangeet is a graceful stream with its story. Sometimes, sandy bed. Its meeting with Tista provides a picturesque of the view.

Darjeeling is the best destination for those who want an exclusive view of the grandeur and majority of the towering snow capped Himalayans. From memorous points in the town one gets views of the mountain ranges that the scarcely rivalled in any other parts of the world. The bridle paths leading to Ghoom ridge offer delightful scenic beauty places like Senchal 2449 meters, Tiger Hill 2555 meters and Torgen 3070 meters present pleasing views of the mountaineous levelling down to the plains. To the north the Rangpur Valley stands in the foreground and beyond in the Rangeet Valley. Then across the entire northern horizon line up snow capped peaks Kabru 7205 meters, Jami 7590 meters, Siniolecha 6780 meters and many others obviously lorded over by Kanchanjungha 8444 meters.

Places of Interest

Lloyd Botanical garden : Opened in 1865 have a representative collection of the flora of Sikkim Himalayas.

Natural history museum : The museum is within walking distance from Darjeeling Mall or chowrasta.

Art gallery : Arts and crafts of the hill means have been nicely displayed in the two major art galleries of the town 2 kms from Darjeeling on way to Ghoom.

Step Aside : About three minutes walk from the mall will bring the visitors to step Aside where Deshbandhu Chittaranjan Das breathed his last in 1925.

Observatory Hill : The observatory Hill near the mall commands a magnificent view of Kanchanjungha range. Great religious importance is attached to this place by Hindus and Buddhists alike.

Dhir Dham Temple : Situated below the Darjeeling Railway station. Style of Pashupati nath Temple of Kathmandu Nepal.

Himalayan Mountaineering Institution and Zoological Park : 3 kms from the Mall.

Darjeeling-Ranjeet Valley Passenger ropeway: At north point, 3 kms from the Mall is situated Indian first passenger ropeway. This 8 kms. long ropeway links Darjeeling with Singla Bazaar, a beautiful picnic spot.

Labouring Race Course: 8 kms. from Mall, one of the smallest and the highest race course.

Tiger Hill: 11 kms from Darjeeling town. Mount Everest and Kanchanjungha can be seen from here.

Excursions

Syndakphu: 58 kms. from Darjeeling. Unique opportunity for a glorious view of the towering Himalayan peaks.

Ghoon: 6 kms. from Darjeeling at an altitude of 2438 mts. The renowned Buddhist monastary is situated here.

Kurseong: 32 kms. from Darjeeling at an altitude of 1458 meters above sea level. A charming health resort. At a distance of 5 kms. Dom Hill is place of unforgettable charm.

Kalimpong: 51 kms. at an altitude of 1250 meters a quiet hill resort. Journey from Darjeeling is a fascinating experience.

Mirik: 55 kms. Bagdogra, 52 from Siliguri and 49 kms from Darjeeling at an altitude of 1800 meters. Nearest hill station.

Takdah: 26 kms. from Darjeeling at an altitude of 2000 mts.

Mungpo: 49 kms. from Silguri at an altitude of 1253 mts just above the Tirta Valley Road.

Himalayan Treks

Route No. 1. (*a*) Darjeeling Managbhanjang. Tonglu, Sandakphu and Back 118 kms.

(*b*) Darjeeling—Managbhanjang, Tonglu, Sandakphu, Phalut and back 160 kms.

Route No. 2. Darjeeling—Managbhanjang, Tonglu, Sandakphu, Phalut, Ramik, Rimbik, Jhapi, Bijombari and back 149 kms.

Route No. 3. Darjeeling—Managbhanjang, Tonglu, Sandakhu, Phalut, Ramik, Rimbik, Palmajues, Batasi, and back 280 kms. The best seasons to trek in this region are April-May and October-November.

Where to Stay

1. Darjeeling Tourist Lodge, Mall Road, Ph. 2611/13
2. Mapk Tourist Lodge, old Kutcheri Road, Ph. 2092

3. **Shailagarh**, Dr. Zakir Hussain Road, Jalapahar Ph. 2684
4. Tiger Hill Tourist Lodge, Senchal, Ghorm, Ph. 2813
5. Lowis Jubilee Sanitorium, S.K. Pal Road, Ph. 2127
6. Youth Hostel, 16, Dr. Zakir Hussain Road, Ph. 2290
7. Kalimpong Tourist Lodge, Kalimpong, Ph. 384
8. Shangrila, Kalimpong, Ph. 230
9. Siliguri Tourist Lodge, Siliguri, Ph. 21018
10. Traveller's Haven, Jaldapara Wild life sanctuary, Moderniest, Jalpaiguri Ph. 30
11. Tourist Centre, Malbazaar, More, Jalpaiguri

For details please contact :

Tourist Bureau, Govt. of West Bengal,
1. Nehru Road, Darjeeling, Ph. 2050.

ORISSA

BHUBANESHWAR

City of Temples, Capital of ancient Kingdom and the modern State, quintessence of the land of the past and the present, that is Orissa. still reverberates to the echoes of the past amidst its bustling modernity. As one approaches Bhubaneshwar, whether from Air or by Road and Rail one is struck by three magnificeent ancient monuments that Dominates its skyline. These, the soaring spire of the Dwijraj temple, the white dome of the peace pagoda of the Dhauli hill and the park temple of Mahavir Jina in the Khanda Giri hills, epitomise the rise and ascendancy of Hinduism, Buddhism and Jainism during different periods of Orissas history.

How to Reach

Bhubaneshwar is connected by Air with Boeing flights to Delhi, Calcutta, Hyderabad and Bangalore. It has Super Fast Train connections to Calcutta, Madras, Hyderabed, Bombay, Delhi and Trivandrum.

Where to Stay

		Ph.
1.	Panth Niwas, O.T.D.C.	**54515**
2.	State Guest House	**51919**
3.	Hotel Raj Mahal	**52448**
4.	Hotel Pushpak	**50545**
5.	Hotel Kalinga Ashok	**53318**

6.	Hotel Prachi	52521
7.	Hotel Konark	53330
8.	Anarkali	54031
9.	Sworti	54171
10.	Hotel Poonam	53322

Places of Interest

1. Udaygiri and Khandgiri caves
2. Dhauli
3. Parasarameshwar Temple
4. Mukheshwar Temple
5. Rajarani Temple
6. Lingraja Temple
7. Pipili
8. Hirapur Chausath Yogini Temple
9. Nandan Kanan 14 kms
10. Orissa State Museum

KONARK

Built by King Langala Narisimha Deva in the 13th century A.D. in the Golden era of Orissa. This magnificent ruin has its walls sculptures of exquisite beauty covering every aspects of life. Scene of love and war, trade and court transactions, hunting, catching of elephants, sages teaching, child birth amorus dalliances, dancers and mythical figures via with back other for attention on the panels and riches of this immortal work of art. Sura-sundaris, the heavenly damesh, free standing longer than life monoblock female status playing the cymbals and drums flutes and trumpets, adoring the top of the temple and the exquisite couples engaged in myriad modes of amorous union in the most frame depiction of love and sex, with their irresistible and ineffable beauty, prove to be a magical attraction for connoisseurs and Common visitors alike.

Konark is a many splendoured gem of Orissan art. Its beauty is not for description in words. It is to be seen again.

How to Reach There

Air : Nearest Airpart Bhubaneshwar 66 kms

Rail : Nearest Railway station Bhubaneshwar 85 kms

Road : Buses available for Bhubaneshwar and Puri both

Where to Stay

1. Pustha Nivas, Konark. Ph. 21

Places of Interest

1. Sun Temple
2. Archaeological Museum
3. Sea Beach
4. Remains of old Buddhist Vihar at Kusuma
5. Illumination of Konark Temple in the evening

Chilika lake : Chilika is the biggest inland lake in the country. Spreading over 1100 sq. kms. Hundreds of boats sail in the blue expanse of the lake every day. Chilika the queen of nature welcome you with open arms.

How to Reach There

Air : Nearest Airport Bhubaneshwar which is linked with, Delhi, Calcutta, Bombay, Hyderabad, Bangalore by Boeing flights.

Rail : The Calcutta-Madras Rail route of South-Eastern Railways Touch Chilika Lake at Balugaon, Chilika, Khallikote and Rambha. The nearest Railway Station for Barkal is at Balugaon.

Road : The Madras bound National Hill way No. 5 linking Calcutta, Bhubaneshwar Balugaon, Barkal, Rambha, Barhampur, and Vijay runs along the Lake. Buses, Taxis are available at Calcutta, Bhubaneshwar, Puri and Barhampur to Chilika.

Where to Stay

1. Pantha Nivas at Rambha Ph. 46
2. Pantha Nivas and Barkal Ph. Balugaon 60
3. Ashok Hotel, Balugoan Ph. 8, 9

Places of Interest

1. Within the lake : Kalijai Temple

Excursions

1. *Normal Jhar* : 11 kms from Rambha. Picnic spot. Spot for religious worship.
2. *Narayani* : 25 kms from Rambha, picnic spot, natural spring. Temple of goddes Narayani.
3. *Banpur* : 8 kms from Balugaon. Centre of religious activities. House of goddess Bhagwati, Temple of Daksha Prajapati.

4. *Gopalpur on Sea* : 95 kms from Barkul famous sea side resort.
5. *Taptaponi* : 100 kms from Rambha pleasent health resort.

PURI

Abode of Lord Jagannatha one of the four holiest places of India. Puri is place of colourful festivals round the year. Rathyatra is famous festival. Located on the shores of way of Bengal. Puri has one of the forest beaches in the world.

How to Reach

65 kms by State highway from Bhubaneshwar. Puri has direct Rail link, with Calcutta, New Delhi, Hyderabad and Bombay.

Where to Stay

		Ph.
1.	Pantha Niwas of OTDC	2562
2.	Youth Hotel	2424
3.	South Eastern Railway Hotel	2063
4.	Puri Hotel	2124
5.	Pantha Bhawan OTDC	2507
6.	Hotel Prachi Resort	2838
7.	Hotel Vijaya	

Dharamshalas

1. Agga Ram Moti Lal Kothari, Laxmi Bagh
2. Dhanji Moolji Bhatia, Laxmi Bagh
3. Bangla Cibidutt Doodwala Grand Road
4. Ram Chandra Goenka, Grand Road
5. Seth Tolaram Grand Road
6. Sinajmal Bagaria, Grand Road
7. Khemka, Mochi Sahi

Places of Interest

1. Sri Jagannatha Temple
2. The Beach : Colourful Sunrise and Sunset on the beach
3. Bada Danda

Excursions

1. Balighai 5 kms. on the north river Nuanai
2. Baliherachandi : In the view of the Aloknath temple.

ASSAM

Undoubtedly Assam is a most beautiful and attractive region in India. There is greater variety and colourfulness in its natural scenery. Assam lies on the foot hills of the Eastern Himalayas. This shape has an area of 78523 sq. kms. and the sacred river Brahmputra flows through it. Assam is an enchanting pradesh with lush green plains, blue hills, exotic wild life and a rich cultural heritage.

Assam Tourism is mainly based on wild-life tourism. These are temples, of historical relics, beauty of landscape, ranges of hills and peaks, rivers, waterfalls, arts & crafts, folk-songs, folk dances & festivals etc.

How to Reach There

Air Services : Chabua (Dibrugarh) Lilabari (North Lakhun Pur) Rowriah (Jorhat) Saloni (Tezpur) Borjhar (Guwahati) and Kuwfhi gram (Silchar). Guwahati is connected with Boeing services from Delhi, Bagdogra, Patna, Lucknow, Dibrugarh and Imphal and Airbus from Calcutta.

Train Services

1. *Kamrup Express* : Dibrugarh, Guwahati Howagrh.
2. *Assam Mail* : Dibrugarh, Guwahati, Delhi.
3. *Tinsukia Mail* : Tinsukia, Guwahati, Delhi.
4. *Gorakhpur Express* : Guwahati, Barawni, Gorakhpur.
5. *Varanasi Express* : Guwahati, Barauni, Varanasi.
6. *Arunachal Express* : Markongfelck, Rangia, Alipur, Duar.
7. *Barak Valley Express* : Guwahati, Lunding, Silchar.
8. *Cachar Express* : Guwahati, Lunding, Silchar.

Bus Service

All the towns of Assam are well connected with the Bus services of Assam State Transport Corporation's buses like Express. Super Express, and Delux Buses and the H. Q. is at Guwahati (Daltan Bazar).

For Local Visits : Taxis, Auto Rikshaws and Cycle Rikshaws are available in almost all the towns.

Distance

1.	Guwahati to Darjeeling	595 kms.
2.	Guwahati to Calcutta	1128 kms.
3.	Guwahati to Delhi	2160 kms.

4. Guwahati to Madras 1788 kms.
5. Guwahati to Bombay 3104 kms.

Tourism Deptt. of Assam has been forming a transport fleet comprising Mini buses. Ambassador Cars, Jeeps and Station wagons.

GUWAHATI

Known as Pragjyotishpur, today this fast growing metropolis is the principal city of Assam and one of the major cities in Eastern India situated on the bank of Brahmputra. Guwahati is for the most of the tourists the entry point of Assam of the Gateway to North Eastern India.

Where to Stay

1. Tourist Lodge, Guwahati-1 Ph. 24475
2. Stadium Guest House, Dr. B.Bama Road, Guwahati-7 Ph. 23312
3. Circuit House, Near High Court Ph. 23414

Hotels

1. Belle Vue Hotel, Upper Straned Rd. Guwahati-1. Ph. 25314
2. Hotel Nandan, Paltan Bazar Ph. 31281-6
3. Hotel Nova, Fancy Bazar Guwahati-1 Ph. 23258
4. Hotel Kahalsain (Vegetarian) Shiv Market, Fancy Bazar Guwahati, Ph. 24545
5. Hotel Ambassador, Paltan Bazar, Guwahati-6. Ph. 25587
6. Hotel Mayur, Paltan Bazar, Guwahati-7. Ph. 28288
7. Hotel Alka (Vegetarian) Fancy Bazar Ph. 24205
8. Hotel Appolo, Bharalumukh, Guwahati-7 Ph. 27110
9. Hotel Suradevi, Pan Bazar, Guwahati-1 Ph. 25050
10. Hotel Rajdoot, Paltan Bazar, Guwahati-7 Ph. 24335/27732
11. Hotel Madhuban, Paltan Bazar

Places of Interest

1. *Assam State Museum :* Ten minutes walk from Railway station. Opening hours from 9.30 a.m. to 3.30 p.m. Monday closed.
2. *Zoo, Botanical Garden :* Situated on the Zoo Road and 5 kms away from Railway station.
3. *Kamakhya Temple :* 8 kms from Railway station. It

is one of the greatest pithasthans of the Hindus place of Shakti. City bus available from foothill to the temple. Tourist coaches available from Railway Station.

4. *Basistha Ashram :* Hermitage of sage Basistha and also an ideal picnic spot 12 kms from Guwahati. City bus available from Des court.

5. *Nabagraha Temple :* A temple of vice planets, 3 kms from Railway station.

6. *Umananda :* A Shiva temple in the midst of the Brahmputra river. One can go by country boat from Kachharighat.

7. *Swal Kuchi :* 30 kms from Guwahati, famous for Assamese silk on the Northern bank of Brahmputra. Private buses available from Mechkhowe bus station.

8. *Chandubi :* A natural langoon, Picnic spot. 64 kms from Guwahati.

9. *Hajo :* Where religions meet—Hinduism. Islam and Buddhism 72 kms from Guwahati. Private buses are available from Machkhanda.

10. *Daranga :* 100 kms from Guwahati via Ramgir 48 kms Winter Mela held here every year. buses are available from Markhowa.

KAZIRANGA

Kaziranga National Park has already become famous and found a place in the World Tourist Map. This National Park is the abode of the rare one horned Great Indian Rhinocers and is situated over an area of 430 sq. kms. National Park is the natural house of other animals. Visitors are excited and thrilled to get beautiful views of wild buffaloes. Sambers, Swamp Deer, hog deer, wild elephants, tigers, bears, reptiles and lizards. Best season is October to May. Distance from Guwahati 217 kms. Jorhat 97 kms and Golaghat 70 kms. nearest Airport Jorhat 97 kms. Railway Station Farkating Junction. Kaziranga is connected by A.S.T.C. bues.

Where to Stay

1. Tourist Lodge No. 1
2. Tourist Lodge No. 2
3. Forest Lodge, I.T.D.C.

MANAS

One of the Tiger Reserves of India and an Anglers' Paradise

and excellence in scenic beauty spots of Assam. Nestling against the Himalayan foothills of Bhutan Ranges 175 kms. north-west of Guwahati is the Manas Wild Life Sanctuary which is set amidst a scenery of superb magnificance created by the river Manas.

How to Reach There

Guwahati is the nearest Air port 176 kms. Barpeta Railway Station 40 kms.

Where to Stay

1. Forest Lodge (Mathanguri) Ph. 153
2. Tourist Transit camp, Barpeta Road. Ph. 49

SIBSAGAR

One of the historical places of Assam. Capital of Ahom Kings who ruled Assam. The Tocon is built round the Sibsagar Tank at the site of the historical city Rangpur.

How to Reach Sibsagar

Air : Nearest Airport is Jorhat 55 kms.

Rail : Nearest Railway Station Simalaguri 12 kms from Sibsagar.

Road : On National Highway No. 37 distance from Guwahati 34 kms. Jorhat 55 kms. Dibrugarh 85 kms. ASTC and Private buses are available.

Where to Stay

1. Tourist Lodge Ph. 394
2. Circuit House and Dak Bungalow

Hotels

1. Piccole Hotel, near Natya Mandir
2. Kareng Hotel, Temple road Ph. 546

TEZPUR

Beautiful Town situated on the Northern Bank of Brahmaputra. The mighty river going by the side of the town is of superb scenic beauty here. The natural lake inside the town is an added attraction. Several monuments around Tezpur are worth-visiting.

How to Reach

Air : Nearest Airport is Soloni 10 kms

Rail : Connected by N.E. Railway on the North Bank of Brahmputra via Rangia Railway Station Rangapnra 26 kms main line.

Road: Connected by National Highway No. 32 and 190 kms. from Guwahati, Barpetea Road, Nath Lakhimpur.

Ferry: Ferry services are from Silghat (Nowgong District) to Tejpur in the morning and afternoon.

Where to Stay

1. Circuit House and Dak Bungalow
2. Circuit House and Dak Bungalow of Arunachal Pradesh.

Hotels

1. Meghdoot Hotel, Century Road
2. Hotel Blue Star, Jonaki Bldg Ph. 682
3. Hotel Luit Ph. 627

Sight Seeing

1. Bamuni Hills
2. Hazara Tank
3. Da-Parbatia
4. Coke Park
5. Mahabhairava Temple
6. Bhairabi Temple
7. Ruins of Agnigarh

BHALUKPUNG

Situated on the foot hills of Arunachal Pradesh. Full of scenic beauty. Angles' Paradise. Gate way to Bomdila and Taweng of Arunachal Pradesh. Distance from Guwahati 253 kms. and 60 kms. from Tezpur. Private Buses ply to Bhalukpung from Tezpur, taxis are also available.

Tipi is a worth seeing place where there is a very big Orchid House. It is in Arunachal Pradesh 8 kms. from Bhalukpung. Accommodation at Tourist Lodge.

HAFLONG

The lone lovely hill station of Assam. Haflong stands on the height of nearly 300 ft. Borak valley Express and Cacher Express trains are available from Guwahati to Hoflong via Lunding. By road Guwahati to Nowgong 120 kms. to Lanka 65 kms. to Lunding 34 kms to Haflong 132 kms. ASTC Buses are available from Guwahati to Diplic 268 kms. and to Haflong 125 kms. Accommodation at Tourist Lodge, Dak Bunglow and Circuit House.

Places of Interest

'Jatinga' the peak of Haflong hill is full of Blue Vandas' a beautiful sky blue orchid, only blue tree orchid in the world. The bird mystery of the place is a notable feature.

SILCHAR

Silchar is the gateway to Mizoram and Tripura and the only important Town of Surawa Valley. The natural scenery in the entire distance especially in the portions bordering Meghalaya and Mizoram is superb. Silchar is famous for its cane and bamboo products. Silchar is connected by Air from Calcutta and Guwahati, by rail Barak Valley Express and Cachar Express from Guwahati via Lumding, by road A.S.T.C. bus services from Guwahati to Silchar via Shillong, 343 kms. Accommodation at Circuit House, Dak Bungalow. Indian style Hotels are also available.

JORHAT

An Industrial Town. Gateway to Sibsagar, Kazi ranga and the Nagaland States. Jorhat is connected by Air from Calcutta and Guwahati, by Road 312 kms from Guwahati ASTC Buses are available, by rail nearest Railway Station Mariani 24 kms. Accommodation at Transit Camp.

Hotels

1. Hotel Paradise Ph. 821
2. Hotel Eastern Ph. 490/427
3. Hotel Broadway Ph. 192.

MANIPUR

Manipur is called ; 'Little Paradise on earth', 'Switzerland of India' and 'Jewel of India'. The beauty of the surroundings and the softness of the breeze are soothing. Its exotic scenery and mystic atmosphere are nature's masterpieces.

It is the eastermost state of the country and bounded by the State of Nagaland in the north, Assam in the west and Mizoram in the south. On its east lies Burma. The state splits up naturally into two tracts the hills and the plains. The inhabitants of these two divisions have their own different dialects, customers. The meiteis inhabiting the plains are Hindus who speak Manipuri. Most inhabitants of the hills are Christians.

Imphal is the capital of the state and is in the middle which is the centre of cultural, commercial and political activities.

Manipur is best introduced by its world famous Manipur style of Dances and famous for handloom and handicraft products.

How to Reach

Air: Imphal is connected by Air to Guwahati, Bagdogra, Patna and Delhi. It is also connected to Calcutta and Silchar.

Rail: Dimapur on N.E. Railway, 212 kms from Imphal, is the Railhead for Manipur. Regular Buses ply between Dimapur and Imphal.

Road: It is connected by a network of Roads to all important Towns of North-East.

Where to Stay at Imphal

State Tourist Lodge
State Guest House
Comfortable Hotels

Places of Interest at Imphal

1. *Khwairamband Bazar*: In the centre of Imphal, the biggest shopping centre of artistic handloom and handicraft etc.
2. *Shri Gobindajee Temple*: Beautiful golden Temple. Centre of Vaishnavite culture.
3. *War Cemetries*: Two war cemetries dedicated to the memory of the brave soldiers.
4. *Museum*: Near Imphal Pologround famous for its wide variety of customers, implements of war, historical documents etc.
5. *Shaheed Minar*: Stands at Bir Tikendrajir Park in memory of the martyrs who sacrificed their lives against the British.
6. *Zoological Garden*: 6 kms from the heart of the city. Various kinds of birds and animals are kept for public entertainments.
7. *Khonghampat Orchidarium*: 7 kms from the heart of Imphal to the north. More than 110 varieties are grown in the Peak season of April-May.

Excursions

Kaina: 29 kms, a sacred place of Hindus. According to legend, Shri Gobindajee one night appeared in a dream to his devotee Bhagyachandra Maharaj and asked him to instal his image appeared thereby canving out from a Jackfruit tree grown it Kaina accommodation at Kaina Tourist-Home.

Khongljom : 36 kms. on the Indo-Burma Road. A war broke out between Manipur and British India in 1891 and Manipur was invaded from three directions. The British Troops came from Burma were resisted at Khongijom with heavy casualties. A war memorial has been constructed on top of Khaba hill.

Mao : 106 kms. A hill station at an altitude of 1757 mts. Situated half way between Dimapur and Imphal. The climate is embracing.

Moreh : 110 kms. border with Burma, just 5 kms away is Tamu, the Burmese counter part to Moreh. Daily bus service available.

New Churachanpur : 59 kms. distt. Head Quarter of Manipur, South distt. inherited by Tribals.

Waithon Lake : 16 kms. on Indo-Burma road. A picturesque site famous for its pine-apple groves. Accommodation at tourist lodge at the fringe of the lake.

Bishnupur : 27 kms. to the South from Imphal is a picturesque of the Town situated at the foot of the hills that roll down the valley. Bishnupur is known for its historical Bishnu Temple built in 1467 A.D.

Phubala : 40 kms. to the South of Imphal on the Western fringe of Loktak lake. Accommodation at Tourist Home.

Moirang : 45 kms. to the South from Imphal and famous for its early Manipur flock culture. The Temple of Thangjing still preserves the 12th century garments. There is one I.N.A. memorial hall with the statue of Subhash Chandra Bose.

Sendra : 48 kms. from Imphal, 3 kms from Moirang. A small Islet in the middle of Lok Tak. It is viewpoint overlooking the beautiful lake and its surroundings. Accommodation at Tourist House, on the top of the town.

Kabul Lamjo : 53 kms. from Imphal, 5 kms from Sendra only floating National Park in the world. There is a forest Lodge.

Loktak Lake : Biggest fresh water Lake in North-Eastern India lies in the valley of Manipur. Boating facility available.

Ukhrul : 83 kms. from Imphal 1900 meters above from Sea level. District Head Quarters of Imphal-East. It is practically as high and cold as Simla. Other attractions are the Shisol Hill.

MIZORAM

Mizoram in a new name given to the mountainous region earlier known on the Lushai Hills. It was one of the districts of Assam till 1972 when it became a Union Territory. Sandwitched between Burma in the East and South, and Bangladesh in the West Mizoram occupies an area of great strategic importance in the North-Eastern corner of India. It has a total of 1016 kms. boundry with Burma and Bangladesh.

The hills in Mizoram runs from North to South with a tendency to be higher in the East of the Territory and tapering in the North and South. The average height of the hills is about 900 meters. The highest peak in Mizoram is the Blue Mountain with a height of 2065 meters. Mizoram has the most *Variegated* hilly terrain in the Eastern part of India. The hills are steep and are separated by rivers which flow either to the North or South creating deep gorges between the hill ranges.

Mizoram has a pleasant climate. It is generally cool in summer and not yery cold in winter. The entire area is under the direct influence of the monsoon. It rains heavily from May to September. Winter in Mizoram is rainfree and is very pleasant. The skies are wonderfully blue and in the morning the mist forming between the hills gives an enchanting view of wide stretches resembling a vast Lake.

Mizoram has great natural beauty and an endless variety of Landscape and it is rich in fauna and flora. Almost all kinds of Tropical Trees and plants thrive in Mizoram. The hills are marvellous green.

The Mizos are of Mongoloid state and are believed to have migrated from upper Burma between the 17th and 18th century. They came under the influence of the British. Missionaries in the 19th century and most of the Mizos became Christians.

The Mizos are a distinct community and the social unit was the village. Mizo village is usually set on top of the hill with the chief's house at the centre and bachelor's dormitory called Zacolbuk prominently located in a central place. The social in the Mizo Society has undergone tremendous change over the years.

The most colourful and distinctive dance of Mizo is called *Cheraw*. Long bamboo staves are used for this dance, therefore many people call it a bamboo dance. *Cheraw* is a dance of skill and alert minds.

Khullam : This is a dance performed by group of dances. This dance is performed in honour of a visitor or guest.

Chheih Law : It is the dance over a round of rice beer in the cool of the evening.

Aizwal is the capital of Mizoram 180 kms from Silchar which is the nearest Railway Station. The bus journey from Silchar to Aizwal usually takes about 6 hours by delux bus.

Where to Stay

1. Shangrile Hotel
2. Hotel Indian Airlines
3. Broadway Hotel-*cum*-Restaurant
4. Chawthua Hotel
5. Hotel Comfort

Note : For further details place contact : Director of information-Public Relations and Tourist, Aizwal.

ARUNACHAL PRADESH

Arunachal Pradesh is a Union Territory having 9 districts with a population of 4670000 people. The whole of Northern region is under snow during winter months. The main industries are forest based and handicrafts. Capital is Itanagar.

MEGHALAYA

Meghalaya is one of the youngest States of India, carved out of the erstwhile State of Assam. Meghalaya covers 22000 sq. kms. area between the Assam plains on the north and the Bangladesh plains on the South. The scenic beauty of the State is unique. Rolling green hills with streams of sparking water carcading in the valleys make it something to be seen and enjoyed. The subtropical humid climates with heavy rainfall helps nature to keep the hills covered with lush green vegetation Northern slopes of the central high lands rising above 1500 meters elevation have rich temperate to subtropical forests which merge into the forest in the plains of Assam, while the southern part with heavier rainfall is more sub-tropical and has most evergreen forest. The variation in elevation and rainfall patteren goes it a varied type of flora and fauna many of which are not to be seen in any other parts of the country, it is a nature-lovers' paradise.

Shillong is the capital of the Meghalaya. Most picturesque hill station of the country. It is called 'Scotland of the East' situated at an altitude of 1496 Meters above sea level. It is connected with Guwahati 104 kms. the nearest Railhead. Motorable road, Airbus from Calcutta to Guwahati of direct Boeing flight from New Delhi. Mini Bus of Tourism Deptt. of Meghalaya takes tourists to shillong in about 3 hours.

Where to Stay

1. Shillong Tourist Bungalow.
2. Hotel Pinewood Ashok. Ph. 23116 & 43765

Places of Interest in Side City

1. Wand Lake.
2. Lady Hydri Park.
3. Shillong Golf Course.
4. Bara Bazar.
5. Shillong Peak.

Places of Interest Outside City

1. *Cherrapunjee :* 50 kms. from Shillong.
    1. Maws Mai Falls
    2. Mawsmai Caves
    3. Kynnew Falls
    4. Ramkishan Mission
    5. Mawtrop Rock
2. *Mawphlang*—24 kms.
3. *Mawbynram*—56 kms.

Transport

Tourist Taxis and yellow cabs are available in the town. Tourism Deptt. organises tours.

TRIPURA

Tripura is a small State on the north-east, hemmed in almost on all sides by Bangladesh. It has a romance about itself. The antiquity of the land and the charm of its picturesque landscape fascinate one no less than did Hardy's Wessex or Wordsworth's Lake Districts. The undulating green, the murmurring rivulet, the hills, the Jungles, the lakes present to the eyes an object which is a joy forever. Rich to flora and fauna the legendery State of Tripura claims a prominent place in the tourist map of India for her natural beauty spots, for the people with their hoary culture and for the old monuments.

A special mention may be made of Sipahijala—near

Agartata a forest area developed with an artificial lake and Zoological gardens etc., for a peaceful holiday.

Agartala is the capital of Tripura. Kaitashaher is another big town and Udaipur is the previous capital of the State of Tripura.

How to Reach There

Air : Agartala is connected with Calcutta by the Indian Airlines Servics and the Airport is 10 kms. away from the city.

Rail : The nearest Rail head is Dharmanagar on N. E. Railway. It is 51453 kms, from Calcutta Via Guwahati, Luending, Badarpur and Karimganj. Agartala is 200 kms away from Dharmanagar Rail head.

Road : Distance from Agartala to

1. Calcutta 1808 kms.
2. Dharmanagar 200 kms.
3. Guwahati 597 kms.
4. Shilbug 496 kms.
5. Silchar 247 kms.

Agartala is connected by regular Bus services.

Where to Stay

1. Royal Guest Home. Colonel Choumuhami Agartala. Ph. : 526
2. Hotel Minakshi, Hawkers' Corner, H.C. Basak Road Ph. : 1433
3. Hotel Ritz, H. G. Basak Road Ph. : 273
4. Hotel U.K. —do— Ph. : 721
5. Saurastra Hotel—do— Ph. : 173
6. Agartala Club-*cum*-Guest House, Kuajaban. Ph. : 1376
7. Circuit House, Kunjaban Ph. : 41
8. P.W.D. Dak Bungalow

Places of Interest

Ujjayana Palace : Standing in the heart of the town. Two large tanks lie in front of Palace and in the intervening space of beautiful Mughal Garden have been laid out.

Maharaja Bir Bikram College : 3 kms. from Ujjayana Palace the College is situated on a hillock in the eastern extremity of the town.

Laxminarayan Temple : Uma Maheshwar Temple, Buddha Temple, Agartala Museum are some of the worth-seeing places in the city of Agartaia.

Excursions

Sipahijala : Beautiful picnic spot. The forest Bungalow overlooking the lake below, the natural 200 near the place and drive to the spot through forests of rubber. Accommodation at forest Lodre, Sipalifala. Ph. 479/1101.

Tripura Sundore Temple : 56 kms. from Agartala near Udaipur is the Kali Temple built by Late Maharaja Dharya Masikya It is one of the 51 Pithas mentioned in the Tantras. The Temple stands on a small hillock callad Dhaldagai.

Neer Mahal : 56 kms. from Agartala is a lake palace built by Maharaja of Tripura in early part of this Century. It stands in the centre of a vast lake called "Rudrasagar' and hence the structure is given the name 'Neer Mahal'.

Dumbur Reservoir : The water reservior of the Gumti. High Road Project covers an area of 40 sq. kms with an unending spell of luxuriant green vegetation all around. The Dumbur lake stands majestic for her exceedingly charming beauty. The ground of transparent waving water over a vast span and the deep green dots of Islands in the midst are fascinating.

Unakuti : 200 kms. from Agartala. Embedded on a hillock about 45 meters high, 10 kms. from Kailshahar are colossal figures of Hindu Pantheon cut of rocks. Dating back to Buddhist not Hindu period of history, there images include figures of Siva. Hara-Gauri, Panchmukh, Siva, Bishnupada, Kalbhairab, Basudev, Hanuman, Ram-Lakshamana, Ganpati,

Jampoi Hills : Jampoi hills are situated at an altitude of 3000 ft. above sea level and are about 250 kms. from Agartala. Jampoi Hills are a seat of springs.

Temple of Fourteen gods : The Chaturdash Devata Mandir is situated at old Agartala which is about 10 kms. from the modern Town of Agartala.

NAGALAND

For its charming landscape situated on the extreme north-east of India, Nagaland is called Switzerland of India. It is bounded by Assam on the West, Burma on the East, Arunacal Pradesh and Assam on the North and Manipur on the South. The state is endoved with a Kaleidoscopic landscape of blue hills, green valleys, rivers and streams flowing through mountains, deep gorges and narrow valleys

Sixteen odd tribes and sub-tribes in-habitating this small oriental state. Each of the tribes has its own distinctive dialect, customs and traditional dress. Nagaland has seven districts with a population of 7,74,930. Best season for visitors is October to May.

Entry by Permits

I. All foreign tourists desiring to visit Nagaland require Entry permits from the Ministry of Home Affairs, Govt. of India, South Block, New Delhi.

II. Domestic tourists visiting Nagaland require to obtain inner-line permits issued by the Additional Deputy Commissioner, Dimapur, Dy Comm. Kohima. Dy. Comm. Mokakching. Permit fee Rs. 5 from each applicant.

How to Reach There

Air : The only Airport in Nagaland is Dimapur connected with Calcutta via Guwahati, and rest of the country.

Rail : Only Rail head Dimapur on the main line of North Frontier Railway.

Road : All important districts and towns of the State are well connected by the Nagaland State Transport Services. It has a night Deluxe Service from Dimapur to Guwahati.

DIMAPUR

Flourishing commercial town 195 meters above the sea level, gateway to capital.

Places of Interest

Kachari Kingdom : In the heart of the town there is an old relic of the Kachari Kingdom of the medieval period.

In Tanki wild life sanctuary : 37 kms. from Dimapur Hoolock,a rare ape species, is found here. Animals of other varieties like Elephant, Mithun, Sambher, Barking deer, Leopard, Tiger, Sloth beer, Rhenus, Monkey, Wild beer, Ghoral, Flying squirrel, wild dog, civet cat are also found. There are some birds and reptiles available. For the convenience of the visitors there is a forest rest house and a minibus.

Emporium

Naga shawls and handicrafts can be purchased from here.

Where to Stay

Govt. Accommodations

		Ph.
1.	Circuit House	2054
2.	Forest Rest House	2094
3.	Powd Rest House	
4.	Power Rest House	
5.	N.I.D.C. Hotel	

Private Hotel

		Ph.
1.	Hotel Tragopan	2049
2.	Hotel Galaxy	2714
3.	Hotel Amber	2773
4.	Hotel Pilgrim	
5.	Hotel North-East	
6.	Nagaland Tourist Hotel	2274

Restaurant

1.	Plaza Restaurant-*cum*-Bakery	2477
2.	Beerje Restaurant cum Bakery	2547

KOHIMA

Capital and a hill station. 74 kms. from Dimapur 1495 mtrs above sea level.

Places of Interest

War cemetry : In the heart of the Kohima town, the famous Second World War cemetry is a symbolic memorial of the heroes of the Second World War.

Museum : The State museum has a rare collection of articles of different tribes which speak about the history and the tradition of the Nagas.

State Library : There is a good collection of books about the history of the Nagas and various folklores.

Japfu Peak : 15 kms. South of Kohima town, second highest peak 3043 meters above. Best Trekking season November to March.

Dzukou Valley : Valley of eternal charm is situated behind the Japfu peak. A valley of perpetual beauty. 8000 ft., above sea level, 25 kms. from Kohima. The entire valley is overgrown by a type of tough evergreen cave peculiar to its own making the valley appear from a distance as though it was down lawn. The snake-like meandering stream that flows through Dzukou turns into a frozen stream in winter. The valley at this time appears white washed with lagers of snow flakes.

Ohima Village (*Bara Basti*) : It is the second biggest and most popular village in Asia. As you enter the village a large traditional wooden gate with the scimitar of horns of buffalo head pointing to the bravery and valour of the Anganies greets you. Naga stones erected here and there in front of the houses are the memory symbols of grand feats celebrated by the great ancestors.

Sales Emporium : Situated opposite Bus Stand. The Emporium spells varieties of Naga Art and handicrafts items.

Zoological Park : A reflection of the rich flora and fauna of Nagaland is visible at the Zoological Park of Kohima. It exhibits to a visitor some of the rarest species of animals and birds of the world,

Khonoma : 20 kms. west of Kohima. This village has its own tradition of valour and courage. History reveals that Khonoma provided protection to several villages in the port. The Khonoma gate points to the history of the British infiltration into Naga hills.

Dzulakie : A majestic landscape and scenery. 36 kms. from Kohima, this river flows at an altitude of 7000 ft. above sea level The interesting feature of this river is that at one place it flows through a very deep and narrow gorge making it appear and an another place it disappeared and has gone underground.

Peken : 76 km. from Dimapur as an altitude of 1446 meters above the sea level. It is a place of Reliang and Kuki tribes the famous Zeliang dance in pairs is worth-seeing.

Tseminyu : 50 kms. from Kohima at an altitude of 1442 mts Home of Rangmar, 'Ngada' is the popular festival which is celebrated in the last weak of November.

Where to Stay

Govt. Accommodation

1. MLA Hotet, Ph. : 566 Reservation through the legislative Assembly Ph. 2280.

2. V.I.P. Guest House, Ph. 561 Reservation through Dy. Secy Hand.

3. Police Mess, Ph. 417 Reservation. Astt. Inspector General of Police.

Private Hotels

1. Razhu Hotel (Range Rs. 10/- to 161/-)
2. Regal Hotel (Range ,, 15/- to 25/-)
3. West Inn (Range ,, 10/- to 25/-)
4. Evergreen (Range Rs. 10/-)
5. Travel Lodge (Range Rs. 35/- to 30/-)

Restaurant

1. Hotel Embassy
2. Le Boron
3. Mikado

Important Phone numbers

		Ph.
1.	Hospital	2201
2.	Police Station	2233, 873
3.	Enquiry	405
4.	Trunk booking	20

MOKOKCHUNG

Picturesque of the town and distt. Head Quarter at an altitude of 1325.8 meters above sea level commercial and cultural centre. Hand woven colourful shawls namely Tsung Kotepsu (Decorative warrier-shawl) and subangsu (worn by the Rich and warrior alone) log drums and morung depicts about its distinctive culture and tradition of the Ao Nagas. Main festivals are "Moatsu" and "Tsungrenmong" observed during the first week of May and August respectively.

The population of the town is about 20,000. Approachable from Kohima via Wokha which is about 160 kms.

Lunghum : The village is the gems of the legendry spots and history. Situated 17 kms. South-West of Mokokchung at an altitude of 6000 ft.

ASUR RIKHOM, the gate or the dead people which lead to 'Chakrama' means 'Rocky Cliff' is in the centre of the village.

Then we come to a beautiful hillock called 'MATA-YIMIXONG'. In ancient times there was a village on this hillock. From here one can see the whole Ao area, Lotha area, two highest peaks of Saramoti and Japfra and mor district.

Where to Stay

Govt. Accommodation

1. Circuit House Mokokchung Ph. 61
2. Tourist Lodge Mokokchung Ph 145

Private Hotels

1. Madras Hotel Mokokchung
2. Grace Hotel ,,
3. Hotel Citizen ,,
4. Inner circle Restaurant

Mon : Home of Konyak Nagas. District Head Quarter at an altitude of about 900 meters. 354 kms. from Kohima and 280 km from Dimapur. It is interesting to see their totted faces, feathered headgears and traditional earnings. Konyak is an expert Wood carvers. A visit to Angh's palaces at Chui and Wakching are most interesting. Aoling festival is observed during the 1st week of April.

Where to Stay

Government Circuit House Ph. 49.

PHEK : 134 kms. from Kohima district Head quarter, home of Chakhesang, combination of three tribes *i.e.*, Cha of Chekru, Khe of Kheze, sang of Sangtam. It is also the Home of the Pochuri tribes in this District. It is full of varieties of beautiful orchids. The famous rare Blythe Tragopan bird is here. The customer culture of Chakhesang is different from other Nagas Tsukhenyie is their principal festival in March/April.

PFUTSERO : At an altitude of 2134 meters above sea level, beautiful township. One of the coldest hill station in Nagaland. Apples are green in plenty here. 70 kms. border road connects with Kohima. Regular Nagaland State Transport Buses ply on this road.

Where to Stay

1. Govt. Circuit House Phase Ph. 43
2. P.W.D. Rest House, Phek
3. Tourist Hotel, Phek
4. Hotel capital Phek

TUENSANG : Tuensang district is located at an altitude of 1371.60 meters. It is the house of the Chang Yinchungens Khiamunjan, upper Konyaks, Sangtams and phoms 272 kms. from Kohima via Wokha and Mokokchung and 235 kms. via Zunhebito. Regular N.S.T. buses ply on this road.

Their cultural heritage, pattern of dresses are unique and even more colourful than rest of the Nagaland through their dances and songs. They are well built and physically strong people. Their handlooms and handicrafts products are well known and even exported.

Kiphire : 122 kms. from Tuensang and 254 kms. from Kohima, situated at an altitude of 896 meters. It is the Home of Sangtam, Yimchunger and Semer. Saramati, the highest peak in Nagaland is 12600 ft. above sea level which remains snow-capped in winter is not far from here. 'Blythe' Tragopan is found here.

Pungro : 36 kms. from Kiphire, from its lakes, two days trekking to reach Saramati peak, a pass of which falls in Burma

Where to Stay

1. Circuit House Tuensang Ph. 50
2. P.W.D. Rest House Tuensang

WOKHA

District Head Quarter of the Lotha Naga, A picturesque town. 80 kms. from Kohima as well as Mokokchung and 58 kms. from Furkating Railway Station, Assam. There are a lot of eye catching hill top villages around Wokha. Lothas are famous for their colourful dances and folk songs. Tokhu Emong and Pikhuchak are their principal festivals 'Opuuram' and 'Longpenson' are prestigious social shawls, for women and men respectively. Best type of oranges and pine-appeals are found here.

Tyui : Trekking to the top of the Tyui mountain offers exhilirating experience. It is known as abode of spirit.

Doyang Hygro project : The major Hydro Project is 29 kms. from Wokha on the way to Mokokchung Chanpang oil field is another important centre, which is 80 kms. from Wokha.

Liphanyan Governor's Lamp : 43 kms. from Dimapur and approachable from Wokha is located on the foot hill.

The Governor's lamp has an exquisite charm because of its river scene. The Zigzag flow of Doyang river is unique. After swit rush through hills and mountains, Doyong approaches the plains and the water turns blue flowing over a wide bank making a splendid view. A resort for rafting, angling and shikar.

Where to Stay at Wokha

Circuit House, Ph. 26

ZUNHEBOTO

A Distt. H. Q. for the Semas. 150 kms. from Kohima via Chazouba and 8 kms. from Mokokchung at an altitute of 1874 meters. This picturesque town has a charm of its own. Same Tribes are renowned for their colourful war dance and folk sangs. Their ceremonial war dresses are worth-seeing. Tuluni is one of the most important festivals observed in the second week of July every year.

Atoizu Kheloshe Polytechnic : Atoizu is a growing town. Nagaland Polytechnic is located here. The landscape of the town is fascinating.

Where to Stay

Circuit House, Zunheboto Ph. 38

Routes with Distances

1. Dimapur—Kohima 74 kms.
2. Dimapur—Wokha via Kohima 154 kms.
3. Dimapur—Imphal (Manipur State) 216 kms.
4. Dimapur—Mariani-Mokokchung 208 kms.
5. Dimapur—Mon via Jorhat Namtola 286 kms.
6. Dimapur—Amguri 178 kms.
7. Dimapur—Pereu 76 kms.
8. Kohima—Wokha 80 kms.
9. Kohima—Meluri 170 kms.
10. Kohima—Phek 134 kms.
11. Kohima—Zunheboto 150 kms.
12. Kohima—Tuensang via Wokha, Mokokchung. 270 kms.
13. Kohima—Mokokchung 162 kms.
14. Dimapur—Guwahati 292 kms.
15. Dimapur—Zunheboto via Chazouba 225 kms.

SIKKIM

Sikkim is a picture of perfection. It is Himalaya in Heights Himalyan in tranquility and is second to none in its serenity, its show of snowy peaks, its glacial glory at a glance, its appealing scenery with rural homesteads picturesquely parched on the hill side, its forests, its flora and fauna, its lively music and dances, its monasteries and lamas.

Bounded in the North and East by Tibet now in Chinese hands, in the South-East by Bhutan and in the West by Nepal, its borders are gallantly guarded by our heroic armed forces on great heights in, isolation.

Its people are simple, sincere, toiling and spiritual. Their climate may be cold but they are always warm in heart. They are honest, hard working and peace loving all lie in happy harmony.

Fortunately in Sikkim, there is no unemployment, no strikes, no labour problem, no law and order situation, no no pollution and so for no taxes or hardly any to speak of.

Sikkim is a paradise for tourists, walkers, trekkers and mountaineers. It has sufficient number of good and economy class hotels and Tourist lodges.

Sikkim has several fascinating features. It has a range of heights varying from 800 to 28300 feet. It has the world's highest national park and the highest trout hatchery. It has the largest variety of orchides, roses, birds and butterflies. It has the second highest glacier in Asia. It has the hottest springs in the coldest climate.

Sikkim is easy to reach by plane and road, by rail and road, from Bombay to Delhi or Calcutta and then by another IAC flight from Delhi to Bagdogra, Via Lucknow & Patna or from Calcutta to Bagdogra, thereafter by road by bus or Taxi to Gangtoka. Most beautiful Teasta river keeps company up to the hill capital of Gangtok perched at 5600 feet.

Visitor can come by train right up to New Jalpaiguri station and take a vehicle from there Jalpaiguri, Silliguri, Bagdogra all in north of West Bengal State, are all near each other. Many tourists also come to Gangtok via Darjeeling.

WEST SIKKIM

West Sikkim has been recently opened to the tourists. Some of the important tourist interest places are given below :

***Pemayamgtse* : *The Sublime Lotus* : 115 kms. from Gangtok.**

It is the principal Monastary of all the Monasteries of the sect. The annual chaam or Lama dance used to be held in the 12th month of the Tibetan calender (corrosponding to January) in this Monastary. The name of this chaam is Drag-donar, the terrible form of Padma Sambhava. These are almost exclusively performed of the Lamas, dressed in costumes of rare magnificence. Mahakala and Guru Drag-donar are penderoogly marked in blue and red and they are attended by the goddess hamo, and by others marked to represent the tiger, the lion, the monkey, the mythical bird Garuda, the stag, the river monster and the yak.

Yoksame : 40 kms. Yoksam literally means three Lamas'. The first Chogyal Phuntson Namgal of Sikkim was consecreted by the three learned lamas. This is also a Lake known as Kathou lake.

Tso-Shuk-Tso or Khechoepolri lake. 33 kms. from tourist Lodge. This is most serene and sacred lake. Despite the fact that this lake is surrounded by the forest, one cannot see a single leaf or anything floating on the lake. If a leaf falls into it, the birds immediately come and pick it up. It is believed that one gets whatever he or she wishes at the lake. Visitors are required not to smoke or do anything which might disturb that serenity and the sanctity of this second lake.

Rab Dentse Palace Ruin : At a distance of one hour trek are the ruins of Rabdentse Palace. It was constructed after the concseretion of Chogyal Phuntork Namgyal.

Sanga Choeling Monastary. It is situated at about an hours trek from Polling. Climbing up towards the monastary are the ruins of monastary, shukto (stone throne) where Lhatsum chenpo have sat and mediated.

Tashiding Monastery : This beautiful monastary is only a day's trek from Pamayangtse. It is an important place of pilgrimage. There is a forest Bungalow for stay.

Dzongri : Altitude 3939 meters is opened to the Tourists for the first time. Dzongri after the most fascinating close up view of the Khangchendzonda masrif opposite it rises the 6653 meters high Pandiw cloacked in thick ice hood. To the left appears the deep gap of goecha La. To the West our the gentle stopes of Dzongri rise the long out line of the Khangla side.

Where to Stay

1. Pemayangtse Luxury Tourist Lodge Ph. : 73
2. Hotel Vehid, Lyalshing
3. Hotel Yangtrela, Rab dentse.
4. S.P.W D. Rest House, Gyalshing
5. S.P.W.D. Rest House, Pemayangtse
6. Rest House, Yuksaw
7. Rest House, Toshilding

ANDAMAN-NICOBAR ISLANDS

The Andaman and Nicobar group of approximately 300 Islands covering an aiea of 8293 sq. kms. and spread over a length of 700 kms area are located in the Bay of Bengal. The capital town of Port Blair is at a distance of 1255 kms. from Calcutta, 1190 kms. from Madras, and 1200 kms. from Vishakhapatnam. The Islands have a predominantly flat terrain, the highest point not exceeding 732 meters. The population, as per the 1988 census is 1,88,254. The culture is distinctly tropical. The average rainfall is 3180 mm. and the temperature generally varies between 23°C and 31°C. 86 per cent of the area is under reserved and protected forests. 36 per cent of the reserve forest has been marked as 'Primitive Tribal Reserve.

How to Reach There

By sea : From passenger ships namely—MV Andaman, TSS Nancowry, MV Harsh Vardhana and MV Akbar ply between Port Blair and Calcutta/Madras/Vishakhapatnam. The voyage from Port of Call on the mainland to Port Blair takes about three days and the ships normally stay for about three days in Port Blair. About 36 round trips are made to the mainland annually giving an average of one round voyage in every ten days. For further details please contact the following organisation.

1. The Manager, Shipping Corpn. of India Ltd. Nilhat House, No. 13, Strand Road, Calcutta-1

2. M/s KVP Shaikh Mohammed Rowther and Company No. 41, Lingi Chetty, Street, Madras-1.

3. The Manager, Shipping Corpn. of India Ltd. Abardeen Bazar, Port Blair-744101 Andaman.

M/S A.V. Bhanojiraw and Guru Pattabiramayya and Co. Post Box No. 17, Vishakhapatnam.

By Air From Calcutta to Port Blair : Bi-weekly Boeing 737 service of the Indian Airlines between Calcutta and Port Blair throughout the year. The flight takes off from Calcutta at 06.10 hrs. and arrives at Port Blair at 08.00 hrs. The plain returns back to Calcutta on the same day leaving Port Blair at 08.40 hrs. and reaching Calcutta at 10.40 hrs. The fair is Rs. 966/- one way.

From Madras to Port Blair : Biweekly Boeing 737 service between Madras and Port Blair. The Plane takes off from Madras at 6.10 a.m. and lands at Port Blair at 8.1 a m. After a stop over of about 40 minutes, the plane takes off for Madras. Fair is Rs. 976/- one way.

Where to Stay

1. Tourist Houses and Guest Houses of Port Blair. Please contact of Director (Tourism), Andaman and Nicobar Administration, Port Blair for reservation up to three months advance.
2. Andman Beach Resort Ph. 2599 and 2781.
3. Welcome group Bay Island Hotel
4. Youth Hotel
5. Megapore Resort Ph. 2207
6. Bay Island Hotel Ph. 2881 to 91
7. Marine Hill Tourist Home Ph. 2365
8. Carbyris Cave Tourist Home Ph. 2211

Places of Interest

Anthropoligical Museum : This museum displays the tools, implements, models and habitals of the aboriginal tribes in the territory. Their art and handicrafts are other attractions.

Marine Museum : Over 350 species of Sea life are carefully preserved here. The exhibits give an insight into the marine life as found in the Andaman's waters.

Chatham Saw Mill : It is one of the largest in Asia, employing about 1000 workers. There is a show room at Haddo where one can see some of the best species of wood in the world.

Wimco Factory : This is the oldest private factory in these Blanck. Match splints are being manufactured here.

Zoological garden : It is called mini Zoo, it has some of the rare species of animals and birds that are peculiar to these islands.

Chiriya Tapu : Also known as 'Birds Island'. This place is famous for the enchanting view that it presents to the visitors. A beautiful spot for picnic and live fishing. It takes an hour drive from Port Blair by Bus/Taxi.

Wandoor Beach : It is situated on the west coast of South Andaman. It is one of the most famous places for diving, swimming, and picnicing. There is a wooden Jetty at wandoor from where the tourists can board the boat for the nearby islands of Grub, Rodken and Jolly Buoy etc.

Viper Island : Not very far from the Haddo wharf is the viper Island. Before the construction of the famous cellular Jail, this island was used to harbour the convicts. The island had gallows on top of a hillock where the condemned prisoners were hanged.

Corbyn's Cove : Corbyn's case i a palm frenged beach 4 kms. from the Port Blair Air Port. It is an ideal place for swimming, simfing and basking in the sun. Close to the beach is a hotel run by the TCI with 64 beds, as well as Tourist House managed by the Andaman and Nicobar administration, with 8 beds. It is one of the most frequented spots during the weekends.

Sippighat Farm : Situated about 14 kms. from Port Blair It is a great agricultural area demonstration farm spread over area of about 80 acres where experiments are conducted for the improvement of species like clone, nutureg, cinemas and pepper. Once the experiments are found to be successful the cultivators in these islands are informed about the new and improved techniques for the cultivation of these species.

Ross Island : Situated at the mouth of the capacious and picturesque Port Blair harbour, it was the residence of the Chief Commissioner during the British times. It was also the Administrative Head Quarter of the territory during these times. Besides the residence of the Chief Commissioner it also had a church, a swimming pool, Tennis court, a printing press and a cemetry. Spotted deer and peacocks, are seen on the Ross Island in abundance. Visitors are required to take prior permission from the commanding officer, INS Jarawa, Port Blair.

Cellular Jail : It will be no exaggeration to say that the Andaman Nicobar Islands are synonymous with the Cellular Jail. Indeed these islands are known mostly for the Cellular Jail in which Indian revolutionaries were incarcerated during the British times. Declared as a National Memorial on 11th Feb. 1979, the cellular Jail is place of pilgrimage for every Indian. There is also a museum in the Jail where one can see the exhibits and visualise the kind of life that the prisoners led during their period of incarceration. It was built in the year 1906 and had 698 cells. On account of the irreparable damage caused to it by an earthquake a portion of the jail had to be demolished. In the place where the demolished portion of the Jail stood new stands the modern G.B. Port Hospital.

Dilthaman Tank : Situated in the heart of the Port Blair town, this tank was once the only source of drinking water in the town. This area has now been developed into a beautiful picnic spot.

Most Important for Foreigner

1. Please ensure that you possess all the travel documents and the restricted area permit issued by the Ministry of Home Affairs Govt. of India.

2. Immediately on arrival at Port Blair Air Port contact the immigration counter near the passenger shed and produce the travel documents.

3. If no permit of any sort was obtained from Govt. of India, obtain permission for visiting the Municipal Area and the islands of Jolly Buloy and cinque from Immigration officer at Port Blair (Ph. 2577).

4. For visiting snob, Red skin, guide and Boat Island you may obtain necessary permission from the Chief Secretary Andaman Nicobar Admn.

5. If interested, contact the chief wild life warden and obtain necessary permit for photography, investigation and filming inside a sanctuary or National Park (Ph. 2721).

6. Obtain transit pass for transporting any wild animal trophy/article, outside this territory, from the deputy conservator of forests, wild division, Port Blair (Ph. 2233)

7. Contact the Harbour Master for sailing programme of the ferry vessels or listen to the local News Bulletin. All India Radio, Port Blair, at 7.5 a.m. and 7.5 p.m. (Ph. no. at Marine Deptt. 2528).

Very Very Important

8. Do not plan a visit to the island without obtaining necessary travel documents and permission from the Govt. of India, Ministry of Home Affairs New Delhi.

9. Do not individually visit the following Islands as they are only allowed for visit by organised groups :

   1. Red Skin Island
   2. Snob Island
   3. Grub Island
   4. Boat Island

10. Do not stay in the Islands for purpose other than tourism unless specifically permitted by the Govt. of India, Ministry of Home Affairs, New Delhi.

11. Do not visit places/areas, which are not covered by the permit.

12. Photography in the areas such as Airport, Govt. Dockyard, Defence, Establishment and Naval wharf. Dhanikaridane, chattans, saw mills or in any reserved areas is strictly prohibited.

13. Transportation of corals, see Fans and Sea Shells, exceeding 10 pieces is prohibited unless specific permits are obtained from fisheries Department.

14. Do not hunt wild animals without a valid licence.

Useful Telephone Numbers

		Ph. Office	*Ph. Residence*
1.	Chief Secretary	2427	2700
2.	Deputy Commissioner (Andamans)	2702	2765
3.	Superintendent of Police	2571	2640
4.	Dy. Director (Tourism)	2694	
5.	Public Relations officer	2694	
6.	Tourist Information Centre and Tourist Home	2380	
7.	Warden, Youth Hotel	3509	
8.	Indian Air Lines,	2208	
9.	Manager shipping Corpn.	2647	2206
10.	G.B. Port Hospital	2756	

IMPORTANT ROAD ROUTES

Bombay to Aurangabad : (664) kms. Via Aianta and Ellora, Nasik, Manmad.

Bombay to Aurangabad : (554) kms Via Shaur, Bhiwandi, Vada. Bulsar, vadodara, Vagira.

Bombay to Banglore : (1035) kms. Thana, Khandala, Lonavala, Surat, Satara, Kolhapur, Belgaum, Dhanwar, Harihar.

Bombay to Calcutta : (2294) kms. Via Nasik, Rahatia, Sendhwa, Indore, Guna, Shiva Puri, Jhansi, Kanpur, Allahabad, Asansol.

Bombay to Calcutta : (2044) kms. Via Nasik, Dhulia, Jalgaun, Nagpur, Jamshedpur.

Bombay to Kanyakumari : (1930) kms. Via Pune, Kolhapur, Belgaum, Dharwar, Bangalore, Mysore, Ooty, Coimbtore, Palghat, Trichur, Cochin, Trivandrum.

Bombay to Delhi : (*i*) (1495) kms. Via Nasik, Dhulia, Sendhwa, Indore, Shivpuri, Gwalior, Agra, Mathura.

(*ii*) (1690) Via Bulsar, Vadodra, Kaira, Ahmedabad, Nadiad, Agothra, Dohad, Ujjain, Udaipur, Jodhpur, Ajmer, Jaipur, Delhi.

Bombay to Darjeeling : (3138) kms. Via Nasik, Indore, Shivapuri, Jhansi, Lucknow, Allahabad, Asansol, Calcutta, Berhampur, Kishan Ganj, Silliguri, Darjeeling.

Bombay to Panji : (674) kms. Via Thana, Pauval, Dasgaon, Halkarnaba, Kudal, Boroer.

Bombay to Hyderabad : (730) kms. Pune, Sholapur, Omargaon.

Bombay to Jaipur : (1170) kms. Via Nasik, Dhulia, Sendhwa, Indore, Dewan, Kota.

Bombay to Khajuraho : (1243) kms. Nasik, Dhulia, Indore, Dewas, Bhopal, Chhatarpur.

Bombay to Kodaikanal : (1496) kms. Thana, Pune, Kolhapur, Belgaum, Dharwar, Harihar, Bangalore, Namakkal, Vattalkander.

Bombay to Kathmandu : (390) kms. Nasik, Dhulia, Indore, Shiv Puri, Kanpur, Allahabad, Patna, Mujaffarpur.

Bombay to Madras : (1592) kms. Via Pune, Kolhapur, Belganm, Dharwar, Harihar, Bangalore, Ranipet.

Bombay to Podicherry : (1280) kms. Thane, Pune, Kolhapur, Belgaum, Dharwar, Harihar, Bangalore, Krishnagiri, Tiruvanmalai., Cuddalore.

Bombay to Srinagar : (2282) kms. Via Nasik, Dhulia, Indore Shivapuri, Gawalior, Agra, Mathura, Delhi, Ambala, Jalandhar, Pathankot, Jammu.

Bombay to Shillong, : Thane, Dhulia, Sendhwa, Indore, Shivapuri, Kanpur, Allahabad, Sasaram, Patna, Bhagalpur, Silliguri, Guwahati.

DISTANCE BETWEEN DELHI AND THE FOLLOWING CITIES

Agra	—	203 kms.
Allahabad	—	613 ,,
Varanasi	—	747 ,,
Lucknow	—	502 ,,
Amritsar	—	442 ,,
Almora	—	411 ,,
Mussoorie	—	269 ,,
Nainital	—	315 ,,
Ranikhet	—	354 ,,
Bhakhra Nangal	—	336 ,,
Chandigarh	—	232 ,,
Pathankot	—	480 ,,
Gwalior	—	318 ,,
Khajuraho	—	587 ,,
Jaipur	—	310 ,,
Simla	—	352 ,,
Manali	—	902 ,,
Srinagar	—	876 ,,

IMPORTANT EXPRESS TRAINS WITH ROUTES

Sl. No.	*Name of Train*	*Distance*	*Route*
1.	Janta Exp.	2175 kms.	*Howrah to Bombay V.T. Via.* Asansol, Dhanbad, Gaya, Dehri on Sone, Kiul, Mokamah, Patna, Mughalsarai, Allahabad, Katni, Jabalpur, Itarsi, Ahusawal, Manmad, Nasik, Dadar.
2.	Express 7/8 (up to Nagpur only)	do-	
3.	Mail 3/2	do-	do-
4.	Express 11/12	do-	do-
5.	Howrah Bombay Exp. 30/29	1968 kms.	*Howarah to Bombay V.T.* Via Kharagpur, Tatanagar, Chakradharpur, Raurkela, Bilaspur, Raipur, Durg, Nagpur, Wardha, Akola, Bhusawal, Manmad, Nasik.

IMPORTANT EXPRESS TRAIN WITH ROUTES

Sl. No.	*Name of the Train*	*Distance*	*Route*
1.	Janta Express 41/42, 67/68	2175	*Howrah to Bombay V.T.* Via Asansol, Dhanbad, Dehri on Sone, Mokamah, Patna, Moghul Sarai, Allahabad, Katari, Gaya.
2.	Express 7/8, (Up to Nagpur only)	-do-	*Hawrah to Bombay V.T.* Via. Jabalpur, Itarsi, Bunsawal, Manmad, Nasik, Dadar.
3.	Mail 3/2	-do-	-do-
4.	Express 11/12	-do-	-do-
5.	Howarh Bombay Express 30/29	1968 kms.	*Howrah to Bombay V T.* Via Kharagpur, Tata Nagar, Chakradharpur Rourkela. Bilaspur, Nagpur, Wardha, Akolha, Bhusawal, Manmad, Nasik Rd.

Sl. No.	*Name of Train*	*Distance*	*Route*
6.	Calcutta Mail 2/1	-do-	
7.	Sialdah Jammu-Tawi Express 1751	1926 kms.	*Sialdah to Jammu Tawi* Via Asansol, Dhanbad, Gimth, Gaya. Dehri on Sone, Mughal Sarai, Varanasi, Lucknow, Ambala Catt Ludhiana, Jalandhar city, Pathan-Kot, Jammu Tawi.
8.	Mail 5/6 (up to Pathan Kot)	-do-	*Howrah to Jammu Tawi* Via Asansol, Dhanbad Gomoh, Gaya, Dehri on Sone Mughal Sarai.
9.	Express 9/10	-do-	*Howrah to Jammu Tawi* Via Varanasi, Lucknow, Moradabad. Lausai, Ambala Cantt, Ludhi-ana, Jalandhar, Pathan Kot.
10.	Express 61/62 (up to Dehradum)	-do-	
11.	Express 15/49 (up to Lucknow)		
12.	Express 102/103	1441 kms.	*From Howrah to New Delhi* Via Asansol, Patna, Mughalsarai, Allahabad. Kanpur, Tundla, New Delhi.
13.	Express 7/8	1437 kms.	*From Howrah to Delhi* Via Asansol, Mokamah, Patna, Varanasi, Allaha-bad, Kanpur, Tundla, Agra cauntt, New Delhi, Delhi.
14.	A.C. Express 18/22	1441 kms.	*From Howrah to New Delhi* Via Asansol, Dhanbad. Gaya, Mughal-Sarai. Varanasi, Allaha-bad. Tundla, Agra cantt, New Delhi.

15. Express 101/102	-do-	*Howrah to New Delhi* Via Dhanbad, Kanpur, New Delhi
16. Kalka Mail	1437 kms.	*Howrah to Delhi* Via Asansol Dhanbad, Gaya Dehri on Sone Mughal, Sarai, Allahabad, Kanpur, Tundla, Delhi.
17. Express 11/12	1437 kms.	*Howrah to Delhi Jn.* Via Asansol, Kiul, Mokamah, Patna, Mughalsarai, Allahabad, Kanpur, Tundla, Delhi Jn.
18. Janta Express 39/40	-do-	*Howrah to Delhi Jn.* Via Asansol Kiul, Mokamah, Patna, Mughal Sarai. Varanasi, Allahabad, Kanpur, Tundla, Delhi Jn.
19. Upper India Express 13/14	-do-	*Sialdah to Delhi Jn.* Via Asansol, Kiul, Mokamah, Patna, Mughal-Sarai, Varanasi, Allahabad, Kanpur, Tundla Jn.
20. Mail 3/4	1475 kms.	(*i*) *Howrah to Hyderabad* Via Kharagpur, Cuttack, Bhubaneshwar, Khurda Rd., Vizianagar, Waltair Vijayawada, Hyderabad. (*ii*) From Vijayawada, to Gudin and Madras.
21. Express 45/46		
22. Express 37/38	-do-	*Howrah to Hyderabad* Howrah to Radrm (as above).
23. Jayanti Janta Express	2188 kms.	*New Delhi to Madras* Via Mathura, Agra-Cantt, Jhansi, Bhopal, Itarsi, Nagpur, Belharshah, Kazipet, Vijaywada, Gudin, Madras Central.
24. G.T. Express		
25. Janta Express		